Multimedia Psychotherapy

Multimedia Psychotherapy

A Psychodynamic Approach for Mourning in the Technological Age

Domenico A. Nesci, MD

JASON ARONSON
Lanham • Boulder • New York • Toronto • Plymouth, UK

Domenico Arturo Nesci. Multimedia Psychodynamic Psychotherapy: A Preliminary Report. *Journal of Psychiatric Practice* 15(3): 211-215. Permission courtesy of the *Journal of Psychiatric Practice*.

Calvin F. Settlage. (2001). "Defenses Evoked by Early Childhood Loss," excerpts as they appear in *The Three Faces of Mourning*, edited by Salman Akhtar. Permission courtesy of Jason Aronson, Inc.

Published by Jason Aronson
A wholly owned subsidiary of The Rowman & Littlefield Publishing Group, Inc.
4501 Forbes Boulevard, Suite 200, Lanham, Maryland 20706
www.rowman.com

10 Thornbury Road, Plymouth PL6 7PP, United Kingdom

British Library Cataloguing in Publication Information Available

Library of Congress Cataloging-in-Publication Data

Nesci, Domenico Arturo.
Multimedia psychotherapy : a psychodynamic approach for mourning in the technological age / Domenico A. Nesci.
pages cm
Includes bibliographical references and index.
ISBN 978-0-7657-0913-4 (cloth : alk. paper) -- ISBN 978-0-7657-0914-1 (electronic)
1. Psychodynamic psychotherapy. 2. Group psychotherapy--Case studies. 3. Multimedia systems. I. Title.
RC489.P72N47 2013
616.89'152--dc23
2012038493

The paper used in this publication meets the minimum requirements of American National Standard for Information Sciences Permanence of Paper for Printed Library Materials, ANSI/NISO Z39.48-1992.

Printed in the United States of America

To my wife, my daughter, and my son,
With endless love.
To my dead parents,
With gratitude and nostalgia.
To my patients, my students, and my team,
With hope.
To all my readers, present and future,
Wishing their sky may get bluer and bluer!

Contents

Foreword

I have known Domenico A. Nesci for more than twenty years. I wrote a preface for his outstanding essay on "The Lessons of Jonestown: An Ethnopsychoanalytic Study of Suicidal Communities" in 1999 (Warren R. Procci, past president of the American Psychoanalytic Association wrote the foreword, at that time), and I am honored that he asked me to write a brief foreword for this book. In fact, Domenico and I have worked together on many projects and presentations (in Rome, at the Università Cattolica del Sacro Cuore as well as at UCLA) in our shared field of interest in psycho-oncology.

Dr. Nesci suggested that I describe my impressions and associations to the book itself, to the process of his unique psychotherapeutic method, and to the educational program that he has developed at the Scuola Internazionale di Psicoterapia nel Setting Istituzionale (SIPSI) in Rome to teach others how to make the therapy available to countless people who are suffering from a crisis in grieving the loss of a loved one or being unable to move on in the process of mourning some traumatic experience in the life cycle.

The book achieves the goal as a study tool for students of medicine, psychology, nursing, and social work in their learning the techniques of multimedia psychotherapy. Dr. Nesci uses his own individual cases and the experiences of his graduates as they treat their individual patients, with his supervision. He explains the use of the *ricordino* in Italian culture as a little remembrance of the lost person and how he expanded this traditional experience to his therapeutic process. He describes the painful process of "saying goodbye" to the dying person, trying to find the best time to say it, and often being away from the loved one at the time of death. He wonders if this is "just by chance, or is it an unconscious precognition and escape?"

In a stimulating section of the "Magic of Music," with one of his graduates, he describes how the music chosen by the mourner can evoke emotions and memories that aid in the healing process: "Psychiatry and anthropology seem to move together in the same direction, pointing towards the spiritual aspects that music evokes in the human mind."

The psychotherapeutic process of multimedia psychotherapy is not new. It follows the standard psychoanalytically oriented psychotherapeutic method. It is unique in that it makes use of the technology of the twenty-first century as an adjunct to working through the grief process, recovering lost memories, developing insights, and eventually coming to terms with the loss. Plus, as you will discover, at the conclusion of the therapy, the patient is given an object that is the joint creation of the patient and the artist (who plays the role of the third in the therapeutic setting). This "memory object" is a "psychodynamic montage" that can be replayed over and over again, by the patient, once patient and therapist have seen it and elaborated it in a "screening session."

The educational method to teach the new technique to psychotherapists attracted my greatest attention. The "training group" model illuminates the observation that "multimedia psychotherapy cannot be reduced to a series of pictures, edited with a soundtrack, to become a video." The learning process has a profound emotional impact on each student, as he or she begins to explore the losses that each has experienced during his or her lifetime.

I recall supervising a female psychiatric resident many years ago who was treating a young woman dying of ovarian cancer. She was uncharacteristically late to the appointment, and I began to worry about her. She arrived almost thirty minutes late. "I am so sorry," she said. "I was in an automobile accident. Nobody was injured, but it was my fault. I had to wait to fill out a report." I asked her to tell me what happened. She explained that she had been thinking about our upcoming supervisory meeting and what she would report, when it suddenly occurred to her that her mother had died at a young age from ovarian cancer. She had blocked this memory completely from her mind in association with her patient. She had a "blinding insight" while driving and lost control of her vehicle. Needless to say, this episode had a profound effect upon our supervision as well as her development as a psychiatrist and as a psychotherapist.

I had a similar experience as I read through this part of the book, describing the experiences of the students. I have undergone two great losses in my life. The first was the loss of my mother from colon cancer when I was eleven. I recall three years of her intermittent hospitalizations, my brother's and my dislocations to live with various relatives in distant locations, and my mother's final debilitating terminal phase at home. The experience left me with agonizing migraine headaches for years, and almost, to me, unbearable grief. However, I never was able to show my grieving to the members of my family. To all of them, I was "too good to be true." (How true!) Years later, in discussing this crisis with my father (who lived to be 99+ years old and with whom I was very close), he remarked, "Don't you remember what you said to me after mother's funeral? You said that you had decided to become a doctor and take care of women like your mother so that maybe they wouldn't have to suffer as she did." I have no conscious memory of ever saying that to my father.

My second major loss occurred twenty years later when my infant son suffered an accidental death at the age of two years. It was a totally different experience. I was surrounded by loved ones and my wife, mutually grieving our loss in the company of colleagues, family, and friends. There was open expression of feelings of loss. A dear friend and former fellow resident who was a child psychiatrist met with my two older sons to discuss their feelings of grief. We kept our mourning process in the open. Eventually I got used to the loss, but I never got over it. Reading this book made it possible for me to reopen that chapter in my life and to replay some loving memories of my dear boy. Several years later, with my child psychiatrist colleague Charles Hollingsworth, I published a book entitled *The Family in Mourning*. Part of the book reported our work with a family that had experienced multiple losses of children who died of congenital cardiomyopathy.

I now recognize this work to be my *ricordino*.

Domenico's book is obviously much more than a manual. It is an intimate account of the use of the modern technology to enhance the process of psychotherapy with families in mourning, and probably many more patients suffering from mental disorders. After all, who of us has not experienced the death of a loved one?

However, the most interesting aspect of the book has to do with Dr. Nesci's application of his method to other cases of mourning that do not imply any actual death: "We all have to mourn the 'Paradise Lost' of intrauterine prenatal life, our secret twin (the placenta), the breast, the Oedipal parents, childhood, adolescence, etc." Multimedia psychotherapy thus develops "into a technique that can be used to help everyone work through the critical transformations inherent in the ritual passages of our life cycle."

The clinical part of the book, from chapter 3 to chapter 7, where multimedia psychotherapy is described, step by step, from intake to outcome, is rich with cases where mourning has not to do with any actual death but with the loss of an internal object. For this reason, I would not be surprised if, in the future, multimedia psychotherapy could become the first choice for most patients. In fact, it is also a cost-effective method.

The book is conceived as a manual in order to let all health professionals who work as psychotherapists learn the new technique and apply it with their own patients. Excerpts from sessions are quoted to describe each step of the therapy. At the same time, two theoretical chapters are devoted to explain how and why the "memory objects" created by the multimedia artist are so effective in helping patients to mourn their complicated grief and/or overcome their blocks or inhibitions in normal development.

Finally, a new supervision model (the Clinic and Dreams Workshop) is described, once again through excerpts of this new teaching seminar. The book is written as a "story" in the format of "narrative medicine." It ends opening new horizons: how to use multimedia psychotherapy to make "memory objects for the future," so that a child might see what his/her parents were doing during pregnancy and prenatal life, or to help Alzheimer patients not to lose their capacity to recognize their own relatives.

Robert O. Pasnau, MD
past president, The American Psychiatric Association (APA)
Los Angeles, August 10, 2012

Acknowledgments

Writing this book was not easy. Often, I felt like a barbarian—the word used by the ancient Greek to describe a "stammering man," someone who doesn't know how to speak a language fluently. Fortunately, I was lucky enough to find a wonderful (and patient) editor in Lauren Sunstein, whom I thank wholeheartedly for her work and dedication to the project. Without her help, this book would probably have made sense only to me. So, Lauren, thank you for turning the hiccups of a stammering man into something that could be appreciated by a wider audience!

I also thank the acquisitions editor of Jason Aronson, Amy King, who helped me restructure my manuscript, adapting it to the needs of health professionals and students who practice psychotherapy (or want to practice it in the future).

Another person I am extremely grateful toward is my current psychoanalyst, Elena Caramazza. She helped me to believe in this project and to trust that Jason Aronson actually wanted to publish my book, even if I had no personal "recommendations" or "connections." The Italian collective unconscious is unable to believe that you can do anything without a "godfather" anywhere in the world, but, thankfully, we are wrong!

This leads me to express the enormous gratitude I feel toward Jason Aronson. Through my publisher, I also want to thank America, for its trust in innovation and its belief that everyone who has something valuable to say deserves to be heard.

I am also very grateful toward Ruth Ross (managing editor) and John M. Oldham (editor of the *Journal of Psychiatric Practice*), who accepted the preliminary report of my first multimedia case for publication in their journal, in 2009. Ruth Ross also helped me through the process of getting permission by Wolters Kluwer Health (Lippincott Williams and Wilkins), so that I could reprint my paper in the first chapter of my book.

At a more personal level, I am very grateful to all the American friends who supported me in this endeavor: Jim and Helen Zukin, who saw my first "psychodynamic montage"; Robert O. Pasnau, who accepted to write the foreword and came twice with me to Harbor-UCLA when I presented the preliminary results of my work; Warren Procci, who introduced me both times, at Harbor, and actively participated in the discussion; and Ira Lesser, chairman of the Department of Psychiatry, who invited me and always gave me positive feedback.

Multimedia Psychotherapy was born through the interaction between American and Italian cultures, so I want to say *mille grazie* to my Italian patients, colleagues, and friends who helped me imagine and realize my new technique: Tommaso A. Poliseno, who was always by my side in creating and developing new ideas, and all my students and collaborators at the International Institute for Psychoanalytic Research and Training of Health Professionals (IIPRTHP), at our *Scuola Internazionale di Psicoterapia nel Setting Istituzionale* (SIPSI), and at DREAMS, our nonprofit cooperative formed by our psychotherapists and psycho-oncologists (the best alumni and alumnae of SIPSI and of the courses in psycho-oncology at the *Università Cattolica del Sacro Cuore*, where I have worked since the beginning of my medical career).

Among my Italian friends, Carmelo Arezzo (aka *Meno*) is the one I want to thank in a special way. Without his help, I wouldn't have been able to include the pictures of two wonderful Sicilian carts in my book (courtesy of Vincenzo Arrabbito, better known as *Siranu*). This also gives me a chance to thank my daughter, Valentina, who loved my account of how I was able to find the Sicilian carts at Scicli, and turned it into a short story, "Am I Crazy?" which now introduces the book. I thank Valentina not only for working on that story but also for having convinced me to get an American editor, and for having helped me to find Lauren. I would never have admitted that I needed an editor . . . but I always listen to my children, because young people have the wisdom of being humble, a precious quality that we adults sometimes lose over the years.

This leads me to thank my whole family. The main reason I decided to write my book in English, for American readers, is that my daughter and son both live in California. If Valentina and Filippo choose to remain there, teaching multimedia psychotherapy would be a wonderful excuse for my wife and me to travel to the States and see our children more often.

The person I am most grateful toward is my son, Filippo Arturo, who was in this project from its very beginning. Without him, I would have never even imagined it, and wouldn't have been able to fully understand the importance of the professional relationship between therapist and artist in multimedia psychotherapy. On this regard, special thanks are also due to Giorgio Porcaro, my new multimedia artist, who freed me from my feeling of guilt for having initially exposed Filippo to the transference of my patients through their pictures and music. What is really fun, in our collaboration, is that Giorgio is enjoying discovering his hidden artistic side, editing our patients' "psychodynamic montages," as much as I am enjoying learning some basic computer skills from him. (Before knowing him, computers were incomprehensible for me—more than a "barbarian," I was a caveman!) Giorgio was the multimedia artist of the last video we produced, which was envisioned, for a baby in the womb, by my son and my wife, Simonetta Averna, a gynecologist with special training in Ob. Gyn. ultrasound. So, my last "thank you" goes to my beloved wife, Simonetta, my loyal, sweet, bright, "double," who always encouraged me to dare overcome the Pillars of Hercules and fly overseas to find inspiration in the New World.

Collaborators of Domenico A. Nesci

Domenico Agresta, psychologist, psychotherapist, psycho-oncologist; student at the Scuola Internazionale di Psicoterapia nel Setting Istituzionale (SIPSI), member of DREAMS Società Cooperativa Sociale ONLUS, Rome, Italy.

Simonetta Averna, medical doctor, gynecologist, psycho-oncologist, treasurer of the International Institute for Psychoanalytic Research and Training of Health Professionals (IIPRTHP), vice-president of DREAMS Società Cooperativa Sociale ONLUS, Rome Italy.

Marina Baldi, biologist, psycho-oncologist, master in criminology, director at Genoma Laboratories, Rome, Italy.

Maria Chiara Barbato, psychologist, psycho-oncologist; student at the Scuola Internazionale di Psicoterapia nel Setting Istituzionale (SIPSI), Rome, Italy.

Grazia Cassatella, medical doctor, psycho-oncologist; medico frequentatore at the Istituto di Psichiatria e Psicologia, Università Cattolica del S. Cuore, Policlinico Universitario "Agostino Gemelli," Rome, Italy.

Francesca Dalmastri, medical doctor, psychiatrist, psycho-oncologist, psychotherapist, Sant'Andrea Apostolo dello Jonio (CZ), Italy.

Stefano Daprile, psychologist, psycho-oncologist; student at the Scuola Internazionale di Psicoterapia nel Setting Istituzionale (SIPSI), Rome, Italy.

Marina Delle Cave, psychologist, art therapist; student at the Scuola Internazionale di Psicoterapia nel Setting Istituzionale (SIPSI), Rome, Italy.

Miguel Del Pozo, psychologist, psychotherapist, psycho-oncologist; alumnus of the Scuola Internazionale di Psicoterapia nel Setting Istituzionale (SIPSI), Rome, Italy.

Marcella Fazzi, psychologist, psychotherapist, psycho-oncologist; alumna of the Scuola Internazionale di Psicoterapia nel Setting Istituzionale (SIPSI), president of DREAMS Società Cooperativa Sociale ONLUS, Rome, Italy.

Vincenzo Florio, psychologist; student at the Scuola Internazionale di Psicoterapia nel Setting Istituzionale (SIPSI), Rome, Italy.

Cristina Foti, psychologist, psycho-oncologist; student at the Scuola Internazionale di Psicoterapia nel Setting Istituzionale (SIPSI), Rome, Italy.

ChiaraMaria Marra, psychologist, psychotherapist, psycho-oncologist; student at the Scuola Internazionale di Psicoterapia nel Setting Istituzionale (SIPSI), Rome, Italy.

Alessia Marzano, psychologist, psycho-oncologist; student at the Scuola Internazionale di Psicoterapia nel Setting Istituzionale (SIPSI), Rome, Italy.

Monica Medici, psychologist, psychotherapist, psycho-oncologist; alumna of the Scuola Internazionale di Psicoterapia nel Setting Istituzionale (SIPSI), member of DREAMS Società Cooperativa Sociale ONLUS, Rome, Italy.

Alessandra Monfeli, psychologist, psycho-oncologist; student at the Scuola Internazionale di Psicoterapia nel Setting Istituzionale (SIPSI), member of the Associazione Genitori Oncologia Pediatrica (AGOP), Rome, Italy.

Filippo Arturo Nesci, multimedia artist, student of film and video, The Art Center College of Design, Pasadena, CA, USA.

Valentina Nesci, BA in communications (The American University of Rome, 2010) MA in journalism (Stanford University, 2011), founder and editor in chief of Write-A-Holic, http://www.write-a-holic.com/, Editor of FLASHBACK–*Rubrica della SIPSI* http://www.doppio-sogno.it/flashback.htm.

Sabrina Podda, psychologist, psychotherapist, psycho-oncologist; alumna of the Scuola Internazionale di Psicoterapia nel Setting Istituzionale (SIPSI), Rome, Italy.

Tommaso Achille Poliseno, medical doctor, psychiatrist, criminologist, psychotherapist, group analyst; Dirigente Medico at the Dipartimento di Salute Mentale ASL RME; co-director at the Scuola Internazionale di Psicoterapia nel Setting Istituzionale (SIPSI); secretary of the International Institute for Psychoanalytic Research and Training of Health Professionals, Rome, Italy; director of the online journal *Doppio Sogno* http://www.doppio-sogno.it/.

Giorgio Porcaro, multimedia artist, IT consultant, Format Systems & Networks, Rome, Italy.

Domenico Scafoglio, anthropologist, professor of anthropology (retired) at the Università di Salerno; Author, with Luigi M. Lombardi Satriani, of "Pulcinella: il mito la storia" and, with Simona De Luna, of "La Possessione diabolica."

Valentina Scopone, psychologist, psychotherapist, psycho-oncologist; alumna of the Scuola Internazionale di Psicoterapia nel Setting Istituzionale (SIPSI), Rome, Italy.

Sara Vendetti, psychologist, psycho-oncologist; student at the Scuola Internazionale di Psicoterapia nel Setting Istituzionale (SIPSI), Rome, Italy.

Am I Crazy?

Domenico A. Nesci, in collaboration with Valentina Nesci

It was 1:00 P.M., and the thermometer hovered around 105° F. I opened the front door of my car and was hit by a tidal wave of sultry, unforgiving heat. The air was heavy, pregnant with sweat and dust. There was not a soul around except my smiling wife, a loyal, optimistic woman, who has been by my side during all my adventures, and my devoted friend Meno, a college buddy who had been reckless enough to accept to accompany me on this quest. As sweat started trickling down their faces and bodies, Meno and my wife looked at me with expectant, hopeful eyes. Although nobody spoke a word, one question lingered in the air around us.

But, before I go any further, let me explain how we had gotten to this sort of hell on earth in the first place.

You see, the thing is, I had just finished writing this book, when I had one of my ideas. More than an idea, it was an intuition. One of those realizations that come to you unexpectedly, when you are thinking about something completely different. I was walking my golden retriever, Eco, when a teenager on a red Vespa cut us off as we were attempting to cross the street. It happened then. Eco barked, and I thought of Sicilian carts, and how relevant they were to multimedia psychotherapy. (Funny how the mind works, sometimes. But I'm sure that there are safer ways to get inspired than almost being run over while taking a walk with your furry companion.)

Since this story revolves around Sicilian carts, I'd better describe them. They are ornate, colorful vehicles that used to be fairly common on the island of Sicily, especially during the 1920s. Each cart depicts a different myth or legend, and storytellers often use them as props to tell their tale. Since this ancient art bears significant similarities to multimedia psychotherapy, I decided, right then and there, that I needed to find a picture of one of those carts and use it as my book cover. There were only a few minor complications I had to deal with. For one, Sicilian carts were almost extinct and, as such, quite hard to find. Additionally, to encounter the last surviving exemplars of this tradition, I would have had to travel almost five hundred miles, to the southern end of Italy.

Which brings us back to Meno, my wife, and I, standing in the sweltering heat, the soles of our shoes melting and fusing with the pavement, in one of the hottest, less-populated villages of Sicily. The place, called Scicli, was a wind-forsaken, yet characteristic, little town stuck in a valley between a few hills. We had driven there from Meno's palace in the nearby city of Ragusa, following his carpenter's advice, "At Scicli, Sicilian carts are a luxury item, just like a Ferrari!"

However, as soon as we reached the square of the ancient, tiny village of Scicli, we realized that finding a cart was not going to be as easy as we had hoped. First of all, the heat threatened to leave us completely dehydrated—and, since Italians aren't exactly the quintessence of practicality, we only had one water bottle between the three of us. Then, there was the question of where to find the carts: we didn't have a name, or an address. . . . There was nothing we could use to find what we were looking for. I was hoping we would spot some carts as soon as we arrived, but, after much driving, it became clear to us that there was no one around. All the shops were closed. There wasn't a single car or bike on the street. The likelihood that we would encounter an elaborately decorated cart in the middle of this nothingness seemed remote at best. It was then that I turned to my friend Meno, and asked *the question*: "Am I crazy?"

After all, who drives all the way to the end of the world, dragging his poor friend and wife in the middle of the desert, just to find a cart for the cover of a book that has very little to do with carts? In this day and age, where you can get any picture you want from the Internet, traveling so far for one single snapshot truly didn't seem like the wisest idea in the world. Mercifully, both my friend and my wife refused to answer my question. Instead, my wife pointed one of her fingers toward the left and said, "I think there's someone inside that shop!"

Indeed, there was a little wine shop on the other side of the square, and its door was open. Meno and I entered and asked whether or not there were any Sicilian carts around there. Without hesitation, the owner of the shop replied: "You need to find Vincenzo Arrabbito, also known as Siranu."

When we left the shop, we had a name, a little more hope, and a general idea of where the storyteller resided . . . but no definite address. Not surprising, we soon got lost inside the meandering, unpaved streets of Scicli, and, once again, I started doubting of my sanity.

Then, finally, we saw, in the distance, the outline of a house. I felt a surge of excitement. Slowly, we approached the house: a simple, tiny structure with a scant patch of yellowing grass courageously growing in front of it. A stout lady with a sagging face was watering what remained of her garden, dust collecting in her wrinkles. As soon as she realized she had company, she gave us an enthusiastic, gap-toothed smile. She was clearly very pleased to see fellow human beings.

"Have you ever heard of Vincenzo Arrabbito?" we asked.

"Siranu?" she replied.

We nodded, in unison.

"Of course!" she said. Then, she pointed one of her hardened fingers toward a hill. "Do you see that bridge over there?" I squinted into the distance and noticed a tiny, fragile-looking bridge that, like we Italians say, looked as though it was being held together by spit. Again, we nodded, and the old lady continued giving us directions.

Ten minutes later (the poor woman really needed someone to talk to) we got back on our trail. We followed the bridge, then found the dried-up stream, which had left a small path beneath it, and followed that up a mountain, huffing and puffing along the way. Pretty soon, we were exhausted and drenched to the bone.

"Should we head back?" I asked sheepishly, feeling guilty about having brought my wife and Meno on a search for unicorns in such burning heat. Meno opened his mouth as if to say something, but, before he could utter a word, a rickety old Fiat came speeding toward us down the dried-up stream. We ducked to the side, and the driver, a burly man with a thick neck and an even thicker Sicilian accent, pressed hard on the brakes of his car. The Fiat stopped inches away from my knees, with a loud shriek.

"Where are you going?" he asked us, seemingly oblivious to the fact he had almost killed us.

"We are trying to find Siranu, but we don't really know where . . ."

"He's here!" the man interrupted us.

We looked at him, wide-eyed. Was that ordinary-looking farmer Siranu? That would have been a disappointment.

"See," went on to explain the farmer. "If you keep going up the hill, you will find a half-built house. That's where Siranu lives. If the gate is open, it's your lucky day. It means he is home, and all you need to do to meet him is to walk through the gate. If the gate is closed, on the other hand, you will never find him. Nobody knows where he goes or for how long he stays there, so I wouldn't recommend waiting—or looking for him, for the matter."

Very reassuring, I thought. We thanked the man and kept slowly making our way up the hill, the heat burning its way through our shirts. Only my wife kept smiling—she loves sunbathing, and had already taken off her hat so she could absorb as much of the sun's light as possible.

When we reached Siranu's house, we didn't even realize that it was a house. There were a bunch of pillars sticking out of the dry earth, like lampposts. Other than that, there was no sign that something resembling a house was going to be built there any time soon.

"Where does he live?" muttered my wife. "Underneath the sky? I understand that it's hot, but . . ."

Walking further, we eventually found a small shack behind the foundations of the unfinished building. There was a small gate in front of the shack. It was open. We all took a deep breath and looked at each other, our eyes filled with relief. Then, one by one, we crossed the gate.

There was no one inside. As the minutes passed and no one showed up, I started fearing that we had come all the way there for nothing. We walked further, and encountered a large warehouse. Inside it, there were a lot of weird objects, some made of wood, some of metal. I couldn't understand what the purpose of any of them was.

"Look!" Meno called out to us, triumphantly pointing toward one of the objects. In the midst of all the junk and knickknacks, there was a large, accurately decorated wheel. It had probably belonged to a Sicilian cart. A good sign.

"Great! But we need an entire cart," I pointed out.

"Ha. You are looking for Sicilian carts?" asked a jovial voice from behind us. We turned around to find a pleasant-looking man with round glasses, a round face, and silver hair surrounding the top of his head, like a halo.

"Are you . . . Siranu?" I asked, not daring to get my hopes up yet.

"In flesh and bone!" he announced, proudly. "Well, actually, I'm his son. My name is Franco Arrabbito," he said, wiping both hands on his filthy, discolored pants, and shaking mine energetically.

"Will you show us your Sicilian carts?" we asked, unable to contain our excitement. Franco beamed with happiness, a glitter in his tiny eyes. However, he didn't answer our question. Instead, he beckoned us to come to another warehouse: "*Venite! Venite!*"

Twenty minutes later, we had the honor to meet Vincenzo Arrabbito, an old, strong man who was the spitting image of his son, with the same narrow nose, round face, and tiny eyes, minus the glasses.

His voice brimming with joy and pride, he showed us the four carts he owned, each featuring a different myth or legend: Moses, Jesus, the French Paladins, and Christopher Columbus. As we took pictures from all sorts of angles and perspectives, Vincenzo explained that each cart had taken over a year to prepare. The care with which they had been decorated was evident: their colors were bright and vibrant, and the characters depicted on them looked almost alive, as if they could jump out of the painting at any moment: a breathtaking sight.

Our mission accomplished, we then proceeded to enjoy the rest of our trip. Vincenzo entertained us with his poetry, and we had the opportunity to pet the beautiful horses that drive the carts. The animals, revealed Vincenzo, had come from France, and had been selected for their size and character. "They need to be big and strong, to be able to pull the cart, yet sweet and calm, since children love to pet them!" he explained.

At the end of our trip, the atmosphere was light, and the heat didn't seem to bother us anymore.

"Thank you very much for coming, said Vincenzo. "You know, nobody cares about us anymore," he complained. "It's wonderful to see that someone still values us and what we are doing."

Franco chimed in, "And we lose a lot of money doing this, too. The government doesn't help us at all."

"We do it because we love it!" added Vincenzo, his watery eyes looking straight into mine. "But, sometimes, I wonder whether or not we are crazy."

"I know exactly what you mean," I said. "This morning, as we embarked on our quest to find a Sicilian cart, I had the same fear."

"But you found the cart!" exclaimed Vincenzo, his cheeks growing red with excitement.

"We found the cart," I repeated. "As a matter of fact, we found four!"

Introduction

My book on multimedia psychotherapy differs from contemporary psychotherapy manuals in several ways: its topic, its style, and the fact that it was written as a work in progress, continually remodeled with the help of my patients, students, and team of collaborators. The multimedia technique I have created is a brand new invention. There is nothing like this in the field of psychotherapy, at the moment. The style I use to present the "story" (chapters 1 and 2) and the features of multimedia psychotherapy (chapters 3–7) is, instead, very close to the classic narrative format of the "old times" of psychoanalysis. Even the theoretical parts of the text (chapters 8 and 10) are often associative, as always happens when you follow the psychoanalytic method, rather than rigidly rational, as manuals usually try to be. Last but not least, the book was not written at all, originally, as a manual. It was written in the space between an oral account of a "story" (the story of how and why it happened that I discovered and developed multimedia psychotherapy) and a complex, labyrinthine, academic text.

When Jason Aronson offered me a publishing agreement, Amy King, the acquisitions editor, politely suggested I should try to integrate the two approaches so that the book could be used as a tool in order to study and apply the new technique: an introductory handbook that any person in the field of psychotherapy (student or experienced therapist) could read and understand as well as an essay providing the theoretical foundations of multimedia psychotherapy within the frame of reference of narrative medicine (Good 1994).

In the end, I took much more time to revise the original text than I had taken to write it. That is why I now see my book as an oil painting, with several overlapping layers. In one layer, I tell the story of how and why multimedia psychotherapy came into my mind and gradually changed from a technique specifically conceived to help a patient mourn her beloved father (who had died of cancer) into a form of therapy that can be useful for any patient who finds himself/herself in crisis at some point in his/her own cycle of life. In another layer appear the ways in which multimedia psychotherapy can be learned and clinical cases be properly supervised. In a third is a series of reflections on the role of the multimedia artist in the therapeutic process, thereby reopening clinical and theoretical perspectives on the future scenario of psychodynamic psychotherapy, inevitably redesigned by my invention. The overall goal of this book is to make my technique available to all psychotherapists engaged in the helping professions (medical doctors, psychologists, counselors, or social workers) as well as to all students in the field.

When I began to conceive the idea of changing my initial text on multimedia psychotherapy from an academic essay into a clinical tool for colleagues and students, I came across a paper in the scientific literature which emphasized that "detailed descriptions of therapist interventions in manual-guided therapies are lacking" (Connolly et al. 1998). So I decided to focus on clinical examples, using transcripts of therapy sessions, supervisions, and workshops in order to give my readers a clearer understanding of what actually goes on in the therapeutic situation of multimedia psychotherapy. Obviously, such an approach is possible since we are dealing here with a "stage I" manual, that is, with a tool that provides only the basic outlines of a therapy in order to disseminate the knowledge needed to carry out "preliminary evaluation of treatments in early pilot studies" (Carroll and Nuro 2002).

In fact, this is exactly what I am interested in: to make it possible for colleagues all over the world to study the new technique, apply it themselves, and help it develop into an approach that can be integrated in the clinical practice of any psychotherapist with a psychodynamic background. Today I see multimedia psychotherapy as a potential new tool in *every* psychodynamic treatment since mourning is at the very core of the human condition. According to Henri Parens, "We all have mourned, do mourn, and will mourn. [. . .] But [. . .] mourning is not one thing. Much of it is not sad or bad; as [. . .] those reactions that result from psychic object losses that occur with normal development progression" (2001).

We all have to mourn the "Paradise Lost" of intrauterine prenatal life, our secret twin (the placenta), the breast, the Oedipal parents, childhood, adolescence, and so on. Thus a method that was shaped with a patient facing a traumatic oncologic mourning has been gradually shifting into a technique that can be used to help everyone work through the critical transformations inherent in the ritual passages of our life cycle. It can even be used to help the parents of a newly conceived baby have a better experience of pregnancy by creating a "memory object" for the future, which will allow their child/teenager/adult to see and "remember" what he/she never actually saw, being still immersed in the uterine night.

This unexpected shift into a universal technique, rather than one to be used only within the limited area of psychosocial oncology, grief, loss, and bereavement, was the main reason I felt I should publish my book now, despite the fact that it is still a work in progress. Actually, as we shall see in chapter 2, multimedia psychotherapy is (and will always be) a work in progress by its very nature. So, I feel it is right to let other researchers and health professionals in the field of psychotherapy share the preliminary results of the clinical work I am carrying out. I feel it is right that they too can further the progress of multimedia psychotherapy working with their patients in their own public and private health institutions.

Let's stop here for now, and let me, my patients, my students, and my team of collaborators begin to tell the story from where it actually began.

ONE

The First Case

In 2009 I published a paper in the *Journal of Psychiatric Practice* under the title "Multimedia Psychodynamic Psychotherapy: A Preliminary Report." The paper was a clinical account of the story of Serena, the first patient I treated with my new technique. Of course, Serena is not the true name of my patient. Less obvious, Serena was not my first patient.

From my present perspective, it is very clear to me that I am the first case I treated, while treating Serena. In fact, I had lost my parents just before she had, and I had the opportunity to review my own denied mourning, since I was her therapist while she was suffering from complicated grief after the death of her beloved father. That is why I think it is good if I add to the text of my 2009 paper a brief introduction about my family roots, so that it might be easier for my readers to understand more fully how and why it happened that I (not another therapist) conceived and developed multimedia psychotherapy.

In so doing, in considering myself a patient as well as a therapist, I don't feel alone, since Freud himself dedicated a significant part of his time to his own self-analysis and taught us that we should never forget to ask ourselves the unconscious meanings of what we are doing as long as we want to practice our "impossible profession" (1937).

FAMILY ROOTS

My parents were born many years ago in southern Italy. I still have vivid memories of the summers I spent in Calabria as a child and teenager in the 1950s and 1960s. In the region near Bova, the ancient Greek language of Griko was still spoken, and storytelling was a traditional activity of the people whose lives moved along so slowly. The ritual of storytelling often took place while walking, as in the philosophical school of Aristotle. The storyteller and the listener would take a stroll together, slowly—very slowly—stopping often—very often—at every few steps. When the storyteller stopped, he would turn and look into the listener's eyes, monitoring any reaction. According to what he saw there, he would decide how to remodel the plot, which motif to introduce, and how to develop it in his narrative. Meanwhile, all around, the air would be thick with the scent of jasmine, lemon, orange, bergamot, and the ever-present sound of the waves of the Mediterranean lapping on the shore (fig. 1.1).

The story of my family is intertwined with the story of storytelling. My paternal uncle, a well-known sound engineer in the movie industry of Rome, Cinecittà, after World War II, often hosted Professor Gerhard Rohlfs from the University of Tübingen, who came to record and save from oblivion the Griko oral narratives recounted by local storytellers. Domenico Minuto (Mimmo), my father's best friend, used to visit us in Rome occasionally on his way from Turin (in the north where he worked) to Reggio Calabria (in the south where his parents were living). Each time he came was a memorable event. He would tell stories, and I would be mesmerized trying to keep up with his imagination. For me, listening to him was like entering the fantastic realm of daydreams. Not only did I follow the story, but I also "saw" and "heard" the images and sounds of his tales.

Figure 1.1. My mother by the sea, near Bova

In Sicily (my mother was born in Messina, the city on the strait separating the Tyrrhenian and Ionian Seas facing Reggio Calabria), there was another fascinating tradition involving men called *cantastorie*. These heirs of the ancient Greek *aoidoi* would sing (not only tell) stories while illustrating the most important episodes with images. Some of these images were also portrayed on the cart of the artists, who traveled around on tour from one town to another (fig. 1.2 and fig. 1.3). So, sights, sounds, and imagination played a central role in my family over the generations.

The first picture I have of my father, Michele, is a photographic plate of him as a little boy, taken by my granduncle Domenico (or by my grandfather, Arturo) in the early1920s. My father graduated in physics and became a photographer and documentarian (fig. 1.4). He was also, for many years, the director of *Note di Tecnica Cinematografica,* the journal of ATIC (Associazione Tecnica Italiana per la Cinematografia e la Televisione). At the end of his career, as professor of editing and film language, he was appointed vice-dean of the Italian School of Cinema "Roberto Rossellini" in Rome.

As a young man, he met Giovanna, my mother, in a photography shop where she was working. He used to call her "Mietta" (implying that

Figure 1.2. A Sicilian cart at Scicli decorated with scenes from the story of Charlemagne and the French Paladins in their fight to defend Christianity from the Saracens. Courtesy of Vincenzo Arrabito aka *Siranu*.

Figure 1.3. Columbus in the New World: side of a Sicilian cart on which the story of the discovery of America is depicted in a series of episodes. Note that even the wheel of the cart is accurately painted! Courtesy of Vincenzo Arrabito aka *Siranu*.

she belonged to him, since Mietta literally means "Little Mine"), and she loved that nickname. When she got pregnant, they ran away from Reggio and moved to Rome, where they got married and my brother and I were born. I have clear memories of our first toys: the discarded plastic cylinders from film spools. Our game was poor and simple, but I remember it as very exciting: we would sing and build towers in different shapes, over and over again. A song to build it up, a song to tear it down, a cathartic outburst of cheers, and the cycle would start over again . . . ad libitum.

My father died in 2007, and my mother followed him a few months later. Their mortal coils rest in the new cemetery of Spoleto, in Umbria, the town of the "Festival of the Two Worlds," where American and European cultures have been meeting every summer since 1958, featuring musical and visual art events in the seventeenth-century Caio Melisso theater, in the ancient Roman amphitheatre, and in the historical square of the Duomo, the old cathedral where the final concert is always applauded before the midnight fireworks.

Figure 1.4. **My father with his camera, in Reggio Calabria**

Eureka!

The idea of using multimedia techniques in psychotherapy began to take shape in my mind while on a plane returning from Asia to Europe, immediately after the death of my parents, two dreamers intrigued by music, photography, and cinema.

Today I realize that I was unconsciously working through my own mourning experience, trying to build a bridge between the realms of the dead and the living, reanimating my deceased parents as internal objects while acknowledging their actual loss in the real external world (Freud 1917). At that time, however, on the flight, I was unaware of this process. According to me, on the conscious level, I was reflecting on the future of psychoanalysis (my idealized love object) and the need to find new ways to introduce and integrate it within the spirit of Eastern cultures in order to help it survive and regenerate itself in the new millennium in our global Technological Age.

Lost in my thoughts, I happened upon a short article in the newspaper I was reading. It reported that there was no longer any space left in Hong Kong for traditional burial places, so a new ritual had been established, encouraged by the local authorities. The dead person was cremated, and his/her ashes were scattered to the wind over the beautiful bay to reach a final resting place in the ocean.

As I was floating in the air, inside the womb of the airplane, the virtual space of the web immediately came to my mind. Why not experiment with a new form of art therapy focused on the need to give birth to new (personalized) mourning rituals? Why not use this innovative multimedia psychotherapy to introduce psychoanalytic methods and thinking in the East, where the need for psychotherapy and the need for new mourning rituals were emerging at the same time? Finally, why not evaluate the possibilities of this new psychotherapy technique in different geographic areas (Europe, America, Asia, Australia, and so on) to explore the ethnopsychoanalytic aspects of a contemporary, personalized, Internet mourning ritual?

What seemed an interesting idea on the plane now looks to me, on a deeper level, as part of the process of working through my own ambivalent feelings about the death of my parents, using sublimation (creativity) and the safe container of a "virtual space" (Internet) for what could not be reanimated as a good internal object and could become a persecutory one instead, something that should be placed somewhere, in a safe space: the World Wide Web.

The website www.thetreeofmemories.it was soon up and running, with my son, Filippo Arturo Nesci, as its webmaster and designer. The container was ready for my patients' (and my own?) "memory objects." Multimedia psychotherapy had been conceived "between Heaven and

Earth" (Frazer 1915). What was actually lost might be found, metaphorically, in another dimension.

SPACE AND TIME

Back at home, in my office, I sat in my transparent Plexiglas armchair facing Serena, one of my patients, a woman in her late thirties. I had known her for many years. She had begun psychodynamic psychotherapy in her twenties, immediately after the death by overdose of a cousin who was addicted to drugs. After that traumatic event, Serena began to suffer from symptoms of anxiety and depression (pounding heart, shortness of breath, fear of dying, sweating, depressed moods, loss of interest and enjoyment, reduced self-esteem and confidence, ideas of guilt or being unworthy, pessimistic thoughts) and started her treatment (as yet unfinished) involving one session a week. After the first year of classical therapy, the brother of the cousin who had died (also a drug addict) died of an overdose, too. This time Serena was able to deal with her loss better.

However, she decided to continue her therapy anyway since she felt her anxieties still needed to be contained by the setting of psychodynamic psychotherapy. According to Serena, it was her therapy that had enabled her to have a relationship, get married, and have two children. She felt that it would have been impossible for her to experience these situations "alone," as she felt prey to fears of all kinds. In fact, Serena refused psychiatric medications because she was so afraid of becoming "addicted" to a drug.

Then, another death took place in her family, only this time it was her father. He was an athletic man who had been the leader of his family and had cared for all his relatives, including Serena's two cousins. On the other hand, he was an extremely anxious man who lived his entire life with a neurotic fear of financial difficulties. The only moments that he was free from anxiety had been when he was dancing with his wife, Serena's mother, who shared his love for dancing. He was a heavy smoker and died of lung cancer not long after he was diagnosed. Everyone who knew him was surprised by his calm attitude toward the disease and shocked by his extremely quick death. During his last summer, he was still seen as an energetic "young" man in the little village where he lived, so that nobody could believe the sad news of his death a few months later.

It was only after this that Serena was able to recognize and acknowledge to herself, and to me in therapy, that her father had been such an anxious man and that she had always had a very special relationship with him. Nonetheless, Serena was anxious and depressed. Her earlier experiences, mourning the death of her two cousins, could not be compared with this loss and did not appear to be of help to her in working it through. She would see her father in other men, and she would often talk to him in her mind as if he were alive.

She was looking at me now, during our usual therapy session, and speaking, "There is a third dimension . . . not dead or alive . . . and it's less painful. When I think about my dead father, I don't think he's dead. I don't say 'poor him, he died!' No." I associated the patient's third dimension with the Internet and told Serena about my idea of multimedia psychotherapy.

The concept was very simple. It involved making a slide show (a sort of "psychodynamic montage") of the life of the dead person and then posting it on the web so that an "eternal" memory could remain in a "virtual place" where the patient could replay it, share it with selected people, and even change or enrich it at any time.

This was not at all a new idea. "Virtual cemeteries" already existed on the Internet and their efficacy in facilitating mourning has been recognized not only on the individual level but also as a collective psychosocial phenomenon (Sade-Beck 2004). The making of art objects to memorialize someone who has died is a common practice in art therapy and psycho-oncology (Dreifuss-Kattan 1990). The use of photography (Vacheret 2000) and cinema (Senatore 2001) in the setting of individual and group psychotherapy had also been described in the scientific literature.

What was new about the therapy I proposed to my patient was the concept of integrating these experiences. My idea was to create a psychodynamic montage in the setting of individual psychotherapy, during regular sessions in which the rules of the game were changed so that the patient was asked to recover, with the help of relatives and friends, select, and bring in multimedia objects of the dead relative (pictures, drawings, writings, video or audio recordings) and then to freely associate on them just as he or she would do for a dream, a lapse, a screen memory, or a symptom. The whole project was designed for the virtual space/time coordinates of Internet, so reminiscent of the dreamy Freudian scenario of the unconscious mind.

Serena responded enthusiastically and almost immediately started telling me a dream she had had:

> I dreamt about my father. He was a little angry at me. We were at home, my home or his, I can't say, and I was chatting with my mother. Someone else was there too. I don't remember who. I was chatting with him also, astonished. Is he dead or alive? Even in my dream I was unable to locate my father anywhere, among the dead or the living. He was gloomy and said to me, "Let's stop suffering. I am too close to you and too far from my destination. If you really want to help me, you should pray. Let me go!"

It is interesting that the slightly persecutory aspect of her father ("He was a little angry at me") was able to emerge with the memory of the dream only after I had offered a ritual (and virtual) place for him to be "located" (on Internet). Perhaps, in her dream (and in her transference), I was the unknown person who might mediate between her dead father, on one side, and her mother and herself, on the other side, the side of living beings. Maybe Internet could serve the function of Serena's "third dimension" where some of this "suffering" could be imagined and eventually confined, "between Heaven and Earth" (Frazer 1915).

Furthermore, Internet might work like the psychoanalytic couch, promoting associative instead of rational thinking, as I have described elsewhere in discussing the ethnopsychoanalytic meaning of the couch (Nesci 1993) and of the World Wide Web (Nesci, D. A. and Nesci, F. A. 2008) as suspension tools. In psychoanalytic therapy, the couch helps patient and therapist to abandon common sense and rational thinking, to freely associate and enter into an evenly suspended attention, a sort of liminal (intermediate) condition between the world of down-to-earth pedestrian logic and the universe of dreams and the unconscious. Similarly, the World Wide Web allows access to a virtual dimension that can also be experienced as a liminal setting, an intermediate state between the world of solid reality and the universe of abstract imagination.

VISUAL MEMORIES AND INSIGHTS

Serena arrived at the next session with piles of pictures—too many, in fact. Together, we began to look over them. I encouraged her to put them in chronological order and make a selection so as to build a sort of "strip of life." She began with her father's earliest picture, as a baby, and went on with all of the important moments in his life. At the same time, I suggested that she formulate a short text to match each picture (although I no longer do this). During the following sessions, she selected additional pictures and created texts to accompany each one, so that the strip of life was soon completed. The patient told me that some relatives were helping her in this task and that she was relieved because she had finally overcome her reluctance, in the aftermath of her father's death, to look at the many pictures of him that she had at home.

At the same time, she began to remember and discuss some traumatic events that had remained untold during her previous work with me. She recounted the traumatic deaths that had occurred in the lives of both her father (when he was three and lost his beloved eleven-year-old sister who had taken care of him most of the time) and her mother (when she was seven and, without any apparent emotional reaction, watched the horrible agony of her two-year-old nephew, who was burnt to death).

This dramatic return of previously unmentioned memories took place in the midst of our work with the photos. Specifically, it happened when we selected and identified two photos in the strip of life that showed her father at family reunions. In the first, he was with his own relatives, while in the second, he was at a party with his wife's relatives, sitting at the table between the patient's two cousins. Serena's text, written as an imaginary dialogue with her father, said, "Beautiful memories of our family reunions, in which you would never decline to participate, with your own relatives as well as with my mother's relatives. What a great love and support you gave to my cousins who loved you too with the same affect! They adored you."

At the end of the session, we were able to comment on the interesting fact that Serena's parents seemed to have worked through their childhood traumatic experiences in opposite ways, with her father becoming anxious and caring, and her mother apparently fearless and uncaring.

By the end of our work, we had selected forty pictures, and we were both touched by the fact that her father's whole life seemed to have been effectively summarized. Even the two media artists who worked on the project (including my son, Filippo Arturo) told me, after completing it, that they had the same strong feeling of dealing with the life of a good, honest, caring man, who had dedicated his entire existence to his work and to providing moral support to his extended family.

One additional "visual insight" came about two months after the multimedia sessions had ended and the psychodynamic montage had been posted on the Internet. Serena told me that she was finally able to understand why her mother had rejected her at first when she was born. Looking at the pictures on the web, she realized, to her surprise, that she looked very much like her paternal grandmother (a smiling, unsophisticated, overweight woman) and almost nothing like her mother (a very self-conscious, beautiful, slim woman). Needless to say, this insight opened new paths in her psychotherapy, which we are still exploring.

THE SOUNDTRACK

As a soundtrack for her visual memories, Serena chose a song that had been dedicated by an Italian *cantautore* (Jovanotti, a singer-songwriter) to his wife: *A te,* which means "To you." Interestingly, the idea to make a soundtrack came to both of us, patient and therapist, at the same time. Serena had, in fact, drawn words from this song for the beginning and end of the text she wrote to comment on the pictures. Then, during one session, we decided, together, to replace those words with her own, so that she could comment on each picture of her father's strip of life and "talk" to him, in a sort of dialogue, after his death.

Serena began to tape-record herself at home with her children, who interpreted it as a game and began to play with the tape recorder themselves. At the same time, she was also listening to the song over and over again. This resulted in many exhilarating episodes that made everyone laugh and feel unexpected but much-welcome joy while *A te* quite naturally became the soundtrack of the video. The art object crafted in the process of this multimedia psychotherapy had begun to change an uneasy individual mourning experience into moving, emotional, audiovisual memories that could be shared easily within Serena's whole family: the story of a child who lived a simple life, of a young man who was proud of his fiancée, of an adult who enjoyed a successful marriage that produced children and grandchildren. For such a story, *A te* is a very powerful soundtrack indeed, since it is the expression of infinite gratitude toward a love object at a time when the *cantautore* was afraid of losing it forever.

The media team produced two memory objects: a strip of life made with all of the forty pictures selected, each accompanied by a short comment, and a video that we called a psychodynamic montage. It was created by playing with the infinite possibilities offered by technology to frame each photo, to pass from one to the next with transitions, and to zoom or insert movement within each picture. The slide show produced by this artistic endeavor lasted exactly as long as the song. The presentation of the two memory objects (but especially of the video) gave all audiences who saw it the same powerful sensation of grasping a whole life in the time span of a single tune, in the words of a single song, as if they were dedicated by a daughter to her beloved dead father.

CONCLUSIONS

The final memory objects were actually produced by a team of two specialists. Together, they freely edited the pictures and the soundtrack that had been selected during the sessions by patient and therapist. At the end of this process, the strip of life and the psychodynamic montage were shown to Serena, during a session in which I gave her the chance to request changes for anything she might find unacceptable. This proved unnecessary, however, as she immediately expressed her full approval of the media team's work. The two art objects were then posted on a website I had created for this purpose (through The International Institute for Psychoanalytic Research and Training of Health Professionals [IIPRTHP], the Italian nonprofit organization I had incorporated in Rome in 1999 to promote psychoanalytic thinking in health institutions), where the patient and her relatives and friends could access them with a password. Serena also gave me permission to present her memory objects at scientific meetings and to publish and discuss them in scientific journals, university courses, and other similar situations.

Interestingly, subsequent patients (mostly older people) did not want to post their memory objects on the web, but asked instead for a pen drive or DVD as the material container for their psychodynamic montage.

I immediately thought that multimedia psychotherapy might become a cost-effective and well-received tool in health institutions such as hospices and general hospitals, where, as of now, relatives of cancer patients are often left on their own to deal with the deaths of their beloved ones. I also thought that my new technique could easily be taught in Continuing Medical Education (CME) and other training programs. In fact, I presented multimedia psychotherapy at the Department of Psychiatry of the Harbor-UCLA Medical Center with Dr. Robert O. Pasnau (past president of the American Psychiatric Association) and Dr. Warren R. Procci (president of the American Psychoanalytic Association) in Los Angeles on July 21, 2009 (as well as on April 17, 2012), and in the CME program "Creativity and Madness" of the American Institute for Medical Education, in Rome, on April 22, 2010. I also organized a one-year course in psycho-oncology (multimedia psychotherapy) at the School of Medicine of the *Università Cattolica del Sacro Cuore*, where I work, in the academic years 2009–2010 and 2010–2011. At the moment, I teach multimedia psychotherapy at my own school (*Scuola Internazionale di Psicoterapia nel Setting Istituzionale* or SIPSI) in Rome.

Serena is still in therapy (one session every two weeks). However, she has finally begun to take low doses of antidepressant and anxiolytic drugs, which she had refused for so many years out of her neurotic fear of becoming a drug addict. She no longer suffers from most of her disturbing symptoms of complicated grief. My conclusion is that the form of psychotherapy we experienced together allowed for a more rapid elaboration of her mourning process . . . and for the start of my own.

TWO

Multimedia Psychotherapy: Story of a Training Group

My first case in multimedia psychotherapy, Serena, was excited about the work we had done together and encouraged me to train other health professionals so that this new technique could be applied with the growing number of patients suffering from oncologic mourning. An opportunity to do so came very soon, since in that period I was coordinating the master's program in psycho-oncology at the School of Medicine of the *Università Cattolica del Sacro Cuore* (UCSC) in Rome. Among the eighteen graduate students were five women whom I had known for many years: Alessandra, a psychologist whose child had died of a neuroblastoma; Francesca, a psychiatrist who was working as a doctor at a hospice not far from Rome; Marina, a biologist who had taken all my courses in psycho-oncology at UCSC; and Elisabetta and Sabrina, two psychotherapists trained in my School of Psychotherapy (whose program includes many hours of psycho-oncology).

Thanks to the sponsorship of IIPRTHP, the nonprofit organization that manages my private School of Psychotherapy (SIPSI) and promotes the courses in psycho-oncology at UCSC, I was able to invite these women to experience multimedia psychotherapy in a group setting. Elisabetta, who knew my therapy from a presentation I had given at SIPSI and from having read my first paper on the subject (Nesci 2009), volunteered to be the "patient" in this select group of colleagues and work through her own mourning process for the death of her mother, who had died of cancer in 2002. Although Elisabetta was in psychoanalytic psychotherapy at the time, her therapist encouraged her to enter our "training group" to help her work through her loss.

It was only at the end of this successful experience that I realized, with wonder, that together we had done much more than help Elisabetta (and ourselves) to work through her (and our own) mourning processes. In fact, we had created a coherent methodology to train psychotherapists in multimedia psychotherapy and invented the core of a curriculum for this new creative therapy.

Our experience was in harmony with the philosophy of every psychoanalytic training, but it was not such a lengthy or demanding process. A person who wants to become a psychoanalyst (a "candidate") must be analyzed first as a patient within a special setting called "training analysis," under the guidance of an experienced colleague, for many years. In addition, he or she must be supervised individually and participate in clinical seminars conducted by "training analysts," where patients' cases are analyzed in relation to the emotional reactions they trigger in the therapist's mind (countertransference) as well as from other theoretical perspectives. Finally, the candidate must write a paper integrating all of the above.

Our group experience with multimedia psychotherapy was a sort of rhapsodic experience, putting together these psychoanalytic rituals in a new and less demanding way within the safe container of a group setting: a bit of training analysis (Elisabetta was curing herself and learning at the same time), a bit of group supervision/clinical seminars (the five students were in fact discussing clinical experiences in a small group of colleagues), and a bit of writing, since our meetings were oriented towards the students' writing their master's theses in psycho-oncology with my supervision (each one focusing on the experience from her own perspective) as well as contributing to my book on the subject. In short, what made this training group experience particularly interesting was that here we had a group of therapists/patients (including its leader/supervisor) who were able to play both roles at the same time, focusing on Elisabetta's mourning, while reflecting on their own personal mourning experiences.

Before presenting pictures from Elisabetta's memory object and excerpts from the transcripts of our group experience, let me introduce the ritual frame or setting that established the boundaries of our work.

THE SETTING

The group meetings had a tripartite rhythm. Actually, they were structured in the same way as every ritual, anthropologically speaking (van Gennep 1909), where human life is conceived as a series of passages from one (bio-psycho-social) state to the next. Mankind invented rituals to overcome the crisis of each of these transitions, until the last inevitable one, into death. Only later, myths and religions developed to crystallize the meaning of those rituals, which serve as signposts along our existential paths, appearing periodically to the rhythm of the music of life's cycles.

To make possible the passage from one anthropological state (state A) to the next (state B, C, and so on, for example, puberty, marriage, etc.), we need a "pre-liminary" rite (separation from the initial state, i.e., exit from state A), a liminary rite (transition into a neutral, NOT-A/NOT-B state), and finally a "post-liminary" rite (entrance into state B), where the subject is able to adjust thanks to what has been learned and incorporated during the whole process. Only in this way can the change in identity take place without being overly traumatic. This anthropological perspective is important since it parallels the psychoanalytic concept expressed by Henri Parens (2001), who states that mourning is at the core of "the human condition" even in its normal course of development. We all must celebrate the loss of the child in ourselves if we want to give birth to the adult after the transition state of adolescence when we feel we are neither meat nor fish.

Now let's go back to our training group. In our case, the preliminary rite was the working lunch offered by IIPRTHP to help create a sympathetic (*syn* = with, together; *pathos* = deep emotion, as well as traumatic emotion) atmosphere within the group, so that repressed emotions associated with the mourning experience might finally be uncovered, protected by the safe container of the "good" empathic group. From time immemorial, eating together has been a classic ritual to abolish the boundaries between the individual members of a group, to make people vibrate in unison and feel as one.

In our own training group, eating together was "pre-liminary" to mourning together: the preliminary rite. It always took place in the same restaurant, at the hospital cafeteria, at lunch time. After lunch, we had the obligatory espresso in the nearby coffee bar. In this way we were unconsciously following a traditional Mediterranean custom, according to which neighbors and friends join the members of a mourning family and cook for them for a while. It is a sort of reparative ritual where the sense of emptiness triggered by a death is recovered by oral incorporation and group cohesiveness.

The liminary rite, the rite of the limen (Latin for "limit") or of the threshold, consisted of the meeting itself. Actually the limen is the most important mental dimension, the suspended space/time frame (NOT-A/NOT-B) where change can occur. It would begin with a short walk from the cafè to the room where the meeting was to be held. As we walked, we would talk of nothing special, apparently, yet we were unconsciously tuning ourselves for the working through to come, when the door of the meeting room would close and we would be the only people inside. The short walk was a tool—a suspension tool, like the psychoanalytic couch, serving as an instrument to leave everyday reality and reasoning behind. This allowed our unconscious minds to enter the "free floating attention" labyrinthine state of all psychoanalytic work (Nesci 1993) and freely associate on Elisabetta's (and our own) mourning experiences, as well as on her audiovisual memories when she chose to share them with us. Elisabetta's story, the story she was telling us while showing images and evoking sounds, was the "pre-text" (preliminary text) and pretext to let everyone work through his/her own mourning experiences while learning (and teaching) multimedia psychotherapy, all at the same time.

The third ritual, the post-liminary rite, the rite taking place after the threshold, consisted of the individual work each group member did between one meeting and the next. This last step is the most important one: moving on into a new state (state B) from grief (state A) through the process of mourning (the transition state NOT-A/NOT-B).

Now let's go into the meeting room to get an idea of what goes on in there and to feel some of the powerful emotions circulating among us, the members of the training group.

THE FIRST MEETING

by Marina Baldi, in collaboration with Domenico A. Nesci

Marina: My parents divorced when I was very little and my sister was just six months old. We lived with our absent father whom we adored. He was handsome, charming, and intelligent and had this wonderful job in the movies, so he was always traveling. I still have lovely memories of him getting back home from his long journeys in exotic countries. He would sit down in the living room and open his suitcase, taking out all the incredible gifts he had collected for us!

We grew up, and Dad went on being mostly absent from our lives, even though we would talk on the phone every day. Then, in his last two years, he suffered a terrible illness which handicapped him to the point where he was obliged to sit in an armchair all day long: he couldn't even lay down in bed, at all. And yet, he was always calm, never angry, never nervous: what a good character he had! During this time I became closer to him; I idealized him. It was as if I became his daughter all over again.

When he died, two cousins (his sister's daughters) gave us two large bags full of pictures and personal notebooks with all his financial records. It was then that I realized how terribly unfamiliar I was with my own father. I knew no one in the pictures, which forced me to recognize that he had had a parallel life. They showed the life of the father who was not my father, the father who was never with me. I never wanted to see them again. After all, it is through the medium of images that we may come to know the truth.

Domenico: Yes, I agree. The image is important when we are dealing with painful things, those things you don't even think about unless you see them. As the proverb says, "Out of sight, out of mind." It is a primal defense mechanism.

Alessandra: Images also have the opposite power, the power to recover and repair: in the aftermath of my son's death, I made an album with his pictures for myself. I chose the photographs I liked most, very carefully, and reconstructed his life.

Domenico: You made a selection with regard to pain.

Alessandra: Exactly. I chose some pictures of his illness too, but not the painful ones. He suffered from a neuroblastoma, which changed him a lot physically, especially in his last fifteen days. So I always kept one of his earlier pictures with me, and I had a powerful need to see it. By the end of his illness, in fact, there was only the disease on his face . . . and he was in pharmacological coma.

Marina: So, there was only the disease . . . there . . .

Domenico: This makes me associate with my second case in multimedia psychotherapy. He was an obsessive patient whose father died from cancer when he was a teenager. The day this patient was supposed to bring in the photographs, he forgot them. But then, during the session, he told me a disturbing story. Looking at the pictures over the previous days at home, he had realized there was always a particular woman present. In fact, she was his father's lover. This was something my patient always knew, in some way. Yet, at the same time, he never really knew it since the woman had been accepted as a family friend. So, when my patient did his search to collect and select the pictures, he found them and lost them, at the same time . . . and came to the session empty-handed. After working through what had happened, he brought the pictures to the following session, but decided to remove from the psychodynamic montage all the photographs where his father's lover appeared.

Marina: I also sealed up an envelope forever with all the pictures where my father appeared with other women and refused to look at them anymore.

Elisabetta: We don't have any pictures of my mother from the summer of 2001. She was very tired. Her cancer hadn't been discovered yet, and she hadn't told anyone about her symptoms. She was very shy and secretive about herself, which is a typical trait of the insular Sardinian culture.

Domenico: She exited from the scene before . . . She managed not to be photographed since she wanted to leave the memory of a healthy image of herself.

Marina: Probably she was aware, unconsciously, of her situation. I remember a friend of mine who died of cancer when she was thirty-five. I went to visit her one week before her death. She was really beautiful. As she was expecting a visit with her young child, she was putting on make-up since she didn't want to leave the child with the image of a sick mother. I think this is a typical psychological mechanism of mothers.

Domenico: A protective mechanism . . . right . . . Mothers know an image can be painful. I think this is why one ends up being absent "by accident" when his/her parent dies. I knew my father was dying and I didn't go. I knew my brother was there. I knew he was happy to be there, alone, at that moment, while I would feel devastated. So, I didn't go even though I felt he was dying. I "knew" it.

Marina: I arrived immediately after. I suspect that it wasn't exactly an accident that I wasn't there.

Alessandra: Fifteen terrible days, during which I was looking for any way he might . . . I couldn't tolerate the idea of separation. Finally, I decided he had to die. Two hours later he was dead.

Domenico: Yes, he had been waiting for you to be ready.

Alessandra: I didn't feel the pain you're describing. I just felt there was nothing there. There was nothing anymore. However, if he hadn't waited for me to be ready . . . I don't know. I felt something inside myself breaking. Later, I thought, they don't go until you let them go.

Elisabetta: She wanted to talk on the phone, although she couldn't do it anymore. She passed out while dying, so there was no clear death. The night before we had been together on the phone. I could only listen to her deep breathing. She tried to talk, but she couldn't. I was talking to her, encouraging her. "Come on, you'll see!" I was the one who had to bring her joy, while my sister was the one who had to shoulder her anxieties. . . . That year, she had asked me to come visit her at Easter time. This was unusual; in fact, she had never asked me before, "Are you coming or not?" My daughters told me afterward, "We didn't feel pain, tragedy, anxiety. We felt a quiet atmosphere. We realized Grandma was ill, but we felt OK, we were peaceful."

Marina: Try to imagine what an effort she made! It reminds me of the movie *Life is Beautiful*, by Roberto Benigni, where the father of a four-year-old child in a Nazi concentration camp protects his son by convincing him that it is all a game and that if they play well, they will win an American tank in the end. The final scene is really moving. The American army is arriving, and the father saves his son by hiding him in a torture cell and telling him not to come out until all the Nazi guards leave the camp (since this is the boy's great opportunity to reach one thousand points in the game and win the tank). The child comes out, the American tank is there, and he is reunited with his mother, who also survived. His father's love and imagination protected him from the horror of trauma and death.

WORKING AFTER THE MEETING

by Francesca Dalmastri, in collaboration with Domenico A. Nesci

At the beginning of my professional experience as a medical doctor in Palliative Care for cancer patients, I was called to the home of a patient who had just died in a rural area not far from Viterbo, in central Italy. It was 5:00 A.M. when I arrived and found myself face-to-face with an unexpected scenario: all the family members were gathered around the table in the living room, chatting excitedly and selecting, among many pictures, the one that was destined to become the "*ricordino*" (literally "little remembrance" = memorial photo). This is an image of the lost person (before death) that is chosen to be printed and distributed to relatives and friends in the aftermath, with an accompanying sentence, verse, or short text to remember the person in the best possible way, after his or her departure for the last journey to eternal life.

In the following months, I realized that this custom is widespread in the area where I was working. The family members of the dead person discard the pictures that they consider ugly and try to choose the best one, the photo best able to open one's heart, mind, and eyes to the flow of memories. Often the "*ricordino*" begins to represent the person many years before his/her own actual death!

Working as a psychiatrist and psychotherapist, I've been able to make interesting observations of the process through which the "*ricordino*" is chosen by family members who suffered the death by cancer of a beloved person. These relatives/patients express the need to go back over the most significant moments shared in their lives with the deceased persons, mostly through photographic images. They spontaneously select pictures that they find particularly significant in order to recall happy memories, incorporating them in a memorial album or framing them to display in their homes. Not surprisingly, these pictures never show terminal states of the illness.

At that time, I realized clearly that the goal of all these behaviors was to soften the emotions of grief, loss, and mental pain in order to prevent the risk of madness that is inherent in mourning the death of a beloved person. Memorial pictures are essential to hold and handle death agonies by objectifying an image of the person we have lost forever. However, I was unable to fully understand the power of the image at a deeper level, the strength of visual representations that are able to serve as a go-between or "liminal medium" in the process of mourning (as Domenico described it in our group). I didn't know yet how to decode what was going on in the patient's home, the clinical scene, nor how to use it as a precious therapeutic tool.

Some other questions were puzzling me after I read Domenico's preliminary paper on multimedia psychotherapy (Nesci 2009). Mightn't it be risky to remember just the good memories (by selecting only the "best" pictures and discarding the painful memories, the "ugly" photos)? In other words, by encouraging this kind of selection, don't we risk promoting the idealization of the lost person and delaying the mourning process indefinitely? To what extent is it therapeutic to filter mental pain, to keep the painful memories "out of sight and out of mind"? It was only through our training group that I was able to fully realize the difference between discarding a picture, consciously, and repressing a memory, unconsciously.

Curtain's Up!

Last Saturday I had my first meeting with Prof. Nesci and a small group of colleagues from the master in psycho-oncology. Thanks to this lively experience and their personal testimonies, the curtain was raised.

Marina's experience with the discarded pictures of her father's parallel life (a sort of repression that she was able to overcome thanks to the therapeutic function of the training group) led her to this interesting conclusion: "After all, it is always through the medium [*tramite* in Italian] of images that we may come to know the truth." The term *tramite* resonated in my mind according to its etymologic roots, from the Latin *trames* = "passage, path, short cut." This path can be both familiar and unfamiliar, in Freudian terms, *unheimlich* (disorienting), since it can re-evoke ambivalent feelings (love, pain, anger, tenderness). So, one can decide whether (as well as when and how) to walk down that path or not.

A patient (I will call her Melanie) came to my mind. She is in her sixties, a slim young-looking wide-eyed woman whose carefully made-up face conveys a sense of modesty, shyness, and sadness. Her first son was killed by a hit-and-run driver. One month later, her father died and then her husband was diagnosed with a lung cancer on the same day as the funeral. Two years later, her second (and last) son was also killed by a hit-and-run driver.

When her husband became a terminal cancer patient, I was in the team that assisted him at home. Entering the apartment, I felt immersed in a frozen atmosphere. The walls were painted purple and red, respectively, the favorite colors of the two dead sons. The living room, the bathroom, even the bedroom were all flawless, lifeless in fact.

When her husband died, seven years after the death of their first son, Melanie came to me for help. She was unable to perform even the most routine activities in her everyday life. She felt plagued by shame and anxiety and foresaw her future as one of grief, loneliness, and fear. I asked if she would like to show me her family pictures. She told me she didn't have any since after the death of her first son she had hung or framed every picture she had. Then, when her second son died too, she had made a big poster with pictures of them from baptism on, so she could see and go back over their lives. The narrative of their stories shows one son on the right side of the poster, the other on the left, and the family in the center. Other pictures were placed on the tomb to help friends remember and to introduce the dead boys to anyone passing by in the cemetery. No picture was taken after the death of the second son. An old photo of their father was added to the poster after his death.

Melanie was constantly going back over that sequence of images, asking them for advice on what to do and how to manage her life. She confessed to me that she had never accepted her sons' deaths; she just lives with it. "For a mother, it is just too painful." She also told me a few "paranormal" experiences she had had, which convinced her that her sons were somewhere else and that she should accept it and let them "live" that way.

The absence of her dead husband was experienced by Melanie as the loss of a reference point that was essential for her psychic stability. She felt protected by her husband, though not loved. He was jealous and possessive. Timidly, she revealed to me that his illness had been the best period of their life together since he had finally made her feel important to him.

Given that it didn't make sense to work on the pictures again (she had already worked on them in the aftermath of her three losses), I suggested that she look over her husband's papers. The next session she came with two family pictures instead, and a little note found in his wallet that said, "Melanie, the only love of my life." We took this as a starting point to work through her feelings of shame and her quest for identity.

Today, Melanie is expressing the wish to make changes in her home, to remodel her sons' room (where the poster is). Chatting with their images on the wall, asking them for advice on this delicate matter, she is exploring her own separation/individuation issues. Step by step, through their pictures, she is beginning to free herself from her dead love objects. She is letting them die into herself, gradually.

Within our group, Alessandra also made an album after the death of her son. I was very moved, seeing her go through the pictures of her child's short life and recognizing how she made the selection according to her need to protect herself from painful emotions. As she told us, his face was completely distorted by the disease in his final days, so she had placed an earlier picture from when he was healthy beside his hospital bed.

While she was sharing her story with us, I was silently associating with the countless intimate confidences I had listened to, on different occasions, so many times, from my patients' relatives about their uneasiness with the physical changes suffered by their beloved one in the terminal period of the illness. It was not only the pain of the bodily changes, but also of the loss of autonomy, of being confined to bed, of suffering mental impairment. The higher the sociocultural level of the patient, the more severe the difficulty experienced by the family members (mostly by the partners).

Often, in the last days, the patient's relatives ask for their beloved one to be admitted into our hospice. They find the idea of having him/her die at home intolerable. They couldn't live in the house anymore if this fatal event took place within its walls. This deep "secret" anxiety complicates the task of palliative doctors who would like to encourage people to keep their dying relative at home, which was of course the natural way to face death in the past.

From this perspective, the hospice plays a very protective role. Inside the ward, I am frequently asked, "Should I stay here tonight?" The patient's relative asking this uneasy question often makes me feel, in my countertransference, that he/she hopes to receive a negative answer. The very fact that the patient is in the hospice reveals in itself a strong wish/need on the part of the relative not to see the end. So it often happens that relatives who apparently came to live in the hospice to be present at the moment of life's end go out to have a coffee exactly when the patient expires. Is that just chance, or is it an unconscious precognition and escape?

Usually I address this very uncomfortable question, suggesting that the relatives try to find a moment to say goodbye and separate from their beloved one *before* he/she dies. That moment, which should take place before drowsiness, must involve an awareness that it is the last, the final moment of separation. I am emphasizing awareness here, since memories tend to blur and fade with the passing of time and the anguish of grief, and defense mechanisms turn into ineffective pathological protections.

This was happening to me, too.

Like Domenico, I hadn't wanted to be present when my father died and I too had taken care of everything before and after that moment. Just like Domenico, I knew the day my father was going to die. I knew my mother and sister, who wished to be present, were surely there, yet I chose not to go.

Actually, I became aware that I had managed not to be there for my father's death only when Domenico told his story to the group, at which point I found myself feeling relieved from a burden I hadn't known I was carrying. Over time, in fact, I had forgotten the moments when I had decided not to be there at the very end. In the empty space of that repression, my regret and sorrow for not being present at his death insinuated nagging doubts about my not having done enough for him. However, our group experience allowed me to identify with Domenico, as a doctor/son of a dying father, and share his belief/feeling that, when conditions allow a choice, it may be better for a doctor/son or daughter not to be there when the moment comes.

Then, feeling less anxious and guilty, I played the movie of my father's illness back in my mind, recovering memories of his biological testament and of the medical choices that had been carried out according to his will. Finally I remembered I *had* said goodbye to my father the day before he died. We had embraced and said we loved each other. Only two hours later, he began to suffer and was given morphine. Then he lost consciousness.

I had lost all memory of this last goodbye; I had repressed the very idea of loss, and what memories I had were confounded by grief and sorrow. I was experiencing an awkward (as well as useless and burdensome) attempt to replace the loss of my father with my own supposed incapacity to take care of him. Once my memories returned closer to reality, grief and sorrow too took on a different emotional color. Becoming aware at last that I had chosen not to see him die in order to prevent my own "devastation" allowed me, two years later, to start to acknowledge that he was actually dead.

After he died, I had chosen his memorial photo instinctively, with little reflection. Today I realize I look with different eyes at that picture: I now see in it the strength and the weakness of the respected man and beloved father from whom I still take inspiration in my efforts to become a better person.

To finish discussing the process of my working through after the first meeting and before the second, I cannot but recall one last patient (whom I will call Greg). Greg died of prostatic cancer a few months ago, with bone and brain metastasis. Before the tragic progression of his disease, he had been a generous, hearty, playful man, and a profoundly religious one. During the seven long years of his disease, his wife (I will call her Susan) took care of him, forced to witness his piteous psycho-physical changes. In his last weeks of life, Greg suffered from horrific hallucinations that made him disavow Susan, assault her, and call her "bitch." In the end, Susan asked us to admit him to our hospice.

After Greg's death, she suffered from a severe depression. In that period she used to say she had died with her husband. With the passing of time and some antidepressant therapy, she recovered partially, sleeping, eating, and going out again. Nonetheless, she still couldn't think of herself as an independent person, a woman who could exist without her husband. She was unable to find some meaning in her life since she could not share it with Greg.

She also complained that she forgot things. I didn't believe she suffered from a real memory loss, but interpreted her symptoms as consequences of her depression. Inspired by Prof. Nesci's paper on multimedia psychotherapy, I decided to ask her to bring me photographs of her with her husband. She did so enthusiastically and began to recall with me, during our sessions, their life together. Each photo opened the door to endless memories! She was able to recover her relationship in great detail, and even her voice would become more fluent and lively as she was empowering herself more and more through her own personal storytelling about herself and Greg.

Today, she lives with one of her children, surrounded by the love and affection of her extended family. Meanwhile, she is writing her own photo album, which she calls, playfully, "X-ray of a Marriage." Five months after her husband's death, she feels she has a goal. She carries it out secretly, with me, smiling every time she anticipates the moment when she will share it with their children and present it to them as a gift. "When I am dying," she concludes, "I want them to know that I will not be sad, since I will be reunited with their father and be happy again!" By recovering her visual memories of their life together, she now feels better and experiences Greg's absence as more tolerable. It seems she is opening herself up to life once again, slowly and quietly.

The memorial photo, the poster, and the album are all useful tools for a normal mourning process. They allow those suffering from grief and loss to have access once again (after the inevitable immediate traumatic denials, repressions, and disavowals of death) to that virtual space where memories can find a space/time dimension *as if* the beloved person were still alive. In this way, we create extra time to adjust to the reality of his/her death and work through the painful mourning ritual for as long as we need it.

WORKING THROUGH MY MOTHER'S DEATH IN A TRAINING GROUP

by Elisabetta Corona, in collaboration with Domenico A. Nesci

Summer 2001 was special since I went to visit my mother twice, leaving my daughters with her on my first visit and returning once again for another week of holiday. Finally we left her to go back to "the mainland" (as people from Sardinia say when they speak about Italy). My mother did her best to cook for us and spoil us in many ways while we enjoyed our time together, as usual, at a place by the sea called "*sa petra ruia*" in Sardinian dialect (literally "the red rock," from the color of the earth there).

During my work collecting the pictures for multimedia psychotherapy, I realized I had many photos of the last year of my mother's life, but she did not appear in any of them. The training group helped me to understand that this was not by chance. Unconsciously my mother had probably managed to prepare herself to exit from the stage of life leaving a good image of herself; maybe she felt she shouldn't leave an image of herself where her illness could be detected in her changing facial features. That summer, in fact, she was always very tired, especially when she had to walk. I remember very well one hot, humid afternoon when I had suggested we take a walk together by the sea. We crossed the pine wood with difficulty; I had to help her on the Mediterranean dunes, arm-in-arm, until, finally, the blue sea water and the cool breeze gave us some relief.

I thought it was her diabetes, but I was wrong. Something much more serious was looming. In September, she was admitted urgently into the local hospital and diagnosed with incurable colon cancer. The doctors were shocked that she had not discovered it earlier. After her death, one of her best friends came to us full of sorrow and guilt feelings because my mother had confessed to her about a bleeding episode, but they had both ignored it. My mother had a very secretive personality, as one would expect from a respected Sardinian woman. According to the traditional local culture, to talk about such events would have been improper.

On the following Easter holiday, in 2002, my mother asked me explicitly (which was very uncommon for her) to return to Sardinia. Around her, there was now an atmosphere of quiet awareness of her incurable disease, but she was able to protect us from feeling overburdened by it. My daughters told me that during that holiday, "We didn't feel her suffering or any impending tragedy. Or actually, we *did* feel Grandma's suffering, but we were calm anyway."

In my case, the work of collecting my mother's pictures in order to share them with Professor Nesci and my colleagues in the psycho-oncology master's program allowed me to engage in the mourning process and face all the experiences of loss throughout my life. All changes and transformations imply a mourning experience, since we must always lose something to find something new. Always.

Images and Memories

Surprisingly, despite its focus on the theme of mourning, multimedia psychotherapy takes place in an atmosphere lightened by moments of joy and relief. The presentation of the pictures I had chosen of my mother's life aroused intense participation in the group. Our task was to select some of them (forty-two in my case) to build a "strip of life" that summarizes the highlights of my mother's life. Each picture can be associated with a short text, as a comment. Here I will present only ten pictures, a selection from the twenty-one photos I used for my master's thesis in psycho-oncology under the supervision of Professor Nesci, and I will reduce my comments to the theme I want to emphasize here: a mother who liberates herself and, by so doing, liberates her daughters as well.

The first pictures show my mother in traditional dress. In the photographic sequence, one can follow the transition from these images of my mother, rooted in her homeland customs and dedicated to hard work in the fields, to a new look in more modern clothes. (In Sardinia, we refer to not wearing the traditional clothes as "bourgeois wearing," an expression that is usually opposed, in Italian, to "wearing a uniform." This expression makes quite clear how Sardinian people see themselves as a tight unit, an attitude common to islanders in many parts of the world.) The change in dress is one step along a path of emancipation.

From this perspective, the traditional dress takes on a symbolic anthropological meaning, embodying the condition of a woman stifled by archaic cultural restrictions. The change of clothes frees her behavior just as removing a uniform frees the wearer from his/her institutional role. What is interesting here, in this particular process of emancipation, is the fact that it takes place gradually and silently, in the voiceless bodily language of a change of clothes (from fig. 2.1 to fig. 2.6).

The Sardinian dress, now abandoned by my mother, was carefully preserved in order to be handed down to her first niece. Actually it is still in my parents' home, where my father still lives. My mother was able to manage the delicate issue of what to do with this dress (and the precious spherical gold buttons to close the blouse, which seem like two female breasts) in such a way that both my sister and I were allowed not to wear it at our weddings without offending anyone in or out of the family. Long before this, she was also courageous enough to use it as a Carnival costume. On that occasion, the dress, so full of symbolic meanings, was reduced to a mask. Thanks to my mother, we were able to have fun dressing up as Sardinian women, together, wearing traditional dresses at a Carnival party (fig. 2.7). As one can easily see, she is wearing her real

Figure 2.1. My mother in festival dress, in Sardinia

Figure 2.2. My mother with my father on their wedding day

old Sardinian dress, but this time just for fun! Of course, many years had passed, at this point.

Memories and Sounds

The soundtrack is another essential element for the second memory object of multimedia psychotherapy, a video made with the pictures of the strip of life: the psychodynamic montage. The photographs proceed one after the other so that the person's entire life cycle runs within the time (and at the tempo) of a piece of music or a song. When Professor Nesci and the group invited me to freely associate the pictures of my mother with a melody, I felt a kind of disorientation, and nothing came to mind. Then, with the help of the group, pursuing the idea of a suitable music led me to associate with the sound of Sardinian dance music.

In this folk dance, women and men move in a circle, slowly at first, faster when the rhythm is rising, shaping figures of stars and concentric rings. The ritual dance is led by a man who assumes the role of choreographer, deciding the steps for the beginning, the figures for the following

Figure 2.3. A trip to the small Sardinian island of Caprera to visit Garibaldi's monument; the child is my sister. My mother greatly admired the "hero of the two worlds," also known as *El Libertador*—the Liberator—since he helped free many countries in South America and Europe before ending his days here in Caprera, in voluntary exile, feeling utterly betrayed by the Kingdom of Italy.

Figure 2.4. A picnic with my father preparing fresh mussels

passages, and the way it will conclude. While the dance is taking place, anyone who wants can join, but the new dancer must follow the steps being performed at that moment and synchronize with the rhythm.

After this first association, I remembered an old Sardinian lullaby my mother used to sing to me: "*spizza, spizza, pilor de oro*" (which means "comb, comb, hair of gold"), a melody sung to children while patting their heads to help them sleep. From this lullaby, another association emerged in the group with the Sardinian *No potho reposare* ("I cannot rest" or "I cannot sleep"), a love song that recounts the ageless story of two lovers expressing their mutual love as they face separation (a common problem for Sardinians who had to emigrate to find jobs and opportunities on the mainland, or, as we say, on the Continent). The text comes from one of the two twin poems *A Diosu* and *A Diosa* written by Salvatore Sini, a Sardinian poet, in 1915, while the music was composed by a third-generation Sardinian musician (whose family was originally from the Continent) in 1921. Today this song is often sung by contemporary Sardinian singers and groups.

Thus, in the end, the song chosen to be the soundtrack for the video was simultaneously very "old-fashioned" Sardinian and very "modern." Once again, the unconscious thread of associations had brought me to the interplay between ancient and modern, old and new. Perhaps this was a central theme in my mother's life, where the need to belong and the need to move on (women's liberation) interpenetrate and blend together.

Figure 2.5. Changing dress code and wearing "bourgeois" clothes

Figure 2.6. My mother with my father's Vespa

Perhaps this is a central theme in our training group in multimedia psychotherapy as well. We perform a kind of metaphorical "dance," in which everyone can join and work through his/her own mourning experience with the others while learning something new, without sacrificing the roots of our psychodynamic classical training (once again, harmoniously mixing our need to belong to a respected professional tradition

Figure 2.7. My mother and I at a Carnival celebration

with our need to promote its evolution in directions that allow the therapy to answer the emerging needs of our patients).

Multimedia psychotherapy is a flexible setting that places us in new virtual scenarios. The patient, the members of his/her extended family, the therapist, the multimedia artist, and all the students in training groups who are allowed to share the memory objects in order to learn the therapeutic process (not only here and now but also elsewhere in the future, thanks to recording technologies) join in a metaphorical ritual dance that parallels (in concentric rings) the video in which images, sounds, and words, all pulsating to the same rhythm, actually move (and "move" us too!) with the magic of cinema, the factory of dreams.

After I had taken the decision to use the song *No potho reposare* as my soundtrack, one final association occurred to me. There was an important difference in education between my sister and myself. She learned Sardinian as her first language and then had to learn Italian in school as an entirely new language. My mother recognized that this was a problem, so she scolded me every time I spoke Sardinian at home. She did so to prevent me from having trouble at school and to help me in this move toward emancipation. Once again, the change in language, like the change in dress code, was meant to open my mind and my future to a broader world, outside the island enclave of our homeland.

Freudian Slips, Lapses, and Acting Out

In multimedia psychotherapy, pictures are not only collected and selected; when they show something that we don't want to see, they are also discarded. In fact, one always has to keep in mind two different perspectives: on the one hand, unveiling repressed emotions and memories (the individual therapeutic aspect), and on the other, preparing a memory object that might be posted on the institute's website in order to help the process of mourning in those relatives and friends with whom the patient is planning to share the password (the group-individual therapeutic aspect, which Professor Nesci will discuss later in this book).

An interesting example of these complex double dynamics animated the beginning of our second group session, when I brought the pictures and shared them with the training group members. Professor Nesci saw that in some of my childhood pictures, I was in my mother's arms crying.

He pointed this out and asked me whether I would like to discard them. (In my specific case, the memory objects were planned to be visible to everybody, in the public part of the website, to encourage future patients to seek out this new form of psychotherapy.) He was worried I would feel bad thinking that unknown viewers might get a negative impression of my relationship with my parents (fig. 2.8 and fig. 2.9). Moreover, one specific picture I had selected was very "bad" from a photographic point of view (fig. 2.10).

At first I was really surprised since I hadn't seen I was crying in the pictures at all! Then I remembered very clearly that, as a child, I had always hated to be photographed since it meant that I had to stay still. The group members entered in the discussion and observed that, having

Figure 2.8. My first picture: I didn't ever like to be photographed at all!

this information and looking closely at the pictures where I was crying while my mother was smiling, holding me in her arms, none of them felt that the pictures gave a negative image of my mother and her relationship with me. "This is really a caring mother, a Mom who smiles since she knows her little girl very well and knows she's just crying for a whim, for the photo. It is a mother who is able to hold and care properly for her beloved little daughter."

By the end of the discussion, the entire group was deeply moved and unanimously decided that all pictures, including the "bad" one (fig. 2.10) should be displayed in the memory object. Personally, not only was I able to recover lost memories of myself as a child who loved running and moving around freely, who hated to stay still and feel constrained, for example, by the act of being photographed, but, even more important, I felt reassured about my mother's ability to play down, minimize, and take the heat out of any situation. To put it in psychoanalytic terms, I felt reassured she was "a good enough mother" (Winnicott 1951).

Writing my master's thesis, I committed a classic Freudian slip that is deeply associated with this episode: I made a mistake in writing the title of the song chosen for the soundtrack. Instead of writing *No potho repo-*

Figure 2.9. Crying in my father's arms

sare, I wrote *No photo reposare*. The unbelievable thing is that this very slip was repeated by Alessandra in her thesis as well!

Professor Nesci associated all these Freudian slips with another acting out that came to the surface in my thesis. Instead of writing my comments to all the pictures as planned, I stopped precisely at the picture where I first appeared in my mother's strip of life and then skipped to the last image, with my parents by the sea, ending my reflections there. It was only during the work of writing this text that Professor Nesci gave me his interpretation of these unconscious dynamics. I was acting out my childhood hatred for being frozen, constrained, stopped in a picture. "No photo!" I don't want to be photographed. "*No re-posare*!" I don't want to "pose" any more, to exit from the flow of life, which is to me, unconsciously, a perpetual movement.

Work in Progress

An apt metaphor for multimedia psychotherapy is a construction site with a sign saying "work in progress." In fact, you are continually working through your mourning experience, within the therapy (and/or the training group) as well as outside of it. You are working at both an individual level and a group level since an extended family of relatives

Figure 2.10. Crying in my mother's arms

and friends, a sort of primal clan, is invited to share your memory objects and join the ritual dance of the life cycle of that person who lived and died, and whom you want to be remembered. Different aspects come to the fore in different moments in an audiovisual dance where figure and ground play surprising tricks. That is why I don't consider my experience as a patient/student/therapist in this challenging field something that has come to its conclusion.

At the moment, if I should try to summarize my experience, I would say what I said in the last session of our training group: I feel that this work, the construction of my mother's strip of life and psychodynamic montage, are a tribute to her. Certainly, beyond that, these memory objects also celebrate the liberation of my mother, as a woman, from her traditional cultural roles. An anthropological story is being told within the personal story. It is a "moving" documentation of a fight that has been waged silently, peacefully, and courageously by many women in Sardinia, my beloved homeland.

I will end my story with an observation by Professor Nesci, who helped me acknowledge the way it all began. One day, I told him my twin teenage daughters had been admitted to a well-known dance school in northern Italy, and that I was terribly anxious about letting them go. It was there and then that he suggested that I be the "patient" in this new group setting, in the master of psycho-oncology, and I accepted. Today, I know why. I had a deep need for support to be able to let them go to live their own lives. I had to remember and recover a "new" image of my own mother and finally understand more fully what she had done for me, when I was the daughter and she was the parent. She let me go!

Suddenly, my first (discarded) association with dance music for the soundtrack of my mother's video became meaningful to me.

THE SELECTION OF IMAGES: REFLECTIONS

by Alessandra Monfeli, in collaboration with Domenico A. Nesci

The selection of images in multimedia psychotherapy depends on two basic principles: meaningfulness and acceptability. A picture must be meaningful to the individual (patient/student/therapist) to be included as a memory object, but it also must be acceptable to the audience that each individual has in mind. During Elisabetta's work in our training group, I often thought she had selected pictures with a cultural rather than a personal theme in order to make them acceptable to a universal audience. (Professor Nesci's original idea was to make Elisabetta's montage visible on the web to encourage prospective patients to ask for multimedia psychotherapy.) Nevertheless, I actively took part in the discussions. It was only after our meetings, and outside the group, that I allowed myself to reflect on my doubts about the personal meaningfulness of what Elisabetta was bringing into our sessions.

What was personal in the theme of liberation from old habits? At first I couldn't see anything very personal. Interestingly, talking with Elisabetta outside the group, she said exactly the same thing about my contribution to the group meetings. She suggested that I had a resistance to involving myself at a more personal level and sharing more of the emotions associated with my mourning experience after the death of my second child.

Not until I was writing my thesis did I slowly begin to realize that the theme of liberation pursued by Elisabetta was indeed very personal and profoundly linked to the core of her relationship with her mother: she was appreciating the fact that her mother had allowed her to separate, had let her go and relocate away from their native island. This (culturally) acceptable theme (emancipation) was in fact personally meaningful (for Elisabetta) since it had taken shape when she had to let her own adolescent daughters leave her and go north, to another Italian city, to pursue their passion for dance.

It was then, when I understood and acknowledged the personal relevance of her work (dealing with separation-individuation from her daughters), that I began to understand my own work and to uncover, slowly and gradually, the deep associations between Elisabetta's mourning for her mother and my own work of elaboration of my child's death. Actually, in my case, what I was doing was not just working through oncologic death, but something more general and profound: moving on in my own personal development, freeing myself from something (a mental state, a psychological belief, a personal situation) that was paralyzing me. Like Elisabetta's mother, I was fighting my own liberation struggle!

At the end of our work, while writing my thesis, I had a dream that helped me to "see" some unconscious events in my inner world. Here is the dream:

> I am in a building with many interconnecting rooms where activities are taking place simultaneously. I enter one of these rooms through a trapdoor in the floor (though I do not know how I was able to get there). The room is full of people and objects, perhaps sewing machines. I see Francesca (a colleague in our training group). I say something to her and exit. I enter another room, which is empty. I enter through the door this time and a male figure (perhaps a colleague from the master's program) enters immediately after me and begins to hug and kiss me (which I like). Then a lot of people arrive and one of them, pointing his index finger in a peremptory manner, reprimands me saying, "Does your current partner know you're pregnant?" I reply, "I'm not pregnant. I just eat a lot!"

> Then I find out that the building (which in my dream I now see from the outside) consists of two or perhaps more buildings connected at various levels. I see them now from a central perspective and from below. Looking up, I see that they end with terraces covered by a mobile structure made of two layers of curtains: the lower layer is made of lace while the upper layer is made of a dark green waterproof fabric. Someone tells me that I am at the Policlinico Gemelli and that this is the congress that concludes the master in psycho-oncology. Inside each of the rooms of the different buildings, parallel activities are taking place (I immediately think of the room where I had seen Francesca), while on the two terraces, the most important papers will be presented, open only to high-level participants. I reflect on the fact that the whole thing, this multiform arrangement, must have been extremely expensive for the Policlinico Gemelli. Someone answers my thoughts (maybe it's Professor Nesci in person) that it doesn't matter since there will be a much higher economic return.

I sent the dream by e-mail to Professor Nesci. Not until much later, however, several months after the end of the master's program, several months after I had enrolled in SIPSI to be trained as a psychotherapist, sponsored by the same nonprofit organization (AGOP) that had previously sponsored my master in psycho-oncology, did I openly discuss my personal path into the training group with Prof. Nesci, face-to-face.

During our meeting aimed at completing this text, it emerged that, among other things, the dream was revealing that the death of my second child had made it possible for me to begin a process of liberation. In fact, I had started my individual psychotherapy, as a patient, after the death of my child, and what had resulted from my therapy, gradually and very slowly, was a process of separation-individuation (Mahler 1968) that continued to unfold and develop in the training group on multimedia psychotherapy as well as in my actual training in psychotherapy at SIPSI. Like Elisabetta's mother, I also had to leave a mental uniform, a traditional archaic dress, and engage in the expensive task of changing habits, wearing a dress for every different situation, adjusting to the changing circumstances of life in my inner and outer environments.

The association between Elisabetta's mother's evolution (made possible by her daughters) with my own emancipation (made possible by my son's illness and death) appeared clearly in my mind. Tragic as it is, let me put it in a few words: children can help their parents to grow, not just when they come to life but even when they die.

Death confronts us with separation and obliges us to face it and work it through.

Elisabetta presented us her mother's life as a path in which, gradually, at every pause, something changed (the shirt, the dress) or something new appeared (a modern watch on her wrist). Elisabetta's mother was aware that changing habits was a difficult task. In fact, her husband

(Elisabetta's father) had explicitly told her, "If you take off the traditional gown, the Sardinian dress, you will need more than one dress to replace it!" At the same time, being a tailor, he was ready to help her practically. As in my dream, making new "multiform arrangements" is expensive. Freud taught us that there is an "economic" aspect at work in human development. Discovering something new (in fact, rooms and buildings in dreams often represent mental places and opportunities, inside and outside us) presents a challenge to find the energy to move on in the path of separation-individuation, to move on in the process of mourning as well as of normal development.

What I have discovered during our training group, and maybe was trying to keep for myself, in a secret room, was the inexorable awareness that the death of my second son had liberated me from all the previous "traps" that had kept me from coming up through the "trapdoor," entering "our adult world" (Klein 1959), and trying to work through its multiform complexity in order to move on in the cycle of life. What I hope to discover, in the future, is that all these "extremely expensive . . . multiform arrangements" will eventually bring, metaphorically speaking, in Freudian terms, "a much higher economic return."

THE MAGIC OF MUSIC: ECHOES

by Sabrina Podda, in collaboration with Domenico A. Nesci

As soon as I completed my four-year training program in psychotherapy at SIPSI, I enrolled in the master's program in psycho-oncology at UCSC, whose coordinators were also the codirectors of my School of Psychotherapy. It was a way to complete my training in psycho-oncology (a discipline that is taught extensively at SIPSI) and, at the same time, to work through my "mourning experience" as a graduate student in psychotherapy, continuing to learn from Prof. Nesci and Dr. Poliseno in a different setting. Graduating in psychotherapy and going into private practice are some of those ritual passages of life that require elaboration.

During the master's program in psycho-oncology , together with four other students (Francesca, Alessandra, Marina, and Elisabetta), I was invited by Prof. Nesci to write my master's thesis on multimedia psychotherapy, a new form of psychodynamic treatment he had originally developed to help relatives of cancer patients to work through their mourning experience. Although I knew I couldn't be present at all the group sessions scheduled for the project (aimed at producing five theses, which would be edited by Prof. Nesci and partially translated into English to be included in his forthcoming book on multimedia psychotherapy), I decided to take the challenge and accept the invitation. Actually, I could hardly have made any other choice: Elisabetta was a dear colleague of mine at SIPSI. What's more, I was grateful to her for helping me work in a community program during my residency, and I knew it was she who would generously be the "patient" in our "training group," presenting her own mourning experience for the death of her mother. How could I not be by her side?

I cannot deny that my associations with the pictures brought to the group by Elisabetta helped me a lot to begin my own inner journey in search of my lost mourning experiences. I prefer to leave that for later, however.

Here and now, I would rather focus on an interesting episode of my own acting out. I was absent from the first two sessions of our training group, when it could be assumed that Elisabetta was going to talk about her mother and recount her story. Of course I received a summary and some excerpts from the other group members, but I missed those first two sessions, during which they also completed the selection of images. I was present, however, at the third meeting, when Prof. Nesci asked us to help Elisabetta choose the music for the soundtrack of her memory object. Although I'd had "real" reasons that made it impossible for me to participate in the first two sessions, today I recognize that I also had an unconscious motivation: to allow Elisabetta to feel more comfortable and open herself more freely, thanks to my absence. The fact is that Elisabetta and I both come from Sardinia, an island where people are all very reserved and don't like to open up about private things and personal emotions, especially if other Sardinians are there to watch and listen.

The Third Meeting

At the beginning of the third meeting, Prof. Nesci encouraged us to help Elisabetta in her search for music to use as the soundtrack of the memory object we were trying to produce. I immediately felt personally involved since I spontaneously associated with sound memories of my own childhood, adolescence, and adult life. What a powerful natural magic links memories and sounds!

In his book *Il pensiero del cuore* (Gaita 1971) the Italian psychiatrist and musician writes that music communicates in a way that cannot be translated into words insofar as it automatically calls forth emotions and affects that follow different paths from those of language. Music manages to pass through our bodies, evoking "the mother, the god, the myth of cosmos and the universe" without speaking any words at all. Gaita describes music as "sensorial" and "evocative," rather than "representative," of the maternal object.

In *The Golden Bough: A Study in Magic and Religion* (Frazer 1915), the famous Scottish anthropologist emphasizes the magic power of music.

> We cannot doubt that this, the most intimate and affecting of all the arts, has done much to modifying more or less deeply the fabric of belief to which at first sight it seems only to minister. [. . .] Every faith has its appropriate music, and the difference between the creeds might almost be expressed in musical notations. [. . .] A different spirit breathes in the difference of the music. (344)

Psychiatry and anthropology seem to move together in the same direction, pointing toward the spiritual aspects that music evokes in the human mind.

I believe that death is something very intimate, deeply associated with everyone's personal sensitivity and spirituality. Whether we conceive of death as just the end of an individual life or as the last "passage" of a mysterious ritual in the life cycle, it is a fact that mankind resorts to music as the universal reminder of what we have lost irremediably and yet go on mourning in our hearts. With the magic of sounds, music alone can answer questions, anxieties, and dilemmas that are unanswerable with words.

Music is profoundly associated with movement, be it a movement of the body, of the mind, or of the soul. The song chosen by Elisabetta within the "ritual dance" of our third training group session bears a double message: "I cannot rest" (*no potho reposare*, in Sardinian dialect, the song's title) implies both the need for movement and, paradoxically, the impossibility of moving out of a stalled, constrained, or frozen state. In fact, the lyrics of the song describe a scene where two lovers are separated by a great distance and cannot reunite although they ardently long to. (We might fantasize that one is in Sardinia and the other on the mainland, divided by the deep and perilous sea.) They really hope to God to be together again forever!

Next follows my associations with a clinical experience, first with Ernest, whom I saw in psychotherapy once a week until he died of cancer, and then with his wife Lydia, in both cases in a unique, personalized setting. The story would not have followed the unusual course it did if multimedia psychotherapy had not already been in Prof. Nesci's mind when I started seeing Ernest.

Ernest and Lydia

Ernest was a cancer patient who had been referred to me while I was in training as a SIPSI graduate student in psychotherapy at the Consultation Liaison-Psychiatry Unit of the Policlinico Universitario "Agostino Gemelli" under the supervision of Prof. Nesci. Our psychotherapy sessions were scheduled once a week and went on for six months during which I saw him as an outpatient of the unit, part of the Italian National Health Service. Lydia would always accompany Ernest to the session and wait for him outside the consultation room, with a warm supportive attitude towards both her husband and myself. When his health went into rapid decline, we had to discontinue therapy quite suddenly. He died shortly thereafter. Lydia called me on the phone two months later, asking me to meet her at their home. I was confused by this request since I had never considered the idea of a home visit, before. Nonetheless, I felt I should meet with her, so I accepted her invitation.

Today I am aware of unconscious countertransference motivations that might have determined my decision. The fact is that when my maternal grandfather, to whom I was deeply attached, developed lung cancer, I took care of him during the whole course of the disease until he breathed his last breath at the age of seventy-six. Naturally, when Prof. Nesci first described Ernest's case, during our team meeting at the hospital when new patients are assigned to the SIPSI students in psychotherapy, I immediately associated him with my grandfather. So I willingly agreed to work with Ernest, even though I was aware that he was destined to die of cancer. Today I recognize that, unconsciously as well as consciously, taking care of Ernest was a way to work through the painful "passage" of my grandfather's death, my first mourning experience.

Ernest was a good-looking, reliable, seventy-six-year-old gentleman whose appearance did not betray the fact that he was taking high doses of painkillers. He was a scholar, author of scientific books and papers, and a member of international scientific associations who had worked with prestigious American universities. What really impressed me, however, was not just his extensive culture but his inner depth, openness, and capacity to engage himself in a psychological encounter in such a dramatic moment of his life. Thanks to these qualities, he was able to overcome the usual initial resistances in a psychodynamic path and face the course of his illness in the best way possible.

Now, let's go back to Lydia's telephone call.

Home Visiting

At the appointed time, Lydia came to open the door and welcomed me with her usual trim and unpretentious look. She was a refined, naturally elegant, trustworthy eighty-year-old lady who had shared about sixty years of her life with her husband. They had met at university when they were very young and had stayed together since then. They had five children. After the birth of their second child, they decided she should stop working as a university researcher in order to look after the children and support her husband's career, full time. They had the same interests, the same passions, and lived a harmonious marriage with absolute solidarity. When he was abroad, doing research or lecturing, she always went with him, helping and encouraging his scientific efforts. In the long years of his fatal disease, they supported each other with mutual, tender, loving care. When his illness degenerated and he became bed-bound, she nursed him at home attentively, well aware of the psychophysical changes that she was watching over, holding his hand, day and night.

In my countertransference, I felt this same affect, which she was now directing at me as if I were the intimate custodian of her husband's last moments. She treated me with freshly squeezed orange juice and sweets from Tuscany, the same kind of sweets she used to relish on her husband in their afternoon breaks. She confessed that she felt lost and disoriented without him. She felt she had arrived at his death unprepared, which filled her with rage against herself. She could have done more, listened to him more, understood him more, asked him the password of his personal computer so that she might continue his unfinished research.

She showed me many pictures that documented their life together. Meanwhile, I listened and observed her gestures very carefully, trying to relax and enter a free-floating-attention state of mind, following the flow of emotions as I had done with her husband during our sessions at the hospital. In effect, I tried to receive and hold her grief while listening.

The image I got was of a union capable of going beyond all limits.

She took me into her husband's office, the place I had imagined so many times when he was talking to me about his work. I was impressed by the brightness of the room and by the fact that every corner and every object "told" something about them. I "recognized" the lamp and the armchair, that creative spot so dear to her husband, where he used to think or rest after his work, up to the last days of his life. At a certain point, Lydia gave me a book saying, "Please take this, my husband really wished to give it to you and was planning to bring it in one of the future sessions."

Nearly speechless, I managed to thank her. I mentioned that during therapy he had talked a lot to me about this last work he had published. Then she took me to his desk, where she began flipping through notes he had written a few moments before his death. She chose one and gave it to me, once again confessing to me how hard it was for her to go on without him. She explained that she spent a lot of time in that room, since he wasn't around anymore. Every evening, she would switch on the lamp beside his armchair and play his favorite music. I asked what it was, and she told me Mozart, especially *The Magic Flute*. At night she left the lamp on as a way to feel that he was still close by.

We agreed to meet again. In fact, we still meet once every month, trying to work through her loss and grief.

An Unusual Therapy

At SIPSI we are trained to focus very seriously on Freud's perspective on the construction of what is called "setting" in psychoanalysis. As is well known (Fachinelli 1983), Freud explicitly wrote that his "technique" (1912, 1913) regarding time, place, and payment (as well as any other element that contributes to the concrete frame of the analytic work) was designed by him for his own personality, not as a rule for all therapists to follow. Nevertheless, psychotherapists generally feel uneasy when they depart from the "classical" (orthodox?) rules. Thus, when I felt distressed at having adjusted the setting of my psychodynamic work to Lydia's needs rather than to the classical rules, I sought out Prof. Nesci for reassurance that what I was doing was "meaningful and acceptable" (as Alessandra writes in her thesis), not only for the patient but also for my professional identity.

During our sessions, I would let Lydia tell me whatever she felt comfortable saying, sharing her memories. When she felt like it, we also read Ernest's writings together and looked at her family photographs. Her "stories" changed gradually, turning into concrete memory objects, which I proposed that she arrange in chronological order, as Prof. Nesci was doing in multimedia psychotherapy, so that the sequence of her life with her husband might be reviewed. She responded enthusiastically, as Prof. Nesci's first patient, since we were actually doing a kind of multimedia psychotherapy, spontaneously, without giving it any title. We both felt the need to concretize our shared work of elaboration, to leave traces of it.

I noticed that when she shared pictures with me, the image served as a creative trigger to recall events and reanimate her storytelling. The narrative was more detailed, the tone of her voice more fluent; her spirit was elated and she no longer seemed depressed. We ended up with the idea of creating a traditional "album of *mémoires*" since that was a familiar medium for both of us. I didn't mention to her the possibility of producing a digital strip of life or psychodynamic montage (Nesci 2009) for Internet. She often smiles to herself, imagining the moment when she will present the album to her sons, daughters, and nephews.

Today, through this psychotherapeutic work of elaboration, Ernest's absence has become more tolerable to Lydia, and she is gradually opening up herself to life once again.

It is a rebirth. She has started traveling in Europe to visit her relatives again and even attends, on some special occasions, the scientific congresses she used to attend with Ernest. The notes of *The Magic Flute* evoke more reassuring echoes in Lydia's mind now, through the memories of the storytelling we shared in our home sessions as well as through the reflections of her "album of *mémoires*."

AFTERTHOUGHTS

The "training group" experience, as described by my students in the previous parts of this chapter, shows two aspects of multimedia psychotherapy. The first essential feature of the new technique is that it has the potential to take countless shapes. In other words, multimedia psychotherapy cannot be reduced to a series of pictures edited with a soundtrack to become a video (the original psychodynamic montage). Multimedia psychotherapy is in fact a psychoanalytic attitude that enables a psychotherapist to take into account every audiovisual object carried by the patient, exactly like a dream, a lapse, or any other spontaneous communication, and to help the patient associate, remember, and work it through in the sessions. The multimedia objects become the "medium" (Marina) or the "shortcut" (Francesca) that facilitates the common work of patient and therapist and makes it more familiar. Moreover, having in mind the project to produce a concrete memory object, the frequent (paradoxical) inhibition generated by the "golden rule" of asking the patient "to say anything that comes to mind" can be easily overcome. This is an important advantage if we think, for example, of our psychotherapeutic work with older patients.

The second essential feature has to do with the fact that multimedia psychotherapy implies the individual's and the group-individual's perspectives. Each patient, as an individual, has a personal view of what is proper in selecting the pictures (or other multimedia items) and organizing them into multiform memory objects. At the same time, each patient, as a group-individual, has a psychosocial view related to his/her own family/clan/local culture. The individual and the group-individual levels are interconnected and influence each other, as is suggested by the interconnecting rooms and buildings of Alessandra's dream. All the more so when we are confronted with the problem of mourning, of the ritual passages of life and the anxieties they have inevitably triggered in all human beings from time immemorial.

We find ourselves here at the roots of our need for psychotherapy, as in the cases of Alessandra (in the aftermath of the death of her second child) and Elisabetta (confronted with the impending separation from her twin daughters, the "real" mourning process that reawakened her need to further elaborate the prior loss of her mother). Nobody goes to see a therapist when he/she is happy, healthy, and full of hope. If we ask for psychotherapy it means we feel lost, disoriented, anxious, or depressed. In order to clarify the importance of this distinction between individual and group-individual levels of the mind in psychotherapy, I would like to pose a radical question: what is psychotherapy?

What is Psychotherapy?

Let me answer this inconvenient question by telling a story. It is the story of a ritual that has been documented in different cultures in different parts of the world, a ritual that was celebrated any time a member of a community disappeared in critical circumstances (a war, an expedition, a hunt, etc.) and was thought to be dead but then, unexpectedly, returned to the village alive. In these cases, the ritual to reintegrate the supposedly dead member of the group consisted of prescribing the "patient" to repeat, one after the other, all the rites of passage he/she had overcome before getting lost. The rites of birth, childhood, adolescence, adulthood, had to be reenacted very carefully so that, in the end, the member could be readmitted to his/her previous social role and identity.

The idea underlying this ritual is illuminating. If group members had gotten lost and were unable to find their way to the village/homeland, it is because something went wrong in their rites of passage. This meant that the subjects had not received the training needed (in the liminal transitions through the NOT-X/NOT-Y states) to fully reach the state in which they got lost. If a group member gets lost at stage D, for example, this happens because something went wrong in the previous rites of passage (from A to B to C to D). By performing all the ritual passages again, the community repairs the member's capacity to keep from getting lost in life, to know who he/she is and where he/she belongs.

To me, psychotherapy is a metaphorical version of this ritual (Nesci 1993). In fact, it requires the patient to go back in time (regress) and re-experience the critical passages of life (in Freudian terms, repeat, remember, and work through) in order to repair, within the suspended space/time coordinates of the therapeutic setting, whatever was damaged or left incomplete in the phases of development. Psychotherapy constructs a liminal setting in order to complete the failed transformations/transitions from one stage to the next in the life cycle.

Of course, psychotherapy is different from the old reintegration ritual since its goal is to let the patient free, once he/she is reintegrated in his/her own Self. The patient of today is not like a member of a prehistoric community. Today we are individuals too, not just group-individuals. In our rapidly changing world, we have to face the challenge of constantly reconstructing ourselves as individuals, for as long as we live.

Multimedia Psychotherapy and the Group-Individual

As we will explore in the following chapters, there is no such thing as an individual in the prehistory of the human race, anthropologically speaking. We are born as group-individuals and only gradually have we progressed and developed to become individual members of human communities, tribes, clans, and families. In the evolution of our species, the individual level is surely the most developed but not the most important level. The individual level is more rational and has to do with words as symbolic shared meanings and the capacity to live as a separate being, while the group-individual level is more emotional and has to do with words as sounds, "orality" rather than "literacy" (Ong 1982), and the need to live in a symbiotic organization where everyone feels part of a broader social body. When we suffer and are in need of help, we need that help on both levels: as individuals and as group-individuals.

When it works effectively, psychotherapy does just that. A "good enough" treatment is one that helps the patient to reach a "good enough" balance between the individual and the group-individual layers of the Self. Multimedia psychotherapy, working directly and indirectly (through the help of the artist) with images and sounds as well as with words, is a re-creative and reparative process (independent of the individual or group setting we choose to use with our patient) because it invariably bridges the gap between individual and group-individual levels of the mind, and thereby contributes to their integration.

Multimedia psychotherapy is able to do this effectively largely because it introduces the triangulation among patient-therapist-artist. Actually, this is one of its unique aspects. The memory objects of multimedia psychotherapy are elaborated by a third person: the multimedia artist. From this perspective, multimedia psychotherapy implies not only a patient-therapist relationship but also a professional relationship between the multimedia artist and the therapist (while in traditional art therapies, the therapist is an artist too and plays two roles within the cure). The real-life presence of the third person in the scenario of multimedia psychotherapy opens its horizon to the group level of mental functioning and requires a deeper understanding of the anthropological concept of the "group-individual" as theorized by Robert Briffault (1927). In fact, Briffault's ideas are absolutely central to our discourse.

> One of the most fundamental and startling differences between the mentality of primitive humanity and the current conception of human nature is the degree, almost inconceivable to us, to which the sentiment of individuality is undeveloped in the primitive mind. [. . .] A savage will not only identify himself with an animal, or a tree, or even a stone; he will say that his son or his brother is "himself," he will tell you with no perception of inconsistency that he is here and that he is at the same time somewhere else. He quite seriously regards any detached portion of his body as a part of himself; his hair, nail-parings, spittle are accounted parts of his person, and what befalls them after they are separated from the body affects him also. [. . .] In the same way an injury to a member of the group to which he belongs, to one who is one flesh with him, is an injury suffered by himself. He resents it not by virtue of magnanimous sentiments, or elevated principles of honor, or sublime ethical faith, but because of the hazy conceptions of individuality which permit his complete identification with the group. He does not think in terms of his ego and his interests, but in terms of the group-individual. (499)

On another occasion, using a bodily metaphor, I defined Briffault's "primitive" human groups as psychologically syncytial (Nesci 1991). In biology, a syncytium is a cell organization where the individual boundaries (membranes) between single members (cells) disappear in order to strengthen the group's ability to implant itself into a given environment.

In nature, this is essential to survival during the very first stages of life. After the first cell of a new human being is born of the fertilization of the ovum by a spermatozoon, it gradually transforms itself, through a series of cell divisions, into a blastocyst, a bubble-like cellular organization containing and protecting the cluster of cells out of which the embryo will develop. In rapid reproductive activity, the outer cells of the blastocyst become differentiated into two layers, one internal and one external (respectively, cito- and syncytio-trophoblast).

The syncytiotrophoblasts have a characteristic that is unique among all human cells. They transform into a syncytium, that is, a multinucleate mass of protoplasm resulting from the fusion of the original cells: a cellular organization with no individual limits, with no boundaries (individual membranes) separating its cells. Because of this, thanks to its external syncytial layer, the blastocyst can easily infiltrate the uterine wall (its environment) and allow the embryonic core to be implanted there.

Interestingly, this is also true if we look at things from an anthropological, evolutionary perspective, since an excess of individuation would have been counterproductive for the survival of the human species during the initial phases of its ecological adaptation. For example, in a syncytial group, if the mother of a baby dies during delivery, all the other mothers will milk and nurse the newborn. Indeed, the syncytial group was the only possible organization for the survival of the first human communities.

Syncytial Mourning . . .

No dynamic equilibrium is perfect, however. The obvious advantages of a syncytial organization (such as the implicit possibility of raising children collectively and compensating for death or any disability of the individual natural mother) could be offset at times by its disadvantages. Above all there was the danger that any internal evil would wreak havoc in the whole structure rather than being limited to one single person.

Anthropological literature seems to confirm this dangerous aspect in the case of the death of a group member as well as of any other collective "mourning" experience, such as famines, epidemics, and so on. Róheim (1945a), commenting on Tylor's studies on funerary rituals (1903) in "primitive" cultures, formulated (and rejected) the "impossible" hypothesis that human groups were originally so fusional in their organization that they were exposed to the danger of collective suicide every time there was a single death in the community.

> Thus the mourners may fast or they may deprive themselves of the staple food; they may lacerate their body or cut their hair, or they may cut their finger joints. Tylor has interpreted these customs as instances

> of sacrificial substitution where the part represents the whole; the amputated finger joint stands for the whole person of the mourner. If this is interpreted as meaning historical sequence it would lead to the impossible conclusion that whole groups of people or even whole tribes were once killed off after every single death. (Róheim 1945a, 35)

Paradoxical as it is, I think this "impossible conclusion" is not impossible at all, as I have documented in my ethnopsychoanalytic study of suicidal communities (Nesci 1999). Here I will only try to make the unconscious dynamics of mourning in the group-individual mind more understandable through an analysis of two prehistoric funerary rituals that provide a dramatic description of what I mean by "syncytial mourning."

In Australia, among the Warramunga, whenever someone in the group was about to die, all the other members would pile themselves on top of him/her in a human mountain. They would then inflict wounds upon themselves and lament incessantly, while crushing him/her to death under their weight, in a sort of prehistoric "heroic treatment" by their own blood and tears and the violent inclusion of the dying member in the human mass of their own bodies. The ritual acted out the impossibility of accepting separation, the need to remain a whole fusional group, in life (rescuing the dying individual) or in death (killing themselves in order to die together). When death finally occurred, the rite would be repeated and the corpse removed from the village. Eventually, the village itself was destroyed and deserted (Spencer and Gillen 1904, 516–519).

The natural death of a single member was experienced as a mutilation of the social body, a bleeding wound inflicted on all the members of the group who did not want to be separated from him and even feared/wished to be dragged into death together with him. In a syncytial culture, precisely because of the absence of limits/boundaries, imitation and dramatization were the prevalent psychodynamic mechanisms of the group-individuals. Everything was thrown into jeopardy when a death occurred. The social body, which had been destroyed symbolically (and, in part, materially), had to be reimplanted elsewhere.

A slightly more developed pattern (based on the dynamics of oral introjection, in addition to imitation and dramatization) can be found among the Duau of Normanby Island.

> In Duau society we have the *susu* (breast), the group of those who are descended from the same uterine ancestor, as the social unit. [. . .] The members of this fictive unit have "one body" and are supposed never to harbour any hostility against each other. But after each death, that is whenever the mother-child unit is disrupted, they are tested by eating *bwabware* which will automatically kill them for any hostile emotions against the members of their own *susu*. (Róheim 1945a, 87)

The poison ordeal after each death was not a rite exclusive to this people. It was so widespread in Africa during the period of the slave trade as to bring about a considerable depopulation (Goldie 1901; Perrot et Vogt 1913; Frazer 1915). Nonetheless, the practice continued until it was suppressed by the European colonizers. The people submitted to it willingly, in fact, convinced that they were demonstrating their own innocence to the dead person and to the group. At that stage of civilization, the disavowal of dying as the natural limit of each individual life contributed to a cultural interpretation of death as murder by magic. Any death represented a sign of hostility within the group and was experienced as a threat of dismemberment for the whole community. If too many deaths or misfortunes were occurring in the community, the entire tribe had to be tested by the poison ordeal. The casualties of this ordeal neutralized the "scandal of limits" (natural death, individuality, in-group hostility). In this way the syncytial group could be regenerated, like a snake that molts its old skin, and then be reimplanted into the womb of the mother (the homeland of the people).

. . . And Its Cure

To prevent such tragedies, new beliefs and rituals appeared during the course of the evolution of humankind, all cast in the mold of the double. Whether it be a belief in eternal doubles—the mythical ancestors of the Australian Aborigines, the "Eternal Ones of the Dream," as Géza Róheim called them in his ethnopsychoanalytic study (1945b)—or in an immortal soul (as many believe today), the treatment of syncytial mourning involves shaping something that can cure our anxiety about finitude. Whether it be supported by the idea of resurrection, reincarnation, or time as an eternal return (Éliade 1954), the individual mind is always shaping concrete symbolic objects to work through syncytial mourning and prevent the dangerous self-destructive rituals enacted by the group-individual. Following this evolutionary path, we arrive at the scenario of the *ricordino,* so accurately described by Francesca in her experience with families of terminal patients.

When we mourn, we mourn on both the individual level and the group-individual level. Multimedia psychotherapy is an excellent tool if we keep aware of this complexity. We can use it to help cure our patients not only as rational individuals but also as syncytial group-individuals when they suffer from a critical aspect during a passage in their life cycle and need to mourn the loss of some internal or external "love object" that, on an unconscious level, is part of their own Self.

Mourning and the Production of Memory Objects

While I was working in our training group, with Marina, Elisabetta, Francesca, Alessandra, and Sabrina, I was also teaching my first graduate course in multimedia psychotherapy at UCSC. The feedback I received from the students in the course was provocative. They all thought my technique could be used not only in psycho-oncology but also in any actual death to help the mourning process.

Then I suddenly had an insight. My students were right, but there was even more to it! Isn't it always a "mourning" experience that brings a person to ask for psychotherapy? Shouldn't I try to experiment with multimedia psychotherapy in other situations, unrelated to any actual death? I talked about these questions with my son, Filippo A. Nesci, the multimedia artist, and he encouraged me to try and explore this new dimension. Beyond that, he suggested that we could even make memory objects for newborn babies, since in the womb no one can see what their parents look like nor know what they are doing.

I immediately associated his idea with an ancient ritual custom still carried out by the Australian Aborigines. Whenever a baby is born, they make a *tjurunga*. The *tjurunga* is a sacred object made of wood or stone on which the mythical trail of the ancestor is depicted. Usually they make two such objects. The smaller one is called a "bull-roarer" and can be tied with a string and played to produce sounds. In my association, I saw it as the prototype of our contemporary multimedia objects!

Once again, as in the airplane flying from Asia to my old world (Europe), I had the powerful feeling that what I was trying to develop was meaningful and useful to bridge the gap between our prehistoric unconscious mind and our contemporary awareness, between the group-individual and the individual minds. In other words, I felt it was definitely worthwhile to go on developing multimedia psychotherapy for any type of clinical situation given its potential to promote integration between old and new layers of our Self.

At the same time, my son's idea reassured me that I should not be afraid to imagine and experiment multiform (individual as well as group) settings for multimedia psychotherapy. The development of a new technique is justified to meet the needs of patients, so the setting has to be conceived as a work-in-progress itself, as a transitional object rather than as a fetish or immutable set of rules. This "transient" aspect of multimedia psychotherapy inevitably produces anxiety, so I began to develop a workshop (the Clinic and Dreams Workshop) where these new clinical experiences could be shared and supervised by two or three group leaders.

In the following chapters, I am going to present other cases and clinical vignettes to illustrate my therapy, step by step: when and how to offer it, how to work with the pictures, how to choose the soundtrack, how to present the memory object to the patient, and what kind of triangulations are likely to occur among patient, therapist, and multimedia artist. Before we proceed into this clinical part of my work, however, let me end here with one final consideration.

Multimedia psychotherapy offers a concrete metaphor of the intrinsic openness and multiform complexity of the therapeutic process. Actually, once a multimedia object is made, there are a multitude of things the patient can do with it, from handing it on to relatives and friends, as in the case of Susan's "X-Ray of a Marriage" and Lydia's traditional "album of *memoires*," to posting it on the web protected by a password, as in Serena's case, to analyzing it further in other situations, as in Elisabetta's and Alessandra's cases, to ignoring it or leaving it incomplete on the therapist's desk. Regardless, in every case, we as therapists are there to share the multimedia object with our patients and let them use it the way they want or can at that moment of their life. What is precious, for them as for us, is the feeling that we have done something useful and concrete in the course of our psychotherapeutic work, something that reassures not only the individual but also the group-individual that lives inside us and needs to touch and be touched, eternally.

THREE

Multimedia Psychotherapy Step by Step: From Intake to Outcome

In this and the following four chapters, I will review the process of multimedia psychotherapy by describing its phases step by step: the intake, selection of the pictures, choice of the soundtrack, collaboration with the artist, the "screening session" (where the psychodynamic montage is watched by patient and therapist together for the first time) and the outcome. I will do my best to describe what really happens in multimedia psychotherapy using my notes, excerpts from tape-recorded sessions (when I was authorized by the patients to do so), and my memories. At the same time, I will briefly discuss clinically relevant issues (the criteria a psychotherapist should use to decide whether or not to propose multimedia psychotherapy, some innovative features of its setting, the emotional impact of images and music on patient and therapist, etc.) and give some tips to psychotherapists who would like to begin practicing multimedia psychotherapy with their own patients.

THE INTAKE

The intake is the preliminary part of any psychotherapeutic process. It encompasses the way the patient was referred to the therapist, the first meeting, and the subsequent consultations until a therapeutic contract is established and the work of psychotherapy formally begins within a ritual frame that has been agreed upon by patient and therapist. From my ethnopsychoanalytic perspective, the intake is the preliminary ritual; the multimedia sessions (selecting the pictures, choosing the soundtrack, and screening the psychodynamic montage) are the liminary ritual, and whatever takes place after the delivery of the memory object to the patient is the outcome or post-liminary ritual.

The case of Serena (chapter 1) shows how easily multimedia psychotherapy can be introduced to a patient in treatment. Since a therapeutic alliance is already established, it is not difficult to offer the new technique when something happens that makes us think, as therapists, that the use of images and music could enhance the effectiveness of our work and facilitate new insights for the patient.

Here I will focus instead on why and how we might think of offering multimedia psychotherapy to a new patient, a patient with whom a therapeutic alliance has not been developed yet. My experience is that when we are confronted with a mourning issue for an actual loss, it is good to propose multimedia psychotherapy as the first choice. On the other hand, when we face mourning for a problem in the developmental passage from one stage to the next in the life cycle, we should have some screening criteria in mind that help us decide whether or not to discuss the option of multimedia psychotherapy with our patient.

Proposing multimedia psychotherapy does not mean doing it right away. The actual decision is based on the patient's spontaneous reaction to our description of the technique. For example, if the patient says that it would be too painful to review the images of his/her lost love object, or if we feel that there might be too much unconscious hate in their relationship, multimedia psychotherapy should not be started. Instead, it can be left in the background as a possible future option. *Primum non nocere* ("First of all do not harm the patient") is the golden rule of every therapy. Likewise, if we don't clearly see, during the intake, a passage of life that was missed or failed by the patient, it doesn't make sense to propose multimedia psychotherapy at this stage. The clinical cases (and the vignettes) I will present now, show clearly what I am talking about and introduce the screening criteria that should be taken into consideration to decide if multimedia psychotherapy is a good option for our patient.

JOAN

Joan asks for psychotherapy indirectly, preceded by the referral of a colleague, in the beginning of July 2011. The colleague tells me she will call and ask for individual treatment because she cannot bear to live with her hypochondriac anxieties and social phobias anymore. Some time passes, however, between the conversation with my colleague and Joan's call, a typical sign of resistance. Actually, she does not call until the end of the month, at which point she insists on being seen as soon as possible.

Joan is a woman in her forties, mother of a five-year-old boy. She lives with the father of the child, though they are not married as neither of them wants any marital ties. Their child, she tells me, is ill very often. In her narrative, the boy had been ill since birth, suffering continuously from infections of the lungs, ears, and throat or from allergic reactions. He is continually in treatment with antibiotics or antihistamines prescribed by a pediatrician (she tells me she had finally found a good one). Faced with this endless series of problems, her fear of illness had become intolerable. At this point she stops talking.

I experience an intense countertransference (an emotional reaction to her) in the form of a distinct uneasiness. I silently interpret this as the result of her own feelings of uneasiness about becoming a patient. When I ask if she has ever taken any drugs for her anxiety, she tells me her family doctor had suggested that she take anxiolytic medications but she doesn't want to. She is afraid of all psychological dependence, even on a medication. This confirms my feeling that she has a strong resistance against becoming a patient and/or accepting any therapy, including classic psychotherapy.

After a brief silence, Joan explicitly admits she doesn't know what to do here. She knows I am a psychoanalyst, and I expect her to freely associate or say whatever comes into her mind. But she can't, and she doesn't dream or remember her dreams. I ask her where she got her information about how psychoanalytic treatment works, and she replies that many of her friends are in therapy. Feeling her growing distress in the silence that follows (I think she is thinking I am thinking there is something wrong with her), I ask her if she would like me to show her how psychotherapy works by means of a drawing. She looks relieved and asks me to please do so.

I tell her that psychoanalysis, in Freud's words, is an "impossible profession" (1937), just as that of parents, educators, and so on. Then I make a drawing and present an apparently impossible problem just to show (playing a game with words) how (apparently) impossible problems, such as (irrational) neurotic behaviors and inhibitions (such as going to see a psychoanalyst without really wishing to be analyzed) might be resolved by using Freud's associative method, the method of his impossible profession.

I can't remember exactly what I told her, but I do remember her positive reaction when I proposed that she have a look at the method of free association, instead of talking about it. Next I will describe the problem I used in that session since it shows one possible way to introduce and offer multimedia psychotherapy to a patient. The interesting aspect of this clinical vignette is that it offers a figurative rather than a verbal-only introduction to psychotherapy.

The "Impossible" Problem

Here is our (apparently) impossible problem: how can we connect all these nine points (fig. 3.1), drawing only four line segments, without ever detaching the pen from the paper, and never passing over the same segment twice?

The solution is illustrated in the next picture (fig. 3.2), where two additional virtual points (A and B) are drawn outside of our original nine points.

The two external virtual points are essential. In fact, the only way to solve our problem is to think "outside of the box" and exit from the imaginary square border made by the eight outer points. If we use our four lines to connect these eight points, we are doomed to fail since the central ninth point will remain unconnected. To solve the problem we must explore the external space, out of the limits suggested by common sense. As prescribed by the psychoanalytic method, we have to leave commonplaces and familiar thought patterns; we must enter a free-floating attention which allows our mind to ignore borders and become curious about what might become visible from an unfamiliar point of view. Paradoxically, we must focus on the space out there rather than look at the space inside the nine points, here.

Looking now at the four lines in the drawing, we see that our first line segment extends far beyond the imaginary square border to reach virtual point A. To draw this segment, to make this move, some psychological freedom is needed. We must not be afraid of leaving a closed familiar imaginary space (our traditional habits/customs/ideas/beliefs) and nur-

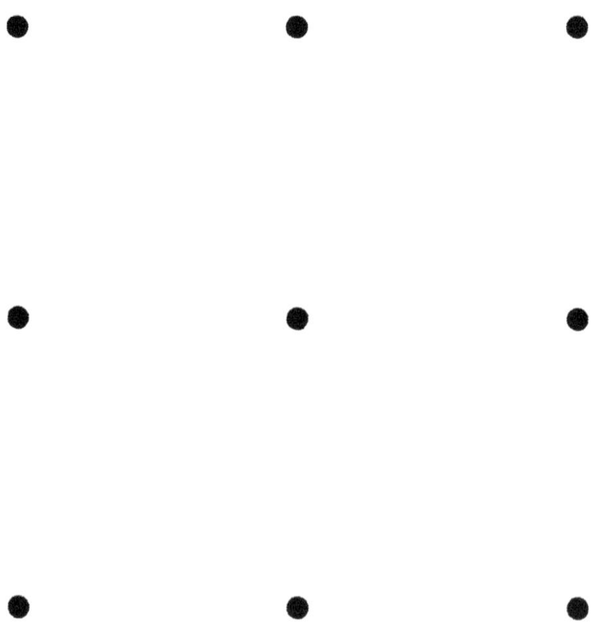

Figure 3.1. The nine points problem

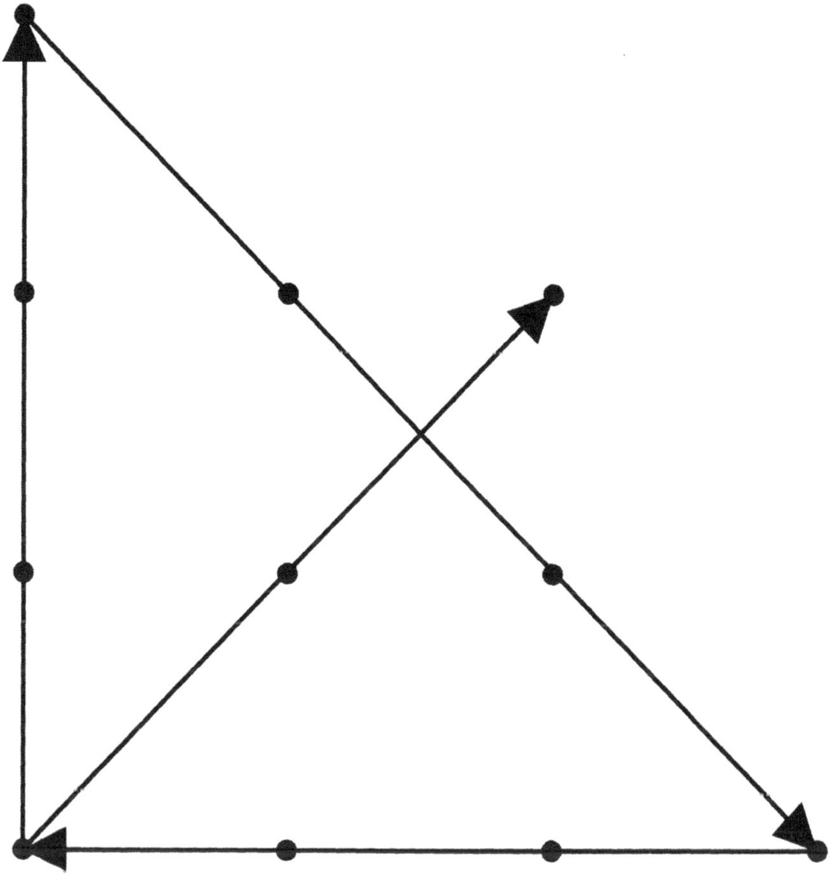

Figure 3.2. The solution of the nine points problem

ture some faith that when a problem seems impossible to solve in the usual way, the best resource is to let our mind follow its own free imagination and look for new paths beyond the here and now.

This does not mean that we enter the external space with no memory (of our problem) and no wish (to solve it). In this regard, I completely disagree with the suggestion that a psychoanalyst should have no memory, understanding, or desire at the beginning of a session (Bion 1967). In fact, it is exactly because we have our goal in mind that we suddenly realize, while exploring the external space with our first line segment, that we are reaching a virtual point from which we can return into our nine points. The diagonal line from point A allows us to touch, with our second segment, two points of the nine we want to connect. Moreover, going outside the imaginary square border again allows us to find the most advantageous virtual point B. This time, encouraged by our previous positive experience, we are less afraid of exploring the external space, and we reach virtual point B. From there, it is not difficult to go back into our nine points and cover one more side of the imaginary square, from B to our starting point. Once back there, the solution to the problem becomes obvious and we can draw our fourth segment, a second diagonal line.

Together, the four lines describe a spiral that moves inside and outside the imaginary square of the nine points, connecting them all. Reading this problem and its solution as a metaphor or allegorical story of the psychoanalytic method offers a possible interpretation of my use of this problem with Joan. I was probably trying to tell her what we were going to do together, in a way she could accept. In fact, not only a picture but any image is "worth a thousand words."

Working in psychotherapy from the perspective of the impossible profession, patient and therapist agree to grant themselves a pattern of continuing oscillation and integration between scouting around (beyond the borders of common sense and familiar places—taking heed of dreams, lapses, symptomatic actions, fantasies, and free associations in a state of free-floating attention) and reflecting (making constructions and/or interpretations) within the safe emotional environment of the therapeutic alliance, always trying to tune in to both the conscious and unconscious levels. In my view, paradoxically, whenever therapist and patient dare to explore the "off limits" areas of denial, repression, and disavowal, they find themselves rewarded by the discovery of new "virtual points" from which symptoms and inhibitions appear quite different and become more manageable. In this way, all the "fixation points," where the patient's libido (or psychosexual energy) had remained blocked due to a failure in the individual's development, can be reached and reconnected. This experience can help us to integrate two different mental patterns: the "primary" and "secondary process" (Freud 1900, 1916–1917).

In psychodynamic therapy, and actually in every complex human endeavor, the "psychoanalytic paradigm" (Nesci, Poliseno, Averna and 2005), based on free association and the acknowledgment of unconscious fantasies and dynamics (Freud 1886–1939), must be integrated with the classical scientific method, based instead on rational observation and experimentation. The two patterns must work together, as in the nine points problem, if we really want to find creative solutions to apparently unsolvable, desperate situations or to address unanswerable questions, such as the meaning of life and death, a question we all ask ourselves conceiving a new baby, mourning someone we love, or just changing our identity in the ritual passages of the life cycle.

Back to Joan's Case

Rereading my notes from Joan's sessions in order to write this chapter, I recognized another possible interpretation of why I had used the metaphor of the nine points problem. In fact, the two virtual points I called A and B might also be interpreted as the external perspectives provided by the images and sounds in multimedia psychotherapy. In other words, being aware of her great difficulty in communicating through the typical verbal pattern, I may have been unconsciously paving the way to offer Joan multimedia psychotherapy. In fact, a few sessions later, after one more long silence, I did tell her about multimedia psychotherapy and suggested focusing our work on the years after her child was born. It was after his birth, in fact, that she felt overwhelmed by his recurrent illnesses and her own hypochondriac anxieties, which were now specifically concentrated on his health.

In the session when I proposed that she bring pictures of that period of time and begin multimedia psychotherapy sessions, she spontaneously told me a recurrent dream from her adolescent years. She was walking along the seashore with a group of people, struggling to communicate with them. The dream came in different versions—people did not listen to her or hear her voice, or she was speechless—but the theme was always the same. Once, with anguish, she even dreamt that her head fell off completely and came to rest on the shoreline, where the land meets the sea . . .

LIZA

Liza was referred to me by her gynecologist. Although there was no problem from a gynecological point of view, she hadn't gotten pregnant after her first year of marriage. Her husband was frequently away from home for professional reasons, and this, along with her growing anxiety about not getting pregnant, led her to request intrauterine insemination, the least invasive of the assisted reproductive technologies. Liza called the same day she was referred to me, and I saw her a few days later in my office.

I find myself with a young woman in her thirties who opens herself up from the very beginning of the first interview. She says she really hopes I can help her because her gynecologist believes her excessive stress may be part of the reason she hasn't gotten pregnant, nor would it allow her to have a healthy pregnancy. She knows she is an anxious person (she is also afraid of sleeping alone), but that doesn't really bother her. What she wants is to have a child. She has a husband and a job but feels handicapped because she doesn't have a child and is not a mother yet, at her age. She cannot wait; she feels she must be pro-active about getting pregnant.

I tell her she should not think about it in such an obsessive way. She agrees and tells me her day is already filled with work and hobbies to distract her. I ask about her hobbies. She says she likes salsa, the Latin American dance. She had stopped dancing, however, approximately three years before. I ask her more about her dance history, and she tells me she began dancing when she was five, studying in her parish with a woman teacher. When she moved to Rome to go to the university, she had a dance partner for seven years. But then, when she was too busy with her engagement, she told him to find another partner, and that was the end of that.

Listening to her story, I think there might be something that she had lost, and possibly repressed, regarding dance and her relationship with her husband, who doesn't dance at all. I tell her about multimedia psychotherapy and its effectiveness when a "life passage" has not been worked through properly. I suggest she might do a memory object with her dance pictures and a musical soundtrack to elaborate that phase of her life. She immediately associates with a video she made (helped by a friend) for her thirtieth birthday. She loves it; it is full of beautiful moments. I tell her this is very interesting and we might look at it in our sessions, but I explain that this is not what I try to do in multimedia psychotherapy. In multimedia psychotherapy, I ask my patient to focus on a passage of life where something traumatic occurred, was repressed, and thereby produced a fixation point, stopping the natural rhythm of life in some way.

She associates with two possible traumas: being left for no reason by her first love at eighteen and being completely rejected by her best friend immediately after graduation. She thinks she has overcome the "first love wound, but not the friendship wound." In fact, Samantha had been a kind of "symbiotic sister" to her. I ask her to tell me more about it. She explains that it was doubly traumatic because she was not even able to talk with Samantha to understand what had happened and why. I think she has an idea about why it happened but it is too painful for her to acknowledge, so I don't question her about this traumatic issue for now; instead, I just ask her to tell me more about their relationship.

Liza tells me a few details that I found quite interesting. "Samantha and I became best friends the very first day I arrived at the nuns' hostel in Rome where we were going to live while studying at the university. She was from southern Italy, like me. We stayed in the hostel for the first nine months of our time in Rome, then we moved and rented an apartment with two other girls." I am struck by this detail of the nine months (the duration of pregnancy) at the nuns' hostel but, once again, keep this observation to myself.

Liza continues, "Samantha spent those years when we were living together in Rome without studying at all. She was always watching television on her king-size bed in the afternoon, or going shopping downtown, going out at night, sleeping in the morning. She spent a lot of money. Her mother came to visit her every month, and they would go shopping together, buying expensive bags (which Samantha collected). She really spent a lot of money on original designer bags!"

At this point I suggest that this friend might be her own double, her disavowed adolescent Self, who didn't want to grow up and become an adult, in strong unconscious collusion with her mother. Liza easily understands my interpretation, so I suggest that she bring in pictures of the two of them so we can focus on the period of her move to Rome and the passages of studying, graduating, and getting engaged—all events that took place while her symbiotic relationship with Samantha was going on. We agree to watch her thirtieth birthday video next time and begin to analyze the pictures of her "friend-story" as well.

At the end of the session, I ask her what her fiancé had thought was the reason for Samantha's refusal to see her. Explaining that the break happened the day after her graduation, Liza said that her fiancé interpreted it at the time as a sign of envy given that Samantha did not graduate and had lost her fiancé as well. At this point I ask her if she "really" has no idea why her first boyfriend left her. Liza tells me that he was twenty-four years old at that time and had just moved to northern Italy to start working; she was eighteen and still living in the south.

The scenario to begin multimedia psychotherapy is already framed in the intake, in the very first session of Liza's therapy, apparently focusing on her relationship with Samantha. At a deeper level, we know that we will focus on Liza's unconscious difficulties in making the ritual passage from being a daughter to becoming a wife and a mother. The exploration of her "Samantha period" will actually be an analysis of her incomplete mourning for her own adolescent Self.

Liza's case taught me that patients might feel motivated to do multimedia psychotherapy when they need "to be active" in the care of their own problem. For such patients, waiting for a dream (or a free association) to come into mind might seem too passive whereas looking for pictures, selecting and bringing them to the sessions, associating the photos with a song or music of their choice, all involve activity. Actually, Liza's case revealed to me still another aspect of multimedia psychotherapy. For Liza, as for all of us, it is easier to analyze our own problems in another person than in ourselves. Bringing Samantha into the therapy, Liza could more easily bring her own disavowed immaturity in her symbiotic sister or "double" instead of being asked to analyze herself and her own immaturity directly.

By the way, a patient's mourning experience is always associated with a love object that the subject has identified as a part of his/her own inner world or as a "selfobject" (Kohut 1971, 1984) from which the natural process of separation-individuation (Mahler 1968) could not take place physiologically, for some reason, somewhere, sometime. The therapeutic path repeats the vicissitudes of the past traumatic relationship (whether it was real or imaginary) within the transference (i.e., in the relationship with the therapist), which helps the patient to remember the original trauma and eventually to work it through. Meanwhile, the psychodynamic montage makes it possible to have a concrete preview of the whole story. Thus, patient and therapist will have a sort of map to navigate the unpredictable waters of the oceanic journey of psychotherapy and the life that awaits them.

SARA

A woman calls me asking for an urgent appointment. Someone at the hospital where I work had given her my home telephone number. I accept since I know that there is a long waiting list for patients followed by the National Health Service.

Sara is a woman in her fifties. She arrives with her husband. Something tells me to let them in together and see what happens instead of asking him to leave. She cries and tells me she feels awful. She cannot sleep, she is full of rage, she has suicidal thoughts, and she is constantly quarrelling with her husband and sons, especially her older son, Paul, who is married and the father of a boy. The second of her two sons, Robert, is married but has no children yet. Sara's husband is retired. She feels empty ever since her "children" joined the army as warrant officers and were assigned to two different military bases in northern Italy. To make matters worse, they often volunteer for dangerous areas where the Italian army is engaged in high risk missions. She is furious with them for this!

I prescribe a medication and offer her an inexpensive treatment with one of the psychologists who is specializing in psychotherapy at my school (once a week in my hospital, where she would pay almost nothing to the National Health Service), with my supervision. However, seeing that she is quite depressed, I give her a second appointment with me, at my office, to monitor her situation.

On her second appointment, Sara comes without her husband. He had given her a ride but doesn't come in so that she can talk more freely. In fact, she talks nonstop. She goes from fragments of her life as a daughter to extensive, detailed accounts of her fights with her sons, mostly with Paul and his wife. She seems better; nonetheless, I give her another appointment since I still hadn't found a psychologist who could take her in therapy at the hospital.

The third time we meet, I notice that she follows the same ritual pattern. It is as if she were split in two parts: one lives in the past, as a daughter (this is the part of her life she brings at the beginning of her sessions); the other lives in a static present, as a postmenopausal mother, a woman without a "man" and without her "children" anymore (this is the part that compulsively returns in the latter part of her sessions).

The awkward "fact" is that the theme is always the same: she is the victim. When Sara speaks about herself as a daughter, she tells a story of psychological abuse by her parents: her father was an alcoholic who betrayed his wife yet was pathologically jealous; her mother was cold and called her "bitch" for no reason at all. When she speaks about herself now, as mother of two married sons and wife of a retired man, she still tells stories of psychological abuse: Robert criticizes her; Paul wants her to sell her apartment in Rome, buy a two-story house in his town in northern Italy, and live with him so she can help, mostly by babysitting his son for free and thus allowing him and his wife to afford a second child. Her husband wants to help their sons, supports their decisions (such as going abroad in dangerous military missions to earn more money), and plays both sides of the fence instead of being on her side in the "fight" with their sons.

An idea occurs to me. Through these inconsolable, grievous lamentations, isn't she celebrating an unconscious mourning ritual for the only "character" in her life she enjoyed enacting? Isn't she mourning for herself as a young wife and mother who can make all the decisions about her children's lives? Isn't this character a sort of selfobject she cannot (or doesn't want to) let go?

I tell her about multimedia psychotherapy and suggest we might focus on her life in the period between her marriage and the marriage of her second son. She responds by opening her wallet and showing me pictures of herself, her children, and her husband, which she always carries around with her. I feel my impression is confirmed: that is the part of her life, the part of herself, she cannot mourn, she cannot let go: she cannot acknowledge that it is over. This is the "unpast" in her life, as I would say, picking up, in a different context, the wonderful expression coined by Scarfone in his paper "A Matter of Time: Actual Time and the Production of the Past" (2006), in which he examines "how the insertion of time into psychic events and structural differentiation form a single process" (807–811).

In multimedia psychotherapy, the music (the soundtrack of the psychodynamic montage) fulfills this role quite concretely, inserting time in such a way as to set the patient's pictures/memories in motion! When I tell Sara about the soundtrack, she surprises me by associating with three songs: one for Paul, one for Robert, and one for herself and her husband together. Music is the magician that seems to let each "child" become himself, a separate individual, and herself and her husband become a symbiotic couple, to stay together and not be separated in this later part of their life. "Next time," she promises, "I'll bring the pictures!"

So what do we learn from Sara's case? A simple truth we already knew: we don't need to suffer from a real death to experience mourning and a need for multimedia psychotherapy. We die every day. It is not only our cells that die; *we* die and change every day. That is why we need so many points of reference, institutions, and rituals. Problems arise when we are unable to accept this. When we are unable to accept, for example, that the successful "young wife and mother of children" or the "young businessman" (who still live unchanged in our unconscious minds) are lost forever and that we have become grandparents in this stage of the life cycle, then we suffer from a syncytial mourning experience! It is the end of our personal world. That is why we need to go back in time more concretely, through images and sounds, in the language of the group-individual that lives inside us all, to repeat the passage again, the critical passage of the exit from that "unpast" X or Y state. In this way, we offer ourselves the chance to live our contemporary state to the fullest instead of wishing a "Warramunga ritual" for all the members of our family, all the while feeling guilty about it and desperately depressed.

SCREENING CRITERIA

These three clinical vignettes suggest the main criteria for therapists to follow when they are considering offering multimedia psychotherapy to a patient.

1. There should be a syncytial mourning experience. Whether it be the birth of a child who is always sick (Joan), the anxiety of being unable to get pregnant (Liza), or the unconscious wish to kill husband and sons and then commit suicide (Sara), the particulars do not really matter. We just need to feel in our countertransference that the patient lives in a regressive scenario where the group-individual needs our care concretely, here and now.
2. There might be an uneasiness or a difficulty in verbal communication. If we think (from details of the patient's history or from our countertransference, as in Joan's case) that the use of audiovisual communication channels might be helpful, then we should follow our intuition and offer multimedia psychotherapy.
3. The patient might have a need for activity and/or an incapacity to wait, as in Liza's case. Multimedia psychotherapy is able to offer instant gratification to these patients' needs. At the same time, it facilitates the construction of the therapeutic alliance so that, if necessary, the psychotherapeutic process can continue along classical lines once the multimedia psychotherapy sessions are over and the patient feels better.

4. There should be the feeling that the patient's subjective time is blocked, as in Sara's case. Multimedia psychotherapy can be offered any time we feel that the patient needs some concrete help for "the production of the past" (Scarfone 2006) so that "ordinary time" can be "inserted" into the repressed (or the "unpast"), and the clock of life can start up again.

FOUR

Selecting the Pictures

Once patient and therapist agree on beginning multimedia psychotherapy, the patient is invited to bring in pictures of the person or period of life they want to explore together. Of course this should be done only if the patient is clearly interested and motivated to do so. As I pointed out previously, if a patient says that it would be too painful to see the pictures of a lost love object or of a past period of his/her life, this might be a contraindication to applying the technique of multimedia psychotherapy. Another contraindication might come from our own countertransference. If we detect the presence of severe unconscious hate feelings toward the lost love object or if we suspect that the patient suffered from extremely traumatic experiences during the period of life we want to help him/her to remember and elaborate, it might be wiser to proceed along classic therapy lines since this would be less painful.

If there are no contraindications, this is the moment to introduce the role of the artist and to show an example of a psychodynamic montage, if the patient asks for it, such as a memory object published on the online scientific journal of IIPRTHP for this purpose (Nesci, D. A. and Nesci, F. A. 2010). This makes it easier for the patient to understand why he/she should bring at least forty pictures and begin thinking about a piece of music that spontaneously comes to mind for the soundtrack since it seems to have a natural association to the person (or life period) we want to review.

During the "picture sessions" (usually one session is not enough to recover the pictures and to work on them), many memories come to life and the emotional climate of the clinical encounter warms up, facilitating the beginning of a strong therapeutic alliance between patient and therapist. The fact that this is a team work with an external helper (the multimedia artist) who will work to concretely produce the memory object reduces the unconscious feeling of shame from which men and women often suffer when they take the role of patients in classic psychotherapy.

I will now present two more clinical cases (Louis and Laurie) and clinical vignettes from Sara's therapy to show in detail what happens in the process of selecting the pictures.

LOUIS

After the successful outcome of my first case in multimedia psychotherapy, I decided to propose my new technique to another long-term patient of mine: Louis, a man I had begun to see when he was in his twenties, suffering from anxiety, inhibitions, phobias, and obsessive neurotic symptoms. Today, he is a married man in his early forties, the happy father of a lively six-year-old daughter, and an officer in the same state institution as his father, though in a different capacity. I still see him, vis-à-vis, in a classic individual setting, but only every other week. When he came to see me the first time, Louis was a young university student who had just recovered from his umpteenth motorcycle accident—a dangerous one, in fact, where he had run a serious risk of death. He had been referred to me by a colleague who feared Louis might kill himself one of these days driving so recklessly through the streets of Rome.

Louis is the third child of Romeo and Mary, born several years after his older sister (Paula) and his brother (Sam). He lost his father to lung cancer when he was fourteen. During the first year of our weekly vis-à-vis classic therapy, it came out that he had been abused as a child by an adult in a public restroom, when his father was still alive. The opportunity to finally talk about this secret trauma, with me, in psychotherapy, helped Louis to gradually moderate his suicidal driving behavior. Nevertheless, he continued to suffer from phobias and obsessive neurotic symptoms that still needed to be constantly relieved by his psychotherapy sessions—a sort of new addiction replacing his old dangerous habits.

I offered Louis multimedia psychotherapy when I noticed that his symptoms recurred on each anniversary of his father's death. Louis responded enthusiastically to my suggestion that he create a memory object for his father in a series of multimedia psychotherapy sessions. He agreed to look for pictures, select the most meaningful ones, and bring them to me so we could work through them together to make a video with the help of a multimedia artist.

At one point, Louis told me he had collected a lot of pictures and would bring them next time, but the following session he arrived empty-handed. Only when he was sitting in front of me did he realize he had totally forgotten about multimedia psychotherapy and left all the photos at home. Being an "expert" patient, he laughed at himself and at his own resistance, conscious and unconscious at the same time! He knew very well what was contributing to this acting out, however. While selecting the pictures and reviewing old home movies he had transferred from 8mm to digital video, he had "discovered" something he already knew but had been denying: his father had a "secret" lover, a woman he pretended was just a colleague at work and who gradually became a "family friend." This is "a very old story," he says. In fact, their liaison went on for about twenty years, but only now Louis feels free to acknowledge it and talk about it, here, with me. Suddenly he changes his expression and says, "You know what? I suddenly remember the face of the man who abused me in the restroom! I could even recognize him! Your system of focusing on pictures really works . . . Doc, you're smart!"

The next session he arrives fifteen minutes late with three DVDs of old family films. We watch them together. His father's lover is always there. Then Louis tells me he had a dream. In this dream, Louis was working at the same job as his father, going on patrol in a northern Italian town infamous for its night life. He had to work sixty-eight hours a week. He associates this number and the nightclub town with sexual activities, with his inhibitions (he interprets sixty-eight as a censored version of sixty-nine), and with his father's extramarital affair.

The following session he is very anxious, afraid that he is becoming impotent. This is one of his obsessive phobias; alternatively, he is afraid to suffer from premature ejaculation. Discussing the pictures in multimedia psychotherapy, Louis explores a series of possible psychodynamic constructions of what happened to his father and what then happened to his children when they grew up (his older sister, older brother, and himself). In fact, both Paula and Sam lost, respectively, their husband and wife because of a lover/colleague at work. Louis feels that they unconsciously repeated something that belonged to their father's past, though reversing the roles (being betrayed and left by their marital partners instead of actively betraying them).

From this perspective, he realizes that his father was neglecting the family (because of his relationship with his lover) exactly as Louis himself is now doing, flirting at the office with women colleagues and neglecting his wife, Louisa, and their daughter. Is it possible that Louis's neurotic sexual fears and inhibitions are a way to protect himself from the risk of destroying his family, of finding himself engulfed in a real long-term extramarital relationship? Is it possible that all his "virtual" relationships (as he calls his multiple flirts) with women colleagues are a way to prevent the danger of a real love affair (a long-term relationship with one lover only), which—he feels now—was responsible for the unhappiness of his original family while the affair was going on and—he believes—for the death of his father after it had come to an end?

After asking himself such questions, Louis thinks back to Candy, his first girlfriend, when he was a teenager. Candy had been abused herself and was afraid of sex. To test his sexual potency (out of his obsessive fears), Louis used to ask her all the time to hold his sex in her hands, in a sort of repetition of what his unknown male abuser had forced him to do, thus reversing the roles of victim and aggressor. "It cannot be just a meaningless coincidence," he says. "It seems like a compulsion to repeat something traumatic. Maybe," he concludes, "Candy accepted my obsessive ritual since it was less traumatic than the real abuse she had experienced, like me, as a child."

In the following session, he tells me he has looked for Candy on Facebook and discovered that she is married and seems to be OK. He is relieved he didn't damage her! This work on the pictures, he tells me, is helping him not only to make peace with his father's death but also to resume and work through other mourning experiences he was afraid to remember.

Louis understands that it would be painful for his mother to see his father's lover again in the psychodynamic montage we are planning to produce with the help of the multimedia artist. Thus he talks about two possible videos: an uncensored one for himself with all the pictures and another one for his relatives. Then he changes his mind and opts for a different solution: only one video and no pictures of his father's lover at all. In this session, he also brings new pictures, beginning with his father at age twenty, and explains that he hopes to recover the pictures of his father's earlier years in southern Italy when he goes there on holiday. Actually, his older relatives refused to lend him their pictures with his father as a child, so he was not able to copy or scan them for multimedia psychotherapy. Interestingly, the repression of Louis's own unhappy childhood parallels the absence of childhood images of his father in the psychodynamic montage, with one notable exception: a picture of the father when he was ten, dressed in his boarding school uniform.

In the next session, Louis shows up with four envelopes. The first contains pictures taken before his parents' marriage; the second contains their wedding pictures; the third contains pictures taken after their wedding, and the fourth contains the most recent ones. He comments on the photos, beginning with the recent ones, while I reflect (silently) on the centrality of marriage in his unconscious life (he often tells me that for him "wedding = funeral").

Finally, in another session, he brings picture number one, a photo of his father as a powerful man at his desk, speaking on the telephone. Louis also tells me he has eliminated the pictures of women with whom he had had sexual affairs from his Facebook profile, leaving only his "virtual" girlfriends. He says he doesn't want to jeopardize his marriage by confusing private and public life as his father had, taking his secretary as his lover and transforming her into a "family friend." For the same reason, Louis refuses to post his memory object on Internet, even if it could be protected by a password. "Nothing is really private on the web," he says, "and this video must remain private." He gives me a pen drive with a Word file describing the pictures (divided in the same way as the four envelopes) in chronological order. He would like the multimedia artist to follow this sequence with the pictures and then save the video onto his pen drive after the final version had been reviewed by us in multimedia psychotherapy.

The Evolution of Multimedia Psychotherapy

This case, my second in multimedia psychotherapy, shows quite clearly something that happens every time. One begins with the conscious agenda of working through a precise mourning experience (in this case the actual death of the patient's father); little by little, however, the elaboration of this mourning experience inevitably brings to light unconscious situations that deal with other ritual passages of life that failed, producing symptoms and inhibitions from which the patient is still suffering. In other words, multimedia psychotherapy began to evolve immediately after my first case (Serena). The lesson I learned from the multimedia sessions with Louis is that my technique is useful to deepen the analytic work in its broader sense. Images from the patient's life help him or her reach new insights and give a different quality to them as well, making them more understandable and emotionally touching for both patient and therapist. In fact, the next case will show that multimedia psychotherapy is able to activate the patient's work of elaboration in a very fast and powerful way.

LAURIE

A colleague at my hospital comes to see me briefly in the interval between one patient and the next. He is worried about his sixty-year-old mother, Laurie, and asks me to see her as soon as possible. About one year before, his grandmother, Laurie's mother Imelda, had died of a massive untreatable hemorrhage in a tragic, bloody scenario in our hospital, all in the space of a single hour. Although Laurie was pushed out of the room by the medical team who were trying to stop the bleeding and resuscitate Imelda, what she had seen was enough to traumatize her. At the time, my colleague tells me, she didn't understand, nor did his father (Laurie's husband). Only now, about one year later, is it clear to everyone, family and friends, that Laurie is depressed and that it has to do with her mother's death. Laurie and her mother had strong blood and affective ties that united them in a way that could hardly be loosened.

The whole family was now in a complex situation: Laurie didn't want to be at home alone, but her husband had to go to work, and her son, the young doctor, had to go abroad for his profession. Moreover, Laurie refused to take any drugs, even though their family doctor had suggested she take antidepressant and anxiolytic medications. I tell my colleague about multimedia psychotherapy and suggest he ask his mother if she would like to see me and try my new form of psychotherapy. I give him my phone number, and I receive a call that same day, directly from Laurie.

I see Laurie in my office at home. She is a small, sweet, respectful woman who immediately has a positive impact on me for her gentle way of introducing herself and telling her story. She seems to know every detail of my brief conversation with her son at the hospital. Before showing me the pictures she has brought, she describes how her mother, Imelda, had had an abortion (first pregnancy) and lost a baby (second pregnancy) immediately after it was born at home. She tells me this story to explain why she herself was born in a hospital, instead of being delivered at home in the small town where they were living: naturally, her mother hadn't wanted to risk losing her third child. After her, Imelda had a fourth pregnancy and gave birth at home, but that baby died also, only two days later. Thus, Laurie is an only child.

Then she tells me another story. She was, and still is, so close to her mother because her father died when she was fourteen. After that, Imelda had to act two roles and "be everything" for her. That is why, when Imelda suffered from kidney stones (Laurie was twenty-eight at the time), she went to talk with a renowned surgeon and asked him to "save her life." The "Professor" was so touched by Laurie's affection for her mother that he agreed to perform the surgery for free (Laurie only had to pay for the clinic and the other doctors in the medical team). I can easily believe her story, since I also feel a paternal countertransference during our consultation.

At this point, I suggest to Laurie that her father's death might have not been worked through, unconsciously, in her past. She doesn't react to this remark, and instead begins to show me the pictures she has brought for our multimedia psychotherapy. Acting out my countertransference, I discard some of her pictures the same way she had just discarded my comment. The pictures I discard show Laurie and/or Imelda with their eyes closed or looking downward. I also discard one poorly framed photo where Laurie's husband appears with his head cut off. My conscious attempt, in that moment, is to try to produce a "good" video in order to replace the traumatic visual memories associated with Imelda's tragic death at the hospital. My acting out (I can see it only now, reflecting on my behavior during the session while writing this part of the book) is probably an unconscious repetition of the defense mechanism Laurie and her mother resorted to in order to overcome the shock of their father/husband's rapid death from cancer many years before.

My mind automatically finds itself immersed in archaic group-individual scenarios, where a husband simply visits and provides food for his wife's maternal group. The idea seems to fit with Laurie's story about her father dying and handing down his pension to his wife and his job to his daughter, providing sustenance but leaving her no memories at all of him as a meaningful, individual, personal presence! A man with a partially cut-off head indeed!

Fragments from a Multimedia Psychotherapy Session: Excerpt 1

In the second session, Laurie brings an envelope full of pictures: old pictures (her mother, her wedding, and the other photos she had brought the first time), new pictures, and an old black-and-white postcard of her mother's hometown. She doesn't open the envelope at the beginning of the session, however.

I will quote here some excerpts from the audiotape recording in order to give a lively firsthand account of the informal spontaneous atmosphere I try to establish in multimedia psychotherapy sessions.

> *Doctor*: I was wondering about some of the pictures you brought here last time . . . about the fact that you and your mother were looking downward or had your eyes closed. Maybe it could signify a wish not to see something (fig. 4.1).
>
> *Laurie*: Not to see what?

Figure 4.1. Laurie and her mother looking downward

Doctor: The dying mother, for example.

Laurie: That's true. Even when my mother was young, I was always telling myself I shouldn't die before her because I had to help her until the very end . . . Maybe you were right last time when you suggested that I had this breakdown after her death because I hadn't worked through my father's death. It's not normal that a person thinks those thoughts of a young mother.

Doctor: Right!

Laurie: I thought I had overcome his death, but after all, I was only fourteen. Old enough to realize he had died but too young to be able to accept it.

Doctor: Yes!

Laurie: My mother managed things very cleverly so that I wouldn't feel the loss of my father so strongly. I remember though she used to tell me to beware of boys who could cheat on me since I had no father to protect me . . . so, maybe she was worried about that. As for me, I was more worried than she was, for sure, at the thought of losing her. I would be lost if she died; for me it would be the end! That's why I went to see the famous "Professor" when she was sick. [She puts an envelope with her pictures on my desk.]

Doctor: So, what did you bring today? [Laurie opens the envelope. I begin to look at the pictures and encourage her to describe them again and comment freely. At a certain point Laurie shows me a picture where she and her mother are at the *Bocca della Verità* (the "Mouth of Truth") in Rome.]

Laurie and Doctor: [at the same time] This is the "Mouth of Truth!"

Doctor: Don't you see you have your eyes shut? (fig. 4.2)

Laurie: Um . . . um . . .

Doctor: [with a singsong tone] You don't want to know the truth . . .

Laurie: [laughing . . . imitating the Doctor's singsong tone] I don't want to know the truth. . . . [resuming a normal tone] Even now, you know? Even now, sometimes, I try hard. I'm a very realistic woman. And yet . . .

Doctor: Yet?

Figure 4.2. Laurie with her eyes shut at the "Mouth of True" in Rome

Laurie: And yet, sometimes I'd really love to put my head in the sand. But I don't do it! With my son, when I see him distressed, I try to [ask him] "What's going on?" On the one hand, I'd like not to know, but on the other, I can't keep myself from asking, "Is everything OK?"

Fragments from a Multimedia Psychotherapy Session: Excerpt 2

I will quote some more excerpts from the same session, focusing on the moments when Laurie brings me the "new" pictures, particularly two meaningful ones.

Laurie: These pictures are new—my son, my husband, and me. This is my mother's village. Here the story begins and ends. . . . My mother is buried here. This is my grandmother with her two children, my mother's brother, and my mother as a little girl. This is the first picture.

Doctor: Not necessarily. We might also begin with Mother Earth, the village. Let's decide later. [Laurie and I put all the pictures in chronological order leaving aside the oldest picture of Laurie's mother (fig. 4.3) and the postcard of the town.]

A picture with Laurie's father allows her to talk about an accident he had on the job six months before his death. Then she shows me a picture of

Figure 4.3. The first picture of Laurie's mother as a child

her wedding but insists on having it back as soon as possible. I notice the difference when she deals with her "normal" pictures and these two "sacred" ones: her "number 1" picture (fig. 4.3) and a "wedding" photo (fig. 4.4).

I decide to scan these two pictures immediately so I can give them back to her right away. As I work on the images with my scanner and personal computer, we chat. I begin with her wedding picture.

Figure 4.4. Laurie and her mother leaving home to go to church for the wedding

Laurie: This is my wedding picture. I've taken it out of my album.

Doctor: Don't worry, if you want I can scan it right now and give it back to you immediately.

Laurie: Yes, thank you. I'd also like to get the old one back now, the oldest picture I have of my mother.

Doctor: Let me work on the wedding photo first. Hmm, it's too large. What if I scan only the central part of the photo and leave out these people around you on either side?

Laurie: That's fine. They don't matter. We don't mind at all about them; the only thing we want is my mother. [Silence, except for the soft noise of the scanner and the computer.]

Doctor: It's really relaxing to work on these old pictures. They bring us back to a different world where time passed at a slower pace.

Laurie: Right! Precisely. I would say a less stressful world.

Doctor: Exactly . . .

Laurie: [A world] where there were troubles, of course, but . . . you know the proverb, "Ignorance is bliss!" We knew less of what was going on all around than today. And it wasn't so bad! Because to know, to be informed, is also a source of stress. On the one hand, it's good, but . . . [I silently notice the interesting association between my elimination of the people around her center of attention—Laurie and Imelda—and her subsequent thoughts on what a blessing it is to ignore "what was going on all around."]

Doctor: I finished that picture. Now let's scan the old black-and white-one. What number shall we give it? Where do we put the town?

Laurie: This is number 1.

Laurie and Doctor: [laughing heartily]

Doctor: This is number 1. We don't care about the town.

Laurie: [laughing] We can even skip it.

Doctor: Let's go back for a moment to the wedding picture. This doesn't look like a church entrance.

Laurie: That's because this is before the wedding. We are leaving the house in this picture. Anyway, you're right. I asked my mother to accompany me to the altar.

Doctor: Not your uncle? Didn't your mother have an older brother? [This would be the traditional way of performing this part of the wedding ritual in Italy, especially in the past.]

Laurie: My mother asked me if I wanted him to take me to the altar, and I said, "No. I want you to do it, just like you always did everything for me, not my uncle."

Tips for Psychotherapists

This case (my eleventh case in multimedia psychotherapy) shows clearly what an intense emotional experience the presentation of the pictures by the patient can be, especially when we are dealing with a new patient, someone who is asking for help for the first time in his/her life and is completely naïve about psychodynamic psychotherapy. Laurie is the first (and only) patient who brought her pictures to her first consultation with me. This happened because of the special circumstances of her son's referral to me at my hospital and his ability (as a doctor) to explain something of my method to her, probably in an attempt to speed up the cure.

I would not recommend proceeding normally in this way, of course. Nonetheless, this clinical experience is useful to show that the sessions to which the patient brings pictures can serve multiple functions and become a tool to

1. be immediately introduced to the patient's story, background, and inner affective world,
2. explore more easily unconscious fantasies and dynamics (such as the emergence of defense mechanisms) since they are displaced onto the media objects, and
3. build a therapeutic alliance.

For example, in Laurie's case it was possible in just a few sessions not only to get positive results (she was able to remain at home alone on the anniversary of her mother's death after only three sessions and without any medication) but also to get a significant amount of information (on her symbiotic relationship with her mother and her massive use of denial) while building, at the same time, a valuable therapeutic alliance. Actually, I think that multimedia psychotherapy makes it easier for the therapist to be in tune with patients because they immediately share a very intimate aspect of their inner world, in the form of their family portraits and stories.

SARA

From this perspective, Sara (whose case was introduced in the previous chapter) is an interesting example because there is such a striking shift from the first consultations, when she literally "vomited up" a boring interminable series of fights (between her and her daughters-in-law, the wives of her two sons; between her and her husband; between her and her two sons—especially Paul, the older one), to the sessions when she brought her pictures for multimedia psychotherapy. The presence of the photos in itself changed the atmosphere of the therapy dramatically, making it more intimate and lively.

Once again, as in Laurie's case, I will quote here some excerpts from the audiotape recording of the final part of a picture session to provide a vivid impression of the atmosphere created by patient and therapist together in multimedia psychotherapy. This time, however, I will introduce the excerpts with a summary of the whole session (Sara's first multimedia psychotherapy session) since it shows so clearly the huge quantity of information that the mere act of bringing pictures and sharing them with the therapist allows the patient to deliver, as well as the intense interactive nature of the multimedia psychotherapy process.

Summary of Sara's First Multimedia Psychotherapy Session

Sara shows me the first picture (with her son Paul as a baby) and tells me her own father died when Paul was only four months old. Her comment is, "As I told you, my father was a useless man." Then she shows me a picture of herself during her first pregnancy. I encourage her to put the pictures in chronological order. As she works, she comments on a picture where her husband is visible with her brother-in-law (her husband's brother), describing him as a "monster" with "a sterile wife." In Sara's words, this is "a woman who is the last of seven children, the daughter of two more monsters, who is married with a monster herself." She adds that her husband is a "monster" too, but a monster "disguised as a sheep."

The following presentation of two more pictures where Sara is visible with her husband and her two sons allows me to ask her to choose one of the two (since they are so similar) and allows her to reply she prefers the second one (where I silently observe she is closer to Robert than Paul and think this preference has a deep affective meaning). Immediately after, she shows me two more pictures that are very similar, since they were shot at the same place and from the same perspective: one shows all four family members (husband, wife, and children) and the other shows herself and her children only. Once again I ask her to choose. She tells me she has chosen them all! So I change my mind and accept them all, putting back the one I had just eliminated from the sequence, the photo where she was close to Paul. While doing this, I think about how we are dealing with her ambivalence toward her love objects, acting out a sort of psychodrama in which, through the medium of her family pictures, we eliminate and then reintegrate her love objects and ambivalent feelings into her affective inner world.

A photo with Paul and her in Venice falls out of one of the two envelopes of pictures she had brought. This leads Sara to tell me about her son's first romance. Paul was engaged and about to marry a young girl. They were both very, very young. Then, one week before the wedding, she left him. He felt completely lost. He was in the army at the time, in northern Italy, far away from home. Paul's commander called his parents and told them to come to try to help their son. They went and took him to Venice for a day to console and distract him. It was there, during that brief visit with his parents, that Paul met another girl . . . who is now his wife!

Now, thanks to other pictures, Sara begins to talk about William (her first grandchild, Paul's son) with a mixture of joy and concern. William is sick. He has a rare disease and might go blind. I feel uneasy. Something makes me act out again. I go on Internet right away (since my computer is on, to record our session) and I discover that the disease, which particularly affects male children, is not really so bad. It can be cured and usually disappears spontaneously by the end of adolescence. I feel better and try to reassure Sara. She confesses she had never done any research about it because she was too scared. What's more, she is not surprised that her daughter-in-law had told her only the bad news about William's illness. (Once again, I silently notice the intensity of countertransference acted out by myself—the therapist—in the multimedia sessions.)

While I am reading about William's disease, Sara spontaneously turns the silver frames on my desk to look at my family pictures: my wedding, my daughter's graduation from university, my son's graduation from high school. I encourage her to do so without considering any complicated interpretation; it seems obvious to me that she wants to look at my family pictures since she is allowing me to look at hers. I reflect (silently, again) on the fact that my own pictures seem to be here in my office as "inanimate objects" (Akhtar 2007) of the setting, and that I should question myself about the unconscious meaning of their presence (which I will discuss later). I identify my wife, my daughter, and my son in the pictures for her. Then Sara reveals some details she had not mentioned when she spoke about her marriage in our first consultation, and asks me to show her an example of the type of video the multimedia artist is going to produce with her pictures.

Actually, earlier in the session, I had told her that other patients had given me permission to show their montage so that other people could learn about this new form of psychotherapy. I turn my computer screen toward her and go online to my institute's scientific journal to show her a video. Sara comments on the different stages of a man's life, illustrated by the pictures, from childhood to the end. She concludes the session saying, "What a wonderful thing!"

Two Fragments from Sara's First Multimedia Psychotherapy Session

I will present now two fragments of the session I have just summarized. These two excerpts have to do with some elements of what we call the "setting" in psychoanalytic psychotherapy, that is, with two variations in the "rules of the game" that patient and therapist play together: talking about therapy with other people (for example, with family members) and introducing multimedia objects of other patients into the sessions. These two changes are normal in multimedia psychotherapy whereas they would be considered "transgressions" in a classic psychoanalytic psychotherapy scenario; therefore, it is important not to disregard them.

> *Sara*: One more issue. I talk a lot with my sons about what I do here, with both Paul and Robert. But someone told me, "No! Poor Paul! You shouldn't do that!"
>
> *Doctor*: Well, you know, most multimedia psychotherapy patients—all patients, in fact—talk about it with their relatives. Some patients even ask for their help to find and select pictures. Actually, I think one of the good things about multimedia psychotherapy is the family's involvement. Who told you that you shouldn't talk about it with your sons?
>
> *Sara*: One of my friends. She's in psychotherapy, and she said it's against the rules. She also told me you shouldn't have seen my husband that first time we met here at your office and that I speak too much about my therapy. We were talking about all this in the car along with another friend of mine who is also in therapy. This other friend explained that she doesn't speak about her therapy at all, not even with her own daughter! So I was the only one who could speak about her therapy: I told them you had never forbidden me to speak. Anyway, I've been thinking I should ask you about this . . . [Since the session is almost over, we count the photos and realize we have only chosen twenty-five, which means we need about fifteen more to have enough for the multimedia artist. Sara tells me she will bring some wedding pictures next time. I tell her that's fine; what we want is to have images and sounds related to the part of her life involving her relationship with her children when they were young and entirely dependent on her.]

Let's go to the second fragment of the session, now.

> *Sara*: I wear the gold ring from my silver wedding anniversary that Paul gave me. He was the only one who could buy the new rings since he was working and had the money; Robert was too young. Paul bought both gold rings, for my husband and for me. I don't wear the old one anymore.
>
> *Doctor*: What about your husband?
>
> *Sara*: He doesn't wear his old one either. We replaced the old rings with the new ones!
>
> *Doctor*: Where did you have the ceremony?

Sara: In the church. I didn't want to, but the priest insisted, "It's a beautiful ritual!"

Doctor: In which church?

Sara: [She says the name of the church, then makes a "digression" about the place where she first met her future husband.] We met in a room of the church where they used to hold meetings for young people. The topic being discussed that day was substance abuse (tobacco, drugs, or alcohol) and addiction. We met on 7/17/71 at 17:00. [She laughs.] When they say that seventeen brings bad luck, I say, "No! To me it didn't." Actually, it was the first day I was able to go out after a long illness . . . after ninety days . . .

Doctor: What illness?

Sara: Hepatitis. And it was the first time my husband went there, too! He was living in a private foster home nearby. He never knew his father and his mother couldn't take care of all of her five children. My husband was lucky to be accepted by that special home whose founder and sponsor is a very important man whom I respect very much. [He created] a wonderful thing! We got married there. The ritual was celebrated by the priest of the foster home. I'd like to bring a photo from my album, but I don't want to take it out.

Doctor: You don't have to. Just bring in the whole album and I'll scan the one you select without detaching the photo, and give it back to you right away.

Sara: You know what? My husband had the same idea and suggested that I bring you the scanned image directly on a pen drive!

Doctor: Feel free to do as you prefer.

SETTING ISSUES IN MULTIMEDIA PSYCHOTHERAPY

Pictures are concrete "inanimate objects" that become parts of the setting (Akhtar 2003) in multimedia psychotherapy. As such, they play a complex role that I will analyze in the theoretical chapters of this book. Here I just want to emphasize some practical issues of their use in therapy.

1. The use of pictures portraying people belonging to the patient's world (relatives and friends) is a powerful tool that allows the therapist to see into this universe concretely. This fact might scare the patient, however, consciously and/or unconsciously. If the therapist wants to practice this form of therapy, he or she should feel

comfortable letting the patient have a look at his/her own inner world as well, by displaying personal concrete objects in the analytic room. In my office, for example, I used to have paintings on the walls and natural or artistic objects (Freud had his antiques collections . . .). I realize now that, since I began to practice multimedia psychotherapy, I have unconsciously introduced four photographs on the wall behind my desk in my office. The symbolic meaning of my choice is interesting, too. The first photo shows an unidentifiable group of people seen from behind (some of my son's schoolmates, their teacher, and some unknown passers-by) in a picturesque narrow street in Rome. It was taken by my son using an original technique and developed by him in the darkroom. The photo was so successful that his teacher at the time congratulated him and encouraged him to study photography. A few months later, my cousin sent me an old picture of one of our ancestors. In fact, it is the first (the oldest) picture of a member of my family. I framed it to match my son's photo, and hung the two on the wall side by side. Finally, I had been unable to find space in my home for two metallic posters of art photographs, each representing a tree, given to me by a friend on my sixtieth birthday, so they ended up in my office too, ostensibly by chance. If we consider that the name of my multimedia psychotherapy website program is "The Tree of Memories," that all my innovations began with the study of "placental leadership" (whose icon is a tree), and that other important progress in my ethnopsychoanalytic explorations has to do with the tale of the "Two Trees," the oldest tale in oral narrative (Bynum 1978), it is obvious that chance has nothing to do with my choice, and that my unconscious induced me to share with my patients both my family history and my personal psychoanalytic path as a therapist and researcher.

2. There is nothing wrong if a patient to whom we propose multimedia psychotherapy asks to see an example in order to really understand what a "psychodynamic montage" is all about. After all, a picture is worth a thousand words. At the moment, one video is available since it was published on the online journal *Doppio Sogno* (Nesci, D. A. and Nesci, F. A. 2010), thanks to a grateful patient and her family who signed a written authorization.
3. The collection and selection of pictures for a psychodynamic montage might require the cooperation of relatives and friends. The atmosphere of multimedia psychotherapy is radically different from the secretive scenario of the so-called classic technique since it openly acknowledges that there is a group (relatives and friends, at a conscious level, and the group-individual in the individual patient, at an unconscious level, and the artist as part of the therapeutic team) that plays an important psychodynamic role in the set-

ting. For example, a patient asked her older sister for a picture of her mother caressing her hair when she was a little girl (she remembered about this photo, but, not without meaning, most family photos were at her sister's home). What she got back was a picture of her mother alone. The patient's image had been cut off by her older sister with the pretense that the frame was not big enough to contain the whole picture. Awful as it was, this fact at least helped the patient to get an extremely important new perspective on her childhood family life, to acknowledge the unconscious ambivalence of her sister toward her, and to try to explore the dynamics of all the situations in which she had been repeatedly "cut off" from her love objects as an adult.

FIVE

Choosing the Soundtrack

As we have seen, the "picture sessions" engage patient and therapist in an intense relationship because the therapist is immediately (and visually) allowed to share people and moments of the patient's life. Talking about someone or something and looking at someone or something are two completely different experiences. When the process of multimedia psychotherapy proceeds to the "music session," we go even deeper in this direction and inevitably touch very sensitive notes in the mysterious chords of human affective life. Three musical pieces, chosen by three of my patients, will help us experience what I am talking about, all the more so if we listen to them while reading the following clinical vignettes.

"COME TI VORREI" (IVA ZANICCI II)

The choice of the music is often associated with explicit verbalizations (and psychosomatic expressions) of emotions by the patient. Laurie's case is a good example. Let's play back together the second part of the session when we discussed the soundtrack of her memory object.

Doctor: What about the soundtrack?

Laurie: My mother used to sing a song often.

Doctor: Really?

Laurie: "Come ti vorrei" ["I want you so much" the Italian cover of "Cry to Me"]. Maybe there was a strong association with my father. She loved this song. Iva Zanicchi was the singer.

Doctor: Right! I remember that song very well. The cry of a woman deserted by her man for some unknown reason.

Laurie: My mother used to sing a lot during the day. She sang everything; she might sing mountain folksongs as well as the songs of her day. She really enjoyed singing. I remember very well she often sang this song, although I would always tell her not to sing it since it made me feel sad. Maybe she sang it thinking about her lost husband . . .

Doctor: Possible . . . quite possible . . . Let's go online and see what year the song was created . . .

Laurie: Internet has opened a whole new world!

Doctor: [reading from websites] Italian singer Iva Zanicchi sings "Come ti vorrei" in 1964. The original song was "Cry to Me" by Bert Russell interpreted by Solomon Burke. So, at that time, both your parents were alive but your father died shortly after the song came out! Let's see what we find by comparing the original version with the Italian one. Wow! Here are the original English lyrics. Let me translate them for you. The song says that when you feel alone since the girl you love isn't there anymore, when you have nobody to cry to and share your pain with, you can cry to me! The singer is a man offering to help relieve the pain of his friend deserted by his woman. Yes, I agree it's a very sad song, beautiful but sad. It's about a mourning situation. In the original English lyrics, there's a definite ambiguity about why the woman isn't there anymore. Let's see the Italian lyrics now. Um . . . interesting . . . The Italian text is similar but very different. Here the singer is a woman, and we have a reversal of the story: she's the one who is deserted. The lyrics say the man left his woman because he's a true man, a real man, a man who will never be subdued.

Laurie: Yes, you're right. The man went away, but he's alive. There's much less ambiguity in the lyrics of "Come ti vorrei." Maybe the woman did something wrong and he just left her. There's no way you would even imagine he died in the Italian song: it's just a love story that ended abruptly for some reason . . . but she wants him back!

Doctor: OK, we have the soundtrack. [. . .] What your mother felt, identifying herself with Iva Zanicchi's "Rock and Soul" voice, is that her man is alive and she can express her deep wish to have him back again. This was probably true for your mother, who was defending herself from the pain of the death of her "love object" by refusing to "see" it, to acknowledge it. Do you remember the comments we made about the pictures where you and your mother are looking down?

Laurie: [completely changing her mood and tone of voice] This song used to just belong to my mother. Now I feel it's mine, too. [Laurie cries quietly.]

Doctor: [after a short silence] Right. Now you also feel her feelings. It's as if it is you now who is singing to your mother "Come ti vorrei" ["I want you so much"], in the true spirit of "Rock and Soul."

Laurie: You know, maybe when my father died, my mother had me, but she felt alone without her husband. Just like me now. I have my son and my husband, but I miss her. In fact, when she was alive, we shared everything together. We were living in the same apartment, spending time together. I never cut my umbilical cord. I shared my whole life with her, but it was never a "sacrifice"; it was really a pleasure to stay with her, to spend time with her.

Doctor: I see . . .

Laurie: When she was alive and my son and husband were out of town, I was always happy to stay with her, just the two of us! I would say, "Now we're free! We can do whatever we want, come and go when we want without having to worry about it being late because they're waiting for us to eat or whatever." It was so good the time we spent together. She loved window-shopping, or just having coffee at a café. She was so happy and lively that I'm finally beginning to wonder why I should be afraid to stay home alone. If I could feel her presence, it wouldn't be a problem at all: it would be wonderful if she would be "here with me" [as Iva Zanicchi sings in her song!].

Doctor: Right!

Laurie: I just had this thought, and everything changed . . . You know? I'm not afraid to stay home alone anymore! My son was abroad and my husband has been in the south for the past two nights. I was home all alone, but I felt perfectly fine!

Doctor: Good! That means your relationship with your mother was basically good, as we've seen working on the pictures, today as well as in our previous sessions. So now you can stay home alone without being afraid; you feel safe . . . at last! I remember your son referred you to me in the beginning because you couldn't stay home alone then.

"IL PRIMO AMORE" (CLAUDIO VILLA)

Bianca is a widow in her eighties. She just lost her husband to liver cancer, and she is depressed. Her "children" obliged her to come and see me at the hospital. She accepted, reluctantly, just to calm them down. I gave her some medications and proposed multimedia psychotherapy at my private office, which was accepted by the whole family during our psychiatric consultation in the National Health Service.

Bianca comes to my office alone for our multimedia psychotherapy sessions, while her daughter waits for her downstairs, not wanting to intrude in our therapy. We select the pictures and analyze them in the first two sessions. In our third session, she chooses the music, which is associated with her own personal memory of her dead husband. She has no hesitation: "Il primo amore" ("One's first love") written by Carlo Buti in 1930 and interpreted by Claudio Villa, a famous Roman singer, in 1959.

Since I don't know the song, I go on Internet and we listen to it together. I notice that the song is subtitled "Angelo," which was Bianca's husband's name! The song tells the story of a man and his first love. The lyrics say that they are still together and sing together (although Claudio Villa is the only one who is actually singing) the old Italian proverb: "One's first love is never forgotten!"

It is obvious to me that Bianca feels as if the singer is her husband, her only love, and that it is he (Angelo) who is singing for her (virtually "with her") and repeating over and over again, "One's first love is never forgotten!" By the way, on the back of one of the photos Angelo had sent Bianca when he was away doing military service as a young man, he had signed "Your great love, Angelo."

Suddenly, as soon as the song is finished and we resume our dialogue, Bianca opens up completely and tells me, without any interruption or prompting, a series of painful events in her life, including the battles she had waged so courageously to protect her family. It seems to me that listening to the song together during the session has changed the atmosphere of our meeting dramatically, making it profoundly intimate, deep, and safe, making the two of us attuned with one another. I feel I have before me the blameless, fearless woman of her past, not the depressed, inhibited eighty-year-old widow of the present who was "obliged" to become a patient in a psychiatric service!

I was profoundly impressed by the strength of her disclosure about so many stressful events in her life right after the music had changed the atmosphere of the session. I felt almost overwhelmed, after the session. So I was not surprised when she called the next week saying she was sorry but she couldn't come to therapy. She had had a fall at home and hurt her shoulder. I told her to call me when she had recovered to set another appointment. One month later, Bianca called back, wishing me Merry Christmas and telling me she would come and see me in the new year. I thanked her and asked her how she was doing. She reassured me that she was fine but very busy with the holiday festivities: she had to cook for her children and grandchildren!

When I finally saw her again, she came with her son and daughter, who wanted to thank me for curing their mother, since she no longer needed the medication I had prescribed at the beginning. My understanding of what happened is that she had fallen down at home because she had been overwhelmed, as I had, by the emotional power of our music session as an activator of memories and of the need to express them. In other words, I think she told me too much too fast and developed a double defense: on the one hand, falling down so as to have all her family members around her, recreating the fusional atmosphere of the syncytial group and, on the other, escaping into recovery to prevent opening up again too much in psychotherapy. Indeed, it would have been too risky and painful for this heroic, old-fashioned lady who had no shoulder to lean on ever since her husband had left her forever.

"SALLY" (FIORELLA MANNOIA)

Frieda, a woman in her fifties with no children and a sad life story, came to my hospital suffering from depression and anxiety. Her father had died of leukemia immediately after she was born. At that time, she was living with her mother and a two-year-old older sister. Although they were poor, Frieda's mother was able to save enough money working as a housekeeper to buy a small apartment for her daughters and herself. Not only was she a victim of mobbing in different forms, but she also had problems with her husband, an ex–drug addict who had suffered from compulsive gambling for a few years, using up all their savings. She became very depressed and risked dying of a serious liver infection. In that period her husband assisted her faithfully, and she survived her ordeal, at which point she tried to renew their relationship. Around then, however, he lent money to a young nephew who was also a drug addict, and never got it back. She was psychologically broken once again and began to have troubles at work, too.

I wrote Frieda a doctor's note so that she could be excused from work for a month. Since her weak liver meant I couldn't give her much medication, I decided to resort to multimedia psychotherapy in a private setting with a low fee and low frequency: one session every two weeks. The idea of trying my new therapy with her had come to mind immediately, considering her premature loss of her father and her failure to solve her need for a paternal figure through her marriage, which, in my view, was an indirect confirmation of a pathological mourning.

As had already happened with Laurie and Bianca, Frieda chose the music for her montage without any hesitation: "Sally," a well-known song interpreted by the Italian pop singer Fiorella Mannoia. The lyrics tell the story of a woman walking down a road alone in the rain, a woman who had a painful life, who suffered "too much." She listens to the rain and it sounds good to her. Finally she seems to be able to find something beautiful in her difficult life: the music of the rain.

Only at a later stage in our therapy, after the psychodynamic montage had been completed by the multimedia artist and we had reviewed it together a few sessions later, did it emerge that Frieda's father had a dependent personality, that he had been unable to fight for his life and his family as he was totally subjugated by his mother and sisters. In fact, Frieda's mother had not been able to marry him for many years because of their opposition. (She was poor and had no education, while he had obtained a university degree and owned some land in their little village on an isolated mountain in central Italy.) Finally, she left the village and moved to Rome. Forced to make a choice, Frieda's father sold his land and married her. He was unable to adjust to the big city or to find work, however, so she became the sole supporter of their family. Then, after the birth of their second child, he fell ill and died in less than a month.

Now let's look more closely at the music Frieda had chosen for her soundtrack. The song ends with a series of lines beginning with "perhaps," as night falls on Sally, and the rain keeps falling, too. Freely translated into English prose, the words say, "Perhaps not everything was lost in Sally's life, perhaps something was saved, perhaps not everything was wrong, perhaps it was right this way! Perhaps, maybe, maybe yes! What can I say? The sound of the rain really is a good noise." It is as if, by choosing this song, Frieda is trying to tell herself that all the painful events she had to endure in her life might be reinterpreted as falling rain, rain whose noise might become music and express some mysterious beauty she could appreciate and even enjoy, paradoxically, as she came closer to the last part of her life cycle ("the night" in the final lines of the lyrics). Like her mother, who had lost her husband but was able to raise her daughters and support herself, Frieda is trying to tell herself that she can turn something bad into something good. In fact, after the end of her multimedia sessions, she began to separate from her husband and nurture some hope to be able to live a more gratifying life.

TIPS FOR PSYCHOTHERAPISTS

Once again, multimedia psychotherapy confronts us with the problem of setting: there is a moment, during the music session, when patient and therapist listen together to some song or piece of music chosen by the patient. What is the therapist's role at this special moment?

1. The therapist must be aware that a "syncytial atmosphere" is very likely to develop in the music session if the song is actually played.

In other words, the therapist has two options here: going on the web to find the lyrics and discuss the background of the musical piece with the patient, or listening to it together with the patient as well. The second choice changes the atmosphere of the session, inducing a regression to the group-individual levels of the mind or, in Freudian terms, to "primary process" (Freud 1900), because music speaks a universal language that directly evokes unconscious emotions and affects.

2. In each case, however, the therapist has to consider the need to do extra work outside of the session on the audiovisual materials of multimedia psychotherapy, alone and/or with the multimedia artist when they meet to discuss the psychodynamic montage.
3. The song must be analyzed not only by considering the meaning expressed by the lyrics and the music, but also by putting it into historical perspective so that a possible connection between the song (and/or its singer) and events in the patient's life can be found and discussed. When a song is a "cover," we should take into account the chance that it is probably disguising some repressed contents that can be "recovered" only by knowing the lyrics and sound of the original song.

SIX

Working with the Artist

Having described the "picture sessions" as well as the "music session," we are now ready to explore the artist's work in multimedia psychotherapy. We will do it by reconsidering the cases of Bianca and Frieda from the point of view of the artist. Then we will present two cases (Deborah and Nando) where the artist's interpretation went beyond the chronological order established by the patient during the "picture sessions." By the end, we will begin to appreciate not only the actual work done by the artist editing the images and soundtrack chosen by the patient, but also the unconscious role that the artist is playing in multimedia psychotherapy.

BIANCA

by Filippo A. Nesci, in collaboration with Domenico A. Nesci

When my father gave me the song title and the pictures for the psychodynamic montage of Case No. 0007, we discussed the possibility that Bianca might have chosen the song largely because it had a subtitle (Angelo) that was the name of her dead husband. In fact, my father told me that Angelo was Bianca's first and only love, as the singer (Claudio Villa) sings in "Il primo amore" ("First Love"), a romantic Italian ballad.

If you look at the remix I made and published with my father (Nesci, D. A. and Nesci, F. A. 2010) on the online scientific journal *Doppio Sogno* (http://www.doppio-sogno.it/numero11/OggettoMemoriaVideo.htm), you can listen to the song while the pictures selected by Bianca in her multimedia psychotherapy sessions roll along as a stream of consciousness on the unforgettable nature of one's first love. The lyrics tell the story of a lover who is praising his first and only woman. The song was chosen by an eighty-year-old widow as the soundtrack for the psychodynamic montage made with forty pictures representing the most important moments of her husband's (and her own) life: his childhood, his first Communion, their first picture together when they were teenagers, his army life, his job, their wedding, the birth of their two children, the weddings of their children, the birth of their grandchildren, their grandson's eighteenth birthday party, and their own golden wedding anniversary.

Using a well-know software I was able to associate the song with images of the real Angelo, as if he were the lover/singer singing to his woman (Bianca) to confirm that he had been her one and only true love for their whole life. This implicit message is emphasized by my use of the brief text written by Angelo on the back of a picture he mailed her when he was a young man doing military service (fig. 6.1), as my father explained to me when he gave me the pictures and a Word file indicating the order I should follow to make the remix.

In fact, the text on the back of the photo says: "I send you this picture because it is the only one I have here. I hope you will enjoy it anyway. Your great love, Angelo" (fig. 6.2).

Figure 6.1. Angelo during his military service

In this way, the person who sees and listens to the remix inevitably thinks (when I zoom in on Angelo's face) that he is the main character, the "real" Angelo (the man who is singing the song, the man who is in love with his first love, forever and ever) and that Bianca is his only woman.

Actually, I do not zoom in on Angelo's face in the remix. I make a special transition so that after we see his military service photo (fig. 6.1), the photo begins quickly squeezing up from bottom right to top left, giving the impression that I am zooming in on Angelo's face. As the photo disappears, however, it reveals Angelo's message to Bianca on the back (fig. 6.2). At that same moment, the singer is singing "I'm giving you a squeeze" (I'm embracing you), adding one more "new" meaning to the song, the pictures, and the music.

I think this is a very effective example of how a remix, using a song, digital pictures of everyday life, the scan of a handwritten letter on the back of a photo, and some imagination, can produce something new: evoke a feeling that can move an eighty-year-old lady to tears and happiness, helping her to recover from depression and work through her mourning for the loss of her husband after a lifetime spent together.

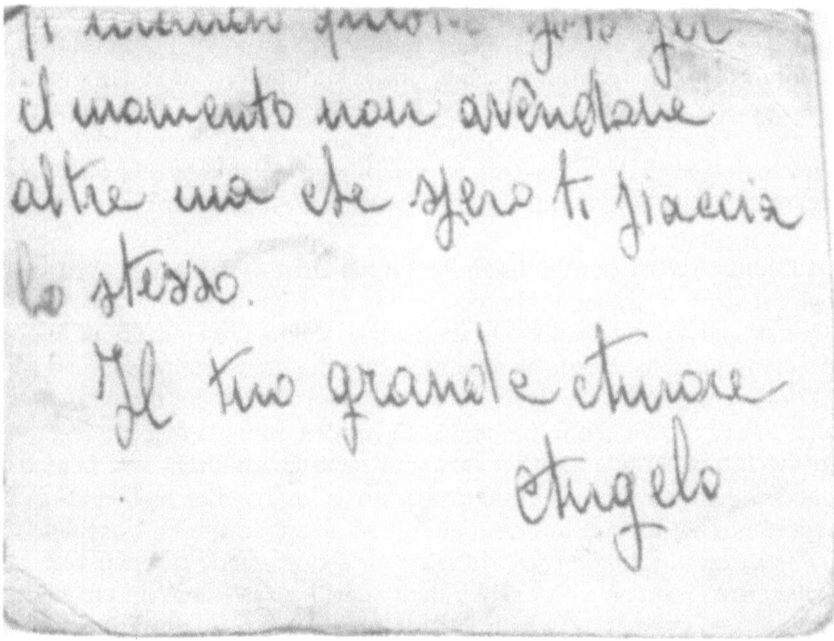

Figure 6.2. Angelo's message to Bianca on the back of the picture

FRIEDA

When I gave my son the pictures and music for Case No. 0010, I was forced to take his emotional reaction into account because, after a few hours of work with the multimedia objects, he told me he didn't want to continue since he was so bored! Then I noticed the name he had just given to the file of the psychodynamic montage: "*mannoio*," which means (if we write it "*m'annoio*") "I'm getting bored!" Clearly my son was playing a word game, associating with the name of the singer (Fiorella Mannoia) of the song chosen by the patient (Frieda). Nonetheless, the song really was boring him to the point that it interfered with his capacity to work on the remix. When we talked about it, he said he felt that my patient must be accustomed to living in an atmosphere of perpetual "lamentation." Otherwise, she would never have chosen that music for her soundtrack.

So, in my next session with Frieda, I shared with her my conversation with the multimedia artist. Actually, what happened was that, at the beginning of the session, Frieda asked me about the artist's reaction to the pictures and the music she had selected, and I told her the truth. She began to laugh, surprising me with her self-irony. "He's absolutely right," she said. "The music really is monotonous and repetitive. I guess I like it because I'm an obsessive person." Then the session took an unexpected path, with Frieda telling me many childhood episodes when she had felt bored with her mother's continual laments about her unlucky fate. Then Frieda went on, "Every family has a sort of motto, and my family's was 'Three women alone,' implying that our problem was the absence of a man. On the other hand," she added, "my husband's family motto is 'Deny, deny, deny . . . everything and always.' In fact, in the past they managed to deny his drug addiction, and today they still deny that the wife of one of his brothers is a male transvestite. They really believe he is a woman."

I think that my candid discussion of the artist's feedback proved very helpful since it probably allowed Frieda to open herself up and reveal "secret" parts of her family life she hadn't been able to talk about in our previous sessions. Frieda also told me that this transvestite is a man she likes very much, a very lively, creative person. She spent the whole session telling stories about him and their serious plan to emigrate together in the future. Frieda and her husband have no children, and her husband's brother, with his trans wife, has no children either. So they think it would not be difficult to eventually go all together, the four of them, to some exotic destination (the transvestite's homeland) to open a small Italian restaurant on a beach, rent their apartment in Rome, and live with their retirement money, which would be sufficient since the cost of living there is very low.

In the same session, Frieda was also able to reveal that she used to yell at her mother when she was old. Of course she didn't want to, but she did it often anyway, compulsively. Frieda remembered a birthday card her mother had given her with some money in the envelope. Her mother had written that she had enclosed more money than on previous birthdays since Frieda had been scolding her less than usual that year. Frieda was moved to tears at this point. She promised she would bring the card and asked me to have the artist add it to the video (with her mother's handwriting). Then she thanked me for the session, saying she had been able to express herself more freely and truly than in our previous meetings.

DEBORAH AND NANDO

When I gave my son the pictures and music chosen by Deborah, a fifty-five-year-old woman whose husband had just died of pancreatic cancer, I never imagined that he would show me a video a few days later with the sequence of the pictures changed from the sequence chosen by the patient. "Why did you change it?" I asked. "I have no idea! Do you like it?" he answered. "Well, I'm surprised!" "OK, but do you like it or not?" "Well, the issue is not if I like it. The question is if the patient likes it." "Right, so why don't you just ask her next time you see her and show her the video?"

I showed Deborah the video in our next session. The music was "Maria Elena," by Santo and Johnny, a piece she had chosen without any hesitation; the pictures were her own, but the sequence was new. Instead of starting with an old black-and-white photo depicting her husband as a baby or a small child, as usually happens in our memorial objects, this psychodynamic montage begins with a family group: Deborah's husband, Deborah, and their only son (born after sixteen years of marriage) in a sequence of four color photos full of sun and joy. The first two pictures portray husband and wife as an adult couple. The third and fourth show them with their son, who smiles happily. In the fourth (which should have been the twenty-eighth, according to the order decided by the patient), the camera zooms in on the child's face, followed by a fast movement that seems to draw the observer directly into the image. Then there is a quick transition to the next photo (the first one, according to Deborah's original intentions), which depicts Deborah's husband many years earlier, at the same age as his son in the previous picture. The effect is extremely powerful: a flashback implying that the boy is the continuation of his father and/or, perhaps, that, paradoxically, the father is reborn out of his own son. After this poetic license by the artist, the following pictures resume the historical sequence of Deborah's husband's life, as organized by the patient, from the second photo to the end.

Deborah was delighted by my son's editing. Apparently she didn't notice the flashback, although it was evident that the chronological order of the pictures had been modified. Her feeling was that the artist had done what she had asked him to do. "It's great!" Then the session took a path I would never have expected. She began to talk about the relationship between her husband and her son. She told me her husband worried excessively about their son's future; for example, when the boy was a teenager, her husband used to look for a job for him in an absurdly counterproductive way.

Recalling that Deborah's husband had begun to work with his own father when he was a teenager, I was able to appreciate the artist's intuition in creating this identity between father and son in boyhood as something poetic and beautiful rather than pathologic and disturbing. While I was thinking this flashback was a wonderful way to help Deborah's son to work through his father's death, Deborah told me she was very sorry that her husband had been unable to have a good relationship with their son until the last months of his life. I took it as a confirmation that what the artist had created in the psychodynamic montage was simultaneously the revelation and the reparation of a pathologic identification between father and son, as if they couldn't both be alive as adults at the same time because of their overidentification. I have the definite sense that the beauty of the flashback in this video comes from the artist's capacity to find an "impossible" solution to these unconscious dynamics through a professional use of audiovisual cinematographic language.

As a matter of fact, Deborah was more realistic about her past by the end of the session. She confessed that it was not true that she had had a wonderful life with her family and her husband. In fact, she had been unhappy: as a child she lived in extreme poverty and was severely restricted by her father, who forbade her to leave the house. Then, after her marriage, she was isolated by her husband, who was always at work and didn't want her to go out of house, just like her father. After completing the memorial object, it seemed that she was finally able to acknowledge her ambivalent feelings toward her father and her husband.

Music without Words

Deborah was my first patient to choose music without words as the soundtrack for the psychodynamic montage. It occurs to me now (reflecting on Deborah's case approximately one year later, as I write this chapter) that this absence of words made my son feel freer to "move" the images from their original positions, according to his own artistic interpretation.

There is only one other patient (so far) who chose music that was not a song with lyrics: Case No. 0008. This patient (Nando, the only child of a widow) lived his whole life as a prisoner of his own mother and suffered a severe depression after her death at age ninety-six. In this case, also, my son edited the psychodynamic montage in a very creative way, using the same pictures several times (without any relation to their chronological order) so as to follow the vertiginous rhythm of the music ("Carmen" by Bizet). In this way, he was also trying to give some zest for life to a man who lived most of his existence controlled by a cold, rigid, castrating mother who was unable to express her own emotions and wouldn't let her son express his freely, either. Deborah and Nando were looking for freedom, which is why they both chose a musical piece without words. My interpretation of what happened is that the artist was able to attune himself with the patients' unconscious (through the pictures, the music, and my verbal and nonverbal communications), which allowed him to take the liberty of moving the pictures from the positions originally chosen by the patients.

THE UNCONSCIOUS ROLE OF THE ARTIST IN MULTIMEDIA PSYCHOTHERAPY

The clinical vignettes summarized here help us to identify the unconscious role played by the multimedia artist. In essence, the artist acts as an intermediary or mediator between patient and therapist. His presence is precious because it allows for triangulations in their unconscious relationship. When I understood the extreme importance of the role of the artist on the unconscious level, I began to look for an artist to replace my son in his work with the multimedia objects. Interestingly, my son felt relieved by this change. This confirms my impression that the artist is exposed to the patient's emotions through the therapist's unconscious countertransference feelings.

In classic psychotherapy, the role of the third is played by the supervisor but, as all psychotherapists know, once training has been completed, there are few opportunities for supervision. Given that multimedia psychotherapy requires the collaboration of an artist, the dimension of the presence of a third party and the opportunity to make triangulations is automatically reintroduced. Moreover, resistances (by patient and therapist) to the artist's "interpretations" (in the editing) are less likely to develop since the artist knows nothing about the patient and works only on concrete audiovisual objects. The patient accepts feedback more easily from someone who is not a therapist, who does not know him/her, and who is trying to make a beautiful memorial object, not to analyze anyone or anything. Even if they never meet personally, patient and artist are motivated to work together, to create something together, and to "meet" through the concrete multimedia objects that represent a precious memory for the patient and a work of art for the artist. The patient is truly interested to see how the artist will interpret his/her images and music, just as the artist is truly interested to get feedback on the meaningfulness (for the patient and the patient's relatives and friends) of what he or she has produced.

By its very nature, multimedia psychotherapy offers an opportunity for a change in perspective. On the positive side, this facilitates a transformation in the unconscious relationship between the patient and his/her inner world objects. Meanwhile, the therapist can also enjoy a positive experience, receiving feedback without feeling judged by another "expert" (student, colleague, or supervisor) since the artist belongs to a completely different field. At the end of the process, when the psychodynamic montage is given to the patient, both therapist and patient feel they have received something valuable and concrete from the artist: a track of the whole process of elaboration. Then the patient can freely decide whether or not to pursue the therapeutic process further with more sessions of classic psychodynamic psychotherapy.

Another positive aspect of the role played by the artist is that the patient's gratitude is not directed toward a single person, but rather toward a whole team that includes himself/herself, the therapist, and the artist, as well as all the other people who contributed by taking pictures, appearing in them, or composing/playing music and writing lyrics. The patient has the feeling of being part of a repairing syncytial group, of having reestablished a harmonious symbiotic relationship with the cultural matrix and the original structure of the group-individual that lives within him or herself. This experience, in fact, plays a therapeutic role in and of itself.

SEVEN

The Screening Session and the Outcome

Watching the psychodynamic montage is the ritual moment in which patient and therapist look at the third. Although it is obviously concrete, like all the "things" studied by Salman Akhtar in the psychoanalytic setting (2003), the music video materializes in the space-time frame of the session as a vivid presence. The main character of the remix, and all the others, appear on the scene as if they were in motion, evoking more-intense "moving" feelings than those induced by the patient's oral narrative or by viewing the still photographs in a picture session. The characters in the montage also look more "real," in part because they unconsciously take "aliveness" from the concrete aliveness of patient and therapist at work in the room. At the same time, the appearances of the therapist, who is actually present, audibly and visibly, are unconsciously compared by the patient with the "lively" motion pictures on the screen, so that the patient can become more easily aware of the illusionary nature of transference. Thus, when the *dramatis personae* of the patient's story appear "live" on the screen, everyone appears more authentic. Patient and therapist get to know who they are more "personally" (or whom they might embody, unconsciously, in the transference) by sharing their own audiovisual experience of the psychodynamic montage as interpreted by the artist through the editing.

Consciously or unconsciously, everyone has the artist in mind. The therapist is anxious about how the patient might react to the video, and the patient is anxious about what the artist did with the "audiovisual doubles" of his/her love objects. While it is obvious that any interpretation may be wrong, in classic psychotherapy it remains abstract, but in multimedia psychotherapy it becomes concrete. Neither the patient nor the therapist is paralyzed with guilt if there is a mistake because it has to do with the artist now, not with them! Their minds are cleared, in some way, by this projection onto the artist. Artists are always free and innocent: whatever they do, it's poetic license! And, in multimedia psychotherapy, it can be changed if "we" don't like it. Patient and therapist will share a "family secret" and be aware of that and of what had been repressed and how it was transformed, covering up the original edition. In fact, even after the screening session, the artist remains available to make any changes requested by the patient. Finally, it becomes absolutely clear that psychotherapy has to do with "constructions" in the analytic work rather than interpretations or historical truth (Freud 1938).

So it often happens that new insights (or new memories) come to the fore after the screening session, as we have seen in the cases of Serena, Elisabetta, and Deborah. The teamwork by patient, therapist, and artist has concretely inserted "ordinary time" into (or "captured in a time net") repressed feelings and memories: the patient's "unpast" (Scarfone 2006), thus allowing the mourning patient to move on.

EXCERPTS FROM A SCREENING SESSION (LAURIE)

Laurie: [with tears welling up in her eyes] It's very beautiful. . . . It's all beautiful.

Doctor: [at the end of the screening] How are you?

Laurie: Fine . . . just fine . . . a few days ago, chatting with my niece, who is a doctor, I was telling her I was getting this help from Dr. Nesci since I took my mother's death so hard . . . I must say that I'm OK now. The memory of my mother is always alive, but I don't have those disturbing flashes of the hospital room anymore . . . of the blood. Not anymore. Now I have a good memory of my mother, a more normal memory, thanks to the path you let me follow with you. I can't say I'm completely at peace about it, though. That moment was truly traumatic; she obviously wouldn't have chosen to die that way . . . but we all have to die one way or another . . . and we all have to accept the destiny that God decides for us. On the other hand, today I can say that even if I couldn't hold her hand at the last moment, I know that I've been with her my whole life. This is a great gift of love. I enjoyed my mother and I hope she also enjoyed her daughter.

Doctor: Right.

Laurie: Also, I had a husband who made this possible. My husband came to our home when we were both teenagers. My mother raised him as her own child, just as she did with me. His parents were living in the countryside, far from the village. Often he would sleep over at my house in the winter so that he could get up early to take the bus to school in the city. After the death of my father, he was sleeping at my mother's house, and I was sleeping in the city to be ready to go to school in the morning. His parents agreed with that. My mother-in-law was a simple but intelligent woman, and she was not jealous at all. She always told my husband and me to treat Imelda with gratitude since she had raised both of us, and our son too! That is why, for him, it was so normal to live with my mother in Rome. She was like a mother for him. This is the missing link I hadn't told you yet in the story chain. I needed to tell you.

Doctor: I see . . .

Laurie: I feel better now. I wonder if you can see it in a tangible way. I have to say that I feel much better, thanks to your help.

Doctor: Yes, I can see that. I'm quite satisfied with the work we've done together.

[At this point, Laurie asks me if I know of a psychotherapist in her mother's native area for a relative who is stressed after a traumatic experience. I tell her about my school of psychotherapy and find an alumnus in the area, looking at my address book in my computer. Then she pays for the video and asks me to thank the artist. I promise I will and ask her what I should tell him since he will surely want to know her reaction.]

Laurie: Tell him I was moved to tears, as you've seen . . . Tell him the movie made me feel so good! I've reviewed the whole "movie" of my life: as a child, as a woman, when my mother accompanied me to the altar to get married, when she raised my child with me. I've seen my life replayed in the video, and it did me a lot of good.

Doctor: Anytime you'd like to see me again, don't hesitate. Just call me.

Laurie: That's exactly what I was going to ask you. Right now everything is fine, but, you know . . . just in case . . .

Doctor: Absolutely, just in case . . . Call me and we'll set up an appointment. Let me know your son's reaction when he sees the video, too!

Laurie: Yes, of course.

We forget to perform the last part of the ritual of multimedia psychotherapy: my giving the pictures back to the patient. I forget, but she also forgets to ask me about it. The next day she calls and asks if she can come to my office to pick them up. I suggest that she send her son to the hospital where I will be the following day. Then, I forget to bring the pictures to the hospital, but it doesn't matter since her son doesn't show up anyway!

A few months later, just before Easter, Laurie called to say she would come to pick up her pictures and greet me for the holiday, which commemorates the resurrection of Jesus from the dead. We meet in my office at my hospital, the place where Imelda died and where Laurie's son first asked me to help her. She presents me with an Easter dove, a symbolic cake of peace.

THE OUTCOME

The process of multimedia psychotherapy (whether it is inserted within a classic therapy or started specifically from the beginning of the cure) seems to be helpful for the patient, independent of its completion. Patients often feel better just working with the pictures or choosing the soundtrack, even before the screening session. Other times they improve only after the remix is seen and analyzed, or in the following sessions. My experience is that in every case multimedia psychotherapy promotes the occurrence of "turning points" in the curative process. I refer to this concept in the sense defined by the Swedish psychoanalyst Böhm (1992), who used this term "to mean a momentary sudden change in quality, depth or direction. It is, to use another image, as if a metaphorical new door to a new unexpected room is opened."

Here I will review two cases: one case (Laurie) where the positive outcome emerged *before* the remix was even produced by the artist (and shared by patient and therapist in the screening session) and one case where it only became evident some months *after* the patient (Nando) had watched the psychodynamic montage for the first time, without expressing any apparent emotional reaction. Significantly, in both cases, the patients mentioned the work with their audiovisual objects during the turning points. In Nando's case, the psychodynamic montage was even played back in the session, for the second time, and watched by patient and therapist together.

Laurie

During one session, Laurie was able to discuss the issue of guilt feelings in the mourning process, thanks to her frequent talks with a friend who had also lost her mother. As always, it is easier to understand ourselves if we are talking about someone else! Just as the therapist works as an auxiliary Ego for the patient, so do our relatives and friends, or even fictional characters (our unconscious "doubles" in movies or narratives of any kind), helping us to see more clearly, protected by a safer distance.

Here is a brief excerpt from Laurie's session *before* the screening session.

> *Laurie*: At times I feel guilty. This is something I talked about with a friend of mine who lost her mother a year before I lost mine. She is an only child, too, like me, and she is only recovering from her mourning now. So we often talk about our feelings when we meet. I feel like her: I feel guilty when I realize that I still think about my mother but I suffer less. Thinking about my mother is not a bleeding experience anymore, so to speak. "Am I forgetting her?" I don't think so . . . Yet, I feel guilty. I am not forgetting; I am thinking/remembering her in a more normal way, perhaps.
>
> *Doctor*: Right. Over time, Mother Nature helps us strengthen our good memories and blunt the painful ones.
>
> *Laurie*: Yes. It's like a wound . . .
>
> *Doctor*: . . . that gradually heals.
>
> *Laurie*: That's still there but isn't bleeding anymore. [I was struck by her use of the metaphor of bleeding from a wound, which was the way her mother had actually died, though of course I didn't say anything in this regard.]
>
> *Doctor*: Exactly.
>
> *Laurie*: I was wondering if what is happening to me in this period regarding the way I think of my mother, after having worked it through here together in our sessions, is normal. You know, I have no doubt that this change happening through our therapy is a change for the better. I mean, I really feel much better now. Still, I was wondering, is it normal?
>
> *Doctor*: It's normal. The normal process of mourning . . .
>
> *Laurie*: You know, I even told my son recently, "I'm feeling much better." [Doctor and patient laugh together.]

Although nobody says it explicitly, the feeling in the session is that "there is no guilt in successfully mourning a person we loved" or, to put it differently, "Separation is possible when a relationship has been good."

Nando

Nando is a seventy-year-old patient who lived his whole life with his mother, who died at ninety-six. He is a very polite, shy person, respectful of the elderly, careful to choose the right words to express himself, and always afraid of offending others or losing his self-control. He was educated by Catholic priests in a private school, where he studied after the death of his father, when he was nine. Now he is retired, after having spent many years working full-time in a public institution.

I see him the first time at the hospital. He tells me the story of several years of depression that has taken a turn for the worse, with the sudden onset of panic attacks that prevent him from driving or taking a plane. I immediately realize that he is unable to make the obvious connection between the death of his mother and his anxious, depressive symptoms, so I propose multimedia psychotherapy to elaborate the death of his mother and complete his mourning process. Nando accepts, although he doesn't "feel" he could be depressed and anxious because of his loss. Only now I realize that I had denied the simple fact that he had been suffering his whole life from the death of his father, long before his mother's death. Of course he is the one who used this defense mechanism to protect himself from mental pain; I just followed him and failed to work through my own countertransference. In his transference, he was able to project onto me not only his unconscious (disavowed) feelings but his defenses, too!

Here I want to emphasize that patient and therapist (Nando and myself) only became aware of this "obvious" fact (i.e., that he had displaced the previous unelaborated grief for the death of his father onto his mourning for his mother) six months *after* the screening session of his mother's memory object had taken place! At the same time, I want to emphasize that during that turning-point session, Nando spoke of the psychodynamic montage, and we watched it again together, realizing that his father never appeared in it at all. Thus began the exploration of this disavowed "room" of his inner world: the loss of his father.

Let's go now into Nando's turning-point session (Böhm 1992). As I mentioned earlier, this session took place six months after the screening session. In this case I didn't use my tape recorder, so I will rely on my notes and my memories.

Nando tells me he had many recurring dreams. This is very unusual for him. Another most unusual thing is that in this series of dreams, he was finally able to be with his mother. In two of them, he dreamt the precise moment of her death. They were together in the hospital room where she died; he was holding her hand and feeling, once again, the warmth of life suddenly fade away from her as she turned dead cold. He was very moved by these dreams. Then, he dreamt of her again in the subsequent nights. In these dreams, however, his mother was alive and happy. She was dressed up as if she were about to go to the opera or the theatre. In one dream, he remembers quite clearly that she was wearing a pair of long earrings that his father had given her as a gift.

Nando wants to talk with me about these unusual dreams. I ask him to freely associate and talk about anything that comes into his mind, and he tells me a story. Once, he came home from work and found his mother reading letters in her bedroom. When he asked about them, she said they were letters from his father, which she read every afternoon when Nando was out. Nando said he would love to read some of them to learn more about his father, but she refused, saying they belonged to her alone and that he should never read them. He was very unhappy, but accepted her point of view and her decision (as he always did). Even now, he would not even consider reading them.

Then he asked me, "What do you think about the earrings?" "Well," I said, "the earrings are a double object. They are associated with your father. They are close to ears/sounds and eyes/sight. Maybe you miss your father . . . a relationship with him . . . We should have done a video for your father, too! It seems as if he still belongs exclusively to your mother." Nando agrees and tells me he doesn't remember whether he had put a picture of his father in the montage or not. (He has only two pictures of him since he gave the third to his nanny, a relative of his father's at whose home he had been living for a few months during his depression after his mother died.) I say I didn't think he had brought me any pictures of his father, but we are not sure, so we decide to watch the video again together. We screen the remix (I have a copy in my computer) and discover that, in fact, he hadn't brought any pictures of his father, so he is not included in the psychodynamic montage at all! I tell Nando he can bring one anytime, and we can ask the artist to add it.

The session ends with an explicit avowal that he suffered from a "double" mourning represented by the paternal earrings in his dream. I reassure Nando that the very fact that he is finally able to dream of his mother, his father, and their strong tie (the earrings) is a good sign. At this point, Nando tells me a vivid memory from his childhood. His father, who was a taxi driver, used to drive Nando and the children who lived in his building for a short ride in his taxi every day at the end of his morning work hours. It was always such a memorable, exciting event! After this session, new "rooms" opened up in the exploration of his inner world.

Now he is enjoying a holiday in Paris, where he was able to fly (taking an airplane again, at last!) with some friends.

CONCLUSIONS

by Domenico A. Nesci, in collaboration with Domenico Agresta, Alessia Marzano, and Sara Vendetti

In order for a psychotherapy to work effectively, it must have strong anthropological roots. If this is so, we should expect people to discover and practice it, spontaneously, even before health professionals "discover" or "invent" it and try to build its scientific theoretical and clinical foundation.

Teaching multimedia psychotherapy to different students in different courses, as well as talking with patients in my countless psychiatric consultations at my hospital, I was deeply impressed by how often people recurred to multimedia objects to overcome difficult passages in their lives. This was the case, for instance, of a young man who had an accident, was forced to stop practicing his sport, and elaborated his "mourning" experience producing by himself a multimedia object of his prior athletic life (Dr. Domenico Agresta told me this story). Now I am no longer surprised when some of my students approach me at the end of a lesson to share stories that echo the many stories posted every day by individuals who fill the Internet with multimedia objects in their efforts to work through things that seem difficult to elaborate through the traditional rituals of our culture.

That is why I want to end this chapter not with one more clinical example, but with a personal experience told by one of my psychotherapy students at SIPSI in Rome. Dr. Sara Vendetti shared with us the story of two adolescents whom she has known for many years. Carla and Dora lost their mother to cancer when they were little. Then, as they grew up and began "playing" with computers, they filled their screensaver with pictures of their lost mother.

Dr. Vendetti's reflections on this original use of the screensaver are quite interesting since they point out unexpected analogies between a mental function and the function of a technological device. As she explained,

> The origin of the screensaver dates back to the late '70s, when technology made it necessary to protect the personal computer screens from the risk of a prolonged display of images or characters (phosphor burn-in). The danger was that an overload in some area of the screen could burn its phosphors and form a "ghost image" due to the permanence of characters or lines in the pixels that should be off. That is why the screensaver enters into operation after a certain period of inactivity of the mouse or keyboard, obscuring the screen or, as in this case, displaying an animation or a series of images in sequence, to protect the screen and extend its life. In an analogous operation, after a period of depressive inactivity, the young artisans instinctively, unconsciously, found a

> solution (a mental screen saver) against the risk of being damaged by the burning power of an indelible ghost (the fixed mental representation of their dead mother). To protect themselves, Carla and Dora effectively created an artistic product, a sort of photographic slide show of their mother, recovering and editing the most meaningful passages of her life and their own family life. They then placed it on a virtual screen (and at the same time, on a mental one), which looks like the sky full of stars, the metaphorical place where their father had told them she had gone, or like the world of our dreams, where we repair ourselves while sleeping, every night, or fantasizing, anytime we need it, every day.

Dr. Alessia Marzano also told an intriguing story, which shows what I and my colleagues at SIPSI mean when we say that multimedia psychotherapy is the new psychodynamic approach for our patients (young and old) in today's Technological Age. I will tell the story in Dr. Marzano's words.

> Flora is an eighteen-month-old girl who was left by her mother for three days when she went to the hospital to deliver her second child. Once during that period, Flora didn't want to eat her dinner since her mother wasn't there to feed her as usual. Then, out of the blue, she asked her aunt to let her see her mother's picture on her cell phone. Specifically, she remembered they had taken a picture of her mother just before she left home to go to the hospital, a picture where her pregnancy was clearly visible . . . and she asked her aunt to show her that picture. Not only that! She turned a toy on the table upside down, so that the cell phone could rest on it and she could look at it while eating. Finally she put her aunt's cell phone on the improvised base and, smiling, said to her, "Ready . . . Din-din now!" And she calmly started eating the babyfood she had been refusing just a minute before!

A technological device had made her mother's image virtually "present" so she could enjoy the illusion that she was actually there feeding her as usual.

In my view, multimedia psychotherapy is the future. Even our offices will change in response to the Technological Age we live in. Besides the chairs and couch of today, we will have screens, loudspeakers, computers, and Internet, so both patient and therapist can freely associate on images and sounds, music and movies, lyrics and art objects the same way we work today on stories, screen memories, and dreams, communicating only through words and silent body language.

EIGHT

Theoretical Reflections on Multimedia Psychotherapy

We have now completed the clinical part of our course. If we look back, we can recall entering the labyrinthine trail of multimedia psychotherapy with Serena (chapter 1), meandering with Elisabetta and the students/patients of the master's program in psycho-oncology (chapter 2), and arriving at the center, thanks to my patients and the clinical vignettes they generously made available for us all to share. We have covered all the essential elements of my technique, step by step: intake (chapter 3), picture sessions (chapter 4), music session (chapter 5), working with the artist (chapter 6), and the screening session and outcome (chapter 7).

Now it is time to reflect, from a theoretical point of view, on what we are doing when we practice multimedia psychotherapy, on why and how it works. It is time to ask ourselves some questions, to give ourselves some answers . . . Once again, I will do it following an associative trail, even if this might arouse some unavoidable feelings of disorientation. To mitigate such feelings, I will anticipate the main ideas we will cover:

1. The memory objects of multimedia psychotherapy are doubles.
2. These doubles can be conceived as "screen memories" (Freud 1901).
3. They can also be seen as "transitional objects" (Winnicott 1951).

In fact, this is the Ariadne's thread I have been unravelling, explicitly or implicitly, during the first part of our course. . . . Now I need only follow it back, here and in the next chapters, to find my way out of the apparent labyrinth of my book.

PRELUDE: MEMORY OBJECTS

On an unconscious level, what are these memory objects we want to produce with the help of the multimedia artist? From our ethnopsychoanalytic approach, as we have already seen, we are working to produce concrete "doubles" in order to replace a lost object (in the inner or outer worlds) or a dead object (inside or outside of ourselves). The healing features of these doubles come from the fact that they are not at all mere copies of the originals. Teamwork produced reparative changes to this inanimate object in order to allow the subject to move on (resetting his or her inner clock so that it is synchronized with chronological time). Unconscious feelings (hate, shame, guilt, etc.) are uncovered more easily while analyzing pictures and music chosen by the patient. This work of elaboration, carried out concretely by a group (the patient, his/her relatives and friends, the therapist, the multimedia artist, the artists who provide the soundtrack, and so on) makes it possible for the dialogue between the individual and the group-individual, within the patient's inner world, to resume.

The work takes place concretely too, at the same time, in the transference/countertransference acting out that occurs in the multimedia sessions, as we have seen. For example, in the case of Sara, when I eliminated and then reintroduced the picture where she was close to Paul, I was acting out and working through the patient's ambivalence toward her first son. I was doing it, unconsciously, via projective identification (Klein 1946) acted out ("moved") by my patient. In that moment, the picture session turned into a sort of psychodrama, a "time machine" where Sara was regressively expelling (and then recovering) her repressed or disavowed emotions, integrating them, and repairing her wounded Self by using me as her "Auxiliary Ego" (Freud, A. 1956).

From Scarfone's point of view, Sara and I were aiming to start up the clock of life again; we were working together to turn the "unpast" into past, to insert chronological time (the time of the session where the drama of ambivalence was revived) into the period of Sara's life that was mummified, frozen, and tragically "actual" (Scarfone 2006) in the compulsive repetition of her unelaborated ambivalent mother-son relationship (in the form of her continual fights with Paul).

Producing the psychodynamic montage for the screening session, the multimedia artist was repeating the process of elaboration in a different setting and with the intermediary of a concrete inanimate memory object (the pictures and music), into which the editing was able to insert a reconstructed chronological time in the bedrock of the repressed, always "actual," unpast (Scarfone 2006). Using the metaphor of our "impossible" problem, we could say that the transference/countertransference dynamics allow patient and therapist to observe the patient's inner world (the nine points) from point A, while the multimedia object by the artist introduces a point B perspective, reinforcing the whole psychodynamic process. That is why we have more opportunities for turning points in multimedia psychotherapy than in classic sessions. The multimedia sessions, even when they are only one part of a classic long-term psychodynamic treatment, become a turning point in themselves.

Shaping Concrete Doubles

As we saw in chapter 2, in central Australia there is a widespread belief in the doubles or spiritual counterparts of human beings (precursors of the soul? of the guardian spirit or angel of our time?). These doubles grow up together with the *rella ndurpa* (the real flesh and blood body), but never grow old and die. They are believed to live underneath the *tjurunga* in a sacred cave, the womb of Mother Earth, and are thus connected symbolically at their birthplace in a dual-unity (Róheim 1945b).

The *tjurunga* is a sacred object with an elongated form, made of wood or stone and covered with carvings. It is considered to be the common body of the human species and of its totemic ancestors (Strehlow 1908–1909). When a child is born, its ancestral home is identified and a *tjurunga* is made and guarded religiously. In many tribes, two different kinds are made: a bigger one (called "body *tjurunga*") and a smaller one, called "bull-roarer." The whole life of a young Aborigine is already traced in the carvings on these *tjurungas*. The body of the ancestor is represented with the cave, the place of origin, and the paths he traveled in the "Dreamtime" (the mythological times of Australian Aborigines, or "the Eternal Ones of the Dream" as Géza Róheim called them). Ernest Jones, one of the first-generation psychoanalysts and Freud's biographer, pointed out that the bull-roarer is the most ancient and widespread sacred object in Australia (1914). When it is swung around on a string or cord, it emits a particular buzzing sound that seems to belong to another dimension.

I would like to emphasize these audiovisual characteristics of the bull-roarer and their powerful emotional effects on the group-individual mind. In fact, the psychodynamic montage of multimedia psychotherapy seems quite similar in its therapeutic reparative functions to the Aboriginal bull-roarer. It condenses a whole life path into a song through a sequence of meaningful images. Thanks to its "double" (audiovisual) nature, it is a powerful memory object. In fact, according to Freud (1901), "Some people remember in visual images; their memories have a visual character. Other people can scarcely reproduce in their memory even the scantiest [visual] outlines of what they have experienced. Following Charcot's proposal, such people are called auditifs and moteurs in contrast to the visuels" (46).

Starting from here, we can begin to reflect on what we are doing when we engage with our patients in multimedia psychotherapy. My theory is that, by producing these concrete doubles/bull-roarers/multimedia objects, we promote the production/elaboration of something that is understandable by the individual as well as by the group-individual, by the "visuels" as well as by the "auditifs and moteurs." I will explore the nature of these powerful memory objects through two psychoanalytic ideas: "screen memories" (Freud 1901) and "transitional objects" (Winnicott 1951). So now, following the path of association, let us discuss the concept of the screen memory (transitional objects will be discussed in the last chapter) and see where it takes us.

From "Screen Memories" to the "Obstetrical Dilemma"

The concept of screen memories was introduced by Sigmund Freud in his book on dreams (1900) and further elaborated by him in the following years, particularly in his work on the psychopathology of everyday life (1901):

> I started from the striking fact that a person's earliest childhood memories seem frequently to have preserved what is indifferent and unimportant, whereas (frequently, though certainly not universally) no trace is found in an adult's memory of impressions dating from that time which are important, impressive and rich in affect. [. . .] As the indifferent memories owe their preservation not to their own content but to an associative relation between their content and another which is repressed, they have some claim to be called "screen memories," the name by which I have described them. [. . .] One is thus forced by various considerations to suspect that in the so-called earliest childhood memories we possess not the genuine memory-trace but a later revision of it, a revision that may have been subjected to the influences of a variety of later psychical forces. Thus the "childhood memories" of individuals come in general to acquire the significance of "screen memories" and in doing so offer a remarkable analogy with the childhood memories that a nation preserves in its store of legends and myths. (Freud 1901, 43–47)

Interestingly, most of the examples quoted by Freud as screen memories have to do with the themes of life and death and with conflicts about ambivalent feelings for the caregiver, the childhood "love object."

According to Goethe's well-known autobiographic narrative, the young Wolfgang (at approximately age four) found himself playing an unusual game when he was left unattended one day. He took a number of pots from the kitchen and quite deliberately threw them all out the window, one after the other. Freud posits the roots of this screen memory in Goethe's ambivalent feelings toward his younger brother, Hermann Jakob, who might have triggered Goethe's jealousy for their mother, until the boy died at age six. Freud's interpretation is based on a series of other childhood memories (one belonging to himself) associated with the mother's pregnancy, the birth of a new baby, and jealousy and homicidal wishes of the older brother toward the next sibling (and his need to work through guilt feelings for the actual death of the weaker one).

Here we might follow the psychoanalytic associative method, interpreting this symbolic equation between discarded pots and unwanted siblings in a different and more general way (paradoxically, through another lesser-known Freudian text). A neglected letter in the correspondence between Freud and Jung can be quoted here to give us the uncanny, vertiginous, "double" experience of Freud interpreting Freud. This Freud, however, is the "private" man, writing to a friend (he had a very close relationship with Jung at that time). The Freud of the first symbolic equation (discarded pots = unwanted siblings) is the "public" man, the Freud we all have studied in the standard edition of his complete works. Let's listen to the "private" Freud now.

> The weaker twin, who dies first, is the placenta, or afterbirth, simply because it is regularly born along with the child by the same mother. We found this interpretation some months ago in the work of a modern mythologist [Ehrenreich 1890] totally ignorant of psychoanalysis who for once forgot his science and consequently had a good idea. But in Frazer's *Golden Bough*, Vol. I, one can read that among many primitive peoples the afterbirth is called *brother* (sister) or *twin*, and treated accordingly, that is, fed and taken care of, which of course cannot go on for very long. If there is such a thing as a phylogenetic memory in the individual, which unfortunately will soon be undeniable, this is also the source of the uncanny aspect of the "*doppelganger*" ["the errant double"]. (Freud 1911, 449)

It is from this perspective that Freud interprets the legend of Romulus and Remus (the twins nursed by a she-wolf, who went on to found the city of Rome)—and all stories where two heroes are symbiotically associated, for that matter—as "multiforms" (Bynum 1978) of the vicissitudes of the afterbirth. The weaker hero is the placenta, the smaller twin, the double of the child, who sacrifices itself to let the hero/child live his life of honor and glory, after birth.

So, the discarded pots are not only symbols of every newborn baby the older child wants to throw out the window. As all containers, they might also be symbols of "the former home of all human beings" (the amniotic sac and placenta) that we all want to do away with when we are finally out of the kitchen (the womb). Following this neglected Freudian interpretation, we might try to "err" beyond our nine points and imagine a virtual point A from where it is possible to see that we all have had a weaker sibling who actually died, a secret twin, an afterbirth who was delivered after us and was sacrificed to help our mother produce milk and feed us at her breast. Wouldn't that be an uncelebrated event common to all human beings and associated with "birth trauma" (Rank 1924) resulting from the stress of finding a way out through the delivery canal, an escape from the symbiotic paradise before the placenta gets too old, malfunctions, and turns the uterine environment into a suffocating hell?

This is possible from the perspective of prenatal psychology, but since this approach is rather controversial, I suggest we assume instead another (fully reliable) perspective: the mother's point of view. The trauma is surely here in the mothers' minds, since delivery involved (and still involves) a serious risk of death for them. Originally, this risk was associated with the expulsion of the afterbirth, while now, delivery anxiety has to do mostly with the disproportion between the baby's head and the birth canal. In the course of evolution, in fact, human beings became the only mammals to walk on two legs, freeing their hands to make tools for their survival, which in turn induced the development of a much more complex brain. Thus, in the womb, the baby's head became increasingly large; nonetheless, at the same time, the birth canal became increasingly narrow as the pelvic bones evolved to support the additional weight required of them with the new erect posture (Rosenberg and Trevathan 1995), giving rise to the so-called obstetrical dilemma: how is it possible for such a large-headed baby to come out of such a narrow birth canal?

In this scenario, it is understandable that many women died, and the ones who survived were those who were able to deliver their babies "prematurely." As a matter of fact, only a small percentage of women deliver their babies after forty-two weeks of pregnancy (Averna et al. 1990, Lafuenti et al. 1990, Nesci et al. 1990); most women deliver their babies after forty weeks (ten lunar months), which is now considered the normal length of pregnancy.

Furthermore, the position of the human baby during the transit into the birth canal is such that the mother is unable to help with its delivery and generally need assistance from other people (usually other women), which made human delivery a collective event in the primordial group of mothers.

At our stage of human evolution, the exit of the child from the mother's body is the critical event that resolves delivery anxiety. At an earlier stage of human evolution, however, before the onset of the obstetrical dilemma, it was the expulsion of the placenta that put an end to the mother's anxiety. If the placenta remained partially attached to the womb and was not expelled completely, the primordial mother had no hope of survival. Within a few days, the fragments of the dead placenta would putrefy inside her womb and kill her. Thus the complete expulsion of the placenta brought ultimate relief and aroused the euphoria of catharsis ("*katharsis*" = purification as well as menstruation and the pruning of trees). Only at that moment could the festivities begin for the new mother and the group of mothers who had assisted her.

Originally, the placenta could then be eaten. It was the instinctual prototype of all magical regenerating "filters" or, in a more prosaic vein, of our contemporary birthday cakes. Having surmounted (or collectively repressed, in the course of evolution) the placenta-eating instinct, the mothers of today know that their afterbirth is no longer an edible "fruit" (the fruit of the tree of life); on the contrary, it is now inedible, taboo, sacred (the forbidden fruit of the tree of knowledge of good and evil in the Garden of Eden). They cannot just dismember it, eat it instinctually, and recycle it naturally (Ober 1979). They have to discard the placenta, let it die, and work through the loss. They have to transform it into a cultural object, developing rituals and myths, beliefs and religions, to give some meaning to the banning of the afterbirth from the realm of normal edible objects (Nesci 1991).

Yesterday (prehistoric time), the ritual disposal of the afterbirth and umbilical cord magically protected the newborn baby and exerted a beneficial influence over its life; at the same time, a *tjurunga* was made. If the baby died, its double, who lives in the cave, would visit the mother, and rematerialize in her womb in order to let it be reborn (Róheim 1945b). Today (historical time), we hope to prevent the baby's death. The whole process is delegated to health professionals who assist the mother at delivery (midwives, gynecologists, neonatologists) and freeze the precious stem cells from the umbilical cord immediately after placental expulsion to save the child from future diseases.

Since that prehistoric time when placenta-eating became taboo, the failure in the ritual disposal of the placenta (due to an excess of instinctual oral greed) turned the baby's "twin" into the hostile murderer of both mother and child. By eating the "forbidden fruit," women would commit sacrilege (infringing the taboo of placentophagy) and repeat the "original sin." The discarded placenta, always conceived as the child's weaker twin, might suddenly take its revenge and turn delivery into a collective suicide (death of the placenta, the mother, and the child). This is probably why placenta rituals (Davidson 1985) were practiced all over the world and have survived to this day in so many oral cultures.

It is likely that we so often shape screen memories of a sibling's birth and death because our mothers transferred into us their anxieties about death at delivery (of the mother, the child, and the afterbirth), whether by means of the "private" Freudian symbolic equation: weaker sibling = placenta, by means of his "private" theory of a "phylogenetic memory," or just by transgenerational transference, as most psychoanalysts would say today. In other words, what I am saying, following the "private" Freud, confirms the anthropological equation between the placenta and a little sibling that always comes to light after the baby. I am saying that concrete doubles and screen memories are shaped at the same time by the group of mothers at delivery, from the very beginning, in order to work through their primordial anxieties and mourn this aboriginal loss.

Furthermore, the fathers, who were often the ones to dispose of the afterbirth and to make the cultural concrete doubles (the *tjurungas*), also played a role in this process. In this scenario of delivery as a risky collective event of the first human groups, the fathers had the privilege of a more external point of view. If the mother's female helpers might see the scene from point A, their male counterparts might look at the scene from a virtual point B, which allowed for a more detached experience in the deep emotional state of those stressful moments.

We could say that at the moment of delivery, cultural objects (in external reality) and screen memories (in the mind) both began to be shaped, integrating different points of view in a series of spiral movements. Once again, if we limit ourselves to the subject's and/or the object's perspective, we miss the point. We need to change our position and accept an ambiguous, transitional (in the sense of its intrinsic mobile nature) third point of view, the group-individual's perspective, the multiple perspective of the syncytial group, if we really wish to overcome our unconscious denials, repressions, and disavowals.

Studying economic and ritual objects, Géza Róheim (1945b) came to the conclusion that

> the cultural objects [. . .] have a double aspect. They represent the primary infantile object (parents) and the subject himself. I have called them narcissistic and object-erotic objects, and emphasized their Janus-like aspect from a libido-economic point of view. They stand half-way between the Ego and the object-seeking libido. It is evident that this theory of an "intermediate object" is well fitted to explain the cult of the tjurunga and totemism in general. (99–100)

I agree with him. What is missing in his theory is only the full acknowledgment of the placental imago, the avowal of the syncytial nature of the complex third (the "intermediate object") between the two elements of the symbiotic dual-unity. Actually Janus was not only a two-faced god. By using associative thinking, investigating beyond commonplaces and ideas, we can recover another shape of the god (Nesci, D. A. and Nesci. F. A. 2008): a three-faced one! In this most ancient and uncanny aspect, Janus has three noses and four eyes (fig. 8.1).

At this point, we need to pause to explore a crucial methodological issue through an apparent detour into the fields of prenatal psychology and medicine. In fact I shall introduce here the concept that therapist (mother) and patient (unborn baby) are not alone on the scene in psychotherapy. There is always a third, playing the role and functions of the placental imago, of the group-individual of our unconscious syncytial culture. That is why the introduction of the multimedia artist in the psychotherapeutic team is such a precious acquisition.

Figure 8.1. A three-faced Janus. Courtesy of Renzo Dionigi.

INTERLUDE: THE ULTRASOUND STUDY OF PRENATAL LIFE

by Domenico A. Nesci, in collaboration with Simonetta Averna, and Tommaso A. Poliseno

Alessandra Piontelli, an Italian doctor and psychoanalyst trained in Italy and at the Tavistock Clinic in London, was the first to study early relationships of human beings using the ultrasound scanner (1992), approximately in the same period when we were doing research in prenatal psychology and medicine with an interdisciplinary team (Ancona et al. 1992) at UCSC in Rome. At the beginning of her study, Dr. Piontelli worked with a gynecologist to have the chance to observe fetal behavior; later, however (apparently to overcome practical difficulties in scheduling research sessions with the gynecologist), Dr. Piontelli learned how to use the ultrasound scanner herself. At the same time, she decided to focus on twin pregnancies and study the relationships between twins before and after birth, that is, during prenatal and postnatal life. Interestingly, her research demonstrated a clear continuity between fetal behavior and behavior after birth between the twins.

Meanwhile, our research group in Rome decided to add a gynecologist with training in obstetrical and gynecological ultrasound scanning to our interdisciplinary team (composed of a gynecologist specialized in obstetrical pathology, a neonatologist, a psychoanalyst, a group analyst, a child psychotherapist, a resident in psychiatry, and a technician to record our sessions). Around that time we also decided to focus on high risk pregnancies in the Obstetrical Pathology Unit of our university hospital.

And yet, we were still faced with strong resistance from the staff on the ward. On the conscious level, the doctors in charge of the patients were afraid our research could endanger the already high risk pregnancies, so they told us we couldn't begin our study as all the hospital ultrasound scanners were busy with patient care. One of us had been working full-time at the same hospital for many years, so we knew this was false: a mere pretense. In fact, the scanners were not used at all during the night, which was the time scheduled for research in our protocol.

To overcome this problem, two of us (Dr. Nesci and Dr. Averna, who are husband and wife) purchased a portable ultrasound scanner and managed to get permission to bring it to the hospital at night to do our research without interfering with the unit's medical activities. At that point, nobody dared admit any opposition (unconscious resistance?) to letting our team do the study. So we did it!

Finally, we constructed a "de-medicalized" setting, where, at every session, the pregnant patient's bed was moved by our team members personally, not by the hospital orderlies. The group would go from the ward to the room of Professor Leonardo Ancona (the chairman of the Institute of Psychiatry and Psychology at the time, who allowed us to use it). A green plant, a beautiful butterfly palm (*Dypsis lutescens*), was bought and placed in the room as a living symbol of the healthy placenta (Nesci 1991).

Adjusting our approach to circumvent the resistance of the Obstetrical Pathology Unit clinicians proved productive, since we soon realized that, without being consciously aware of the shift, we had de facto changed our research goal from studying relationships in prenatal life to helping pregnant women (who had lost previous pregnancies) to deliver their new babies successfully. In other words, we found ourselves offering a supportive group to numerous patients in the Obstetrical Pathology Unit, in the form of a research team studying the early relationships of human beings before and after birth. In the end, from among the thirteen high risk pregnancies followed up by our interdisciplinary research team, not one fetus died nor did any mother have medical complications. As a matter of fact, the attitude of the doctors toward our research team changed so dramatically that on one occasion we were asked to enroll a very anxious patient in the research protocol since they now believed it was "therapeutic" for both mother and child.

After a while, something interesting happened within the research team: the psychoanalyst (Dr. Nesci) and the group analyst (Dr. Poliseno) discovered that their wives were pregnant (one being Dr. Averna, the gynecologist specialized in ultrasound scanning). So the research program was discontinued, and two babies were born, one of whom was to become the multimedia psychotherapy video artist (Filippo Arturo Nesci) and the other (Andrea Poliseno), a student in psychology.

TWO OR THREE?

by Domenico A. Nesci, in collaboration with Filippo A. Nesci

Let's return now to the methodological issue we were addressing when we decided to take this interlude: how many faces does Janus have? Two or three? Furthermore, does this metaphor suggest any implications for the choice of constructing a dyadic (patient and therapist) setting rather than a triadic (patient, therapist, and multimedia artist) one for multimedia psychotherapy? To answer this question, we will leave our apparent digression on prenatal life and return to our main topic of multimedia psychotherapy. My second case in this therapy provides an answer.

I have already introduced Louis, a man in his forties affected by an obsessive neurosis, who began psychotherapy about twenty years ago (see chapters 2 and 4). Let me remind you that when Louis began psychodynamic psychotherapy, he was just recovering from a serious motorcycle accident in which he had come very close to dying. Throughout his therapy, he was clearly unable to mourn his father, who had died of cancer when Louis was a teenager. Thus I did not hesitate to propose the new method, especially after the successful outcome of multimedia psychotherapy with Serena. You probably remember that when Louis finally brought in the photos for his father's memory object, he realized that there was always a woman present, officially a family friend but in fact his father's mistress. Patient and therapist worked on this "discovery," coming to the conclusion that it was better to eliminate all the pictures where the woman appeared so that Louis could show the psychodynamic montage to his relatives without any complications. At that point, the images were given to the artist, who prepared the video.

But (and here comes the unanticipated side of the story), in the screening session when patient and therapist were watching the video, Louis noticed a blatant mistake. His parents' wedding had been misplaced by the artist: it did not appear until after the birth of his older brother and sister, immediately before his own birth. This was patently wrong! The therapist suggested that the patient work with this error as if it were a Freudian lapse by the artist. With his long experience in psychotherapy, Louis understood and immediately told me the story underlying the artist's mistake. He explained that when his mother finally realized what was going on, she had a violent fight with her husband's lover, bringing the affair to a dramatic end. The patient was conceived as a tangible sign of his parents' renewed marital bond. Evidently, the artist's "mistake" was actually a meaningful error.

So what is the psychodynamic interpretation of this event?

Transference—the patient's unconscious had been able to communicate with the therapist's unconscious to transmit the information regarding the "real" (psychological) moment when his mother and father had married. Still unconsciously, the therapist transferred this information to the unconscious of the artist, who was able, in his countertransference, to act it out and make the meaningful "mistake."

So now we can answer the question asked above: two or three? In fact, unconscious mental representations associated with repressed (traumatic) emotions need to be triangulated in order to come to the surface and be acknowledged. The whole process of elaboration (working through traumatic memories as well as related unconscious fantasies and feelings) is greatly facilitated by the inclusion of a third person—in this case, the artist. It is highly unlikely that the therapist (were he able to scan the pictures and edit the video) would ever make this type of mistake since he would be too aware of the patient's personal and family history. Furthermore, the patient might easily interpret such an error as a "wise error" or, even worse, he might deny, repress, or disavow it to protect his idealized therapist, or feel guilty if he acknowledged it. To prevent such awkward feelings, he might even consciously decide not to talk about it, thereby losing a precious therapeutic turning point.

On the other hand, there was no way to think the artist might have been aware of the patient's family history since this episode was completely unknown to the therapist himself! The patient (and therapist) had no doubt that this fortuitous mistake was a wonderful example of the workings of transference, as described by Freud (1916–1917): a general phenomenon of human mental life, not just something special that occurs (and belongs) exclusively to patients and therapists. The psychodynamic montage actually worked as an interpretation, or rather as a "construction" (Freud 1938), within the analytic work. In the end, the patient asked to have two videos: an official one with the correct sequence of pictures, which the artist prepared easily, and the "real" psychodynamic one, just for himself to see and reflect upon.

From a psychodynamic point of view, this was a significant event, and one which provided us with the opportunity to discuss the role of splitting in the patient's life. Indeed, there we were acting it out in the production of a double video depicting a double truth: the acceptable one (chronologically correct but psychodynamically false) and the original one (chronologically wrong but psychodynamically true), which included the screen memory constructed by the artist "inventing" the chronological shift in Louis's parents' wedding. Here we were touching the core of the patient's inner world. At the same time, we were establishing the foundations of multimedia psychotherapy under "the sign of three" (Eco and Sebeok, eds. 1983): patient, therapist, and multimedia artist.

From this perspective, we can end our digression with one final hypothesis regarding the unconscious implications of Dr. Piontelli's decision to perform two distinct roles at the same time in her research (learning to use the ultrasound scanner and so becoming the person who makes fetal behavior visible while also being the one who observes that behavior) in order to overcome the resistance she encountered from the doctors (as our research team did). If what was discussed earlier makes sense, we might think that by playing two roles, she found herself missing something of the precious triadic setting. That is why (in my view) her unconscious remedy for the loss of the third point of view was to reintroduce it by studying twins!

In the case of our multidisciplinary research team, we overcame the doctors' resistance by integrating their institutional point of view into our protocol. Empathizing with their concern for the well-being of their patients, we unconsciously organized a protective setting that re-created the psychosocial environment of the group-individual. We were immersed in the "cave" at night, making a double (a *tjurunga*) of the unborn child (tape-recording the ultrasound sessions) and promising to be present to help at the delivery and to visit the mothers afterward in their homes.

Unconsciously, our research team became a new version of the archaic "group of mothers" (Briffault 1927) in its benevolent aspect: the loving mothers, who want the pregnant woman/member to become a mother herself by delivering her baby and thus joining them. Unconsciously, we were repairing the wounds inflicted by its imaginary negative counterpart, the hating mothers (the witches), who do not want the pregnant woman to become powerful in the group structure by having a new baby. In fact, while the power of men in primordial human groups was established by the number of enemies killed in war, the hierarchy within the group of mothers was based on the number of children they had been able to deliver.

Our team was playing the role of the third, of the filter of exchanges, in the dangerous symbiotic scenario of high risk pregnancy. Without realizing the unconscious importance of what we were doing, by shaping a solid research team and filming (recording) our research, thereby producing a concrete double of what was going on, we were performing a propitiatory ritual that probably really did help the medical team to work more effectively and the pregnant women to feel better and more optimistic about their pregnancy.

"One, Two, Three Spells Uberty!"

"One, Two, Three Spells Uberty!" is the title of the first essay (Sebeok 1983) in the intriguing book *The Sign of Three: Dupin, Holmes, Peirce* (Eco and Sebeok, eds. 1983). The expression "esperable uberty" was used by Charles Peirce (1867–1913) with reference to the passage from deduction to induction and abduction. He emphasized the fact that when we make an abduction, although we may be wrong, we may still find something fruitful and highly rewarding: a useful, new discovery. Interestingly, for Peirce, the third, as a logical category, was associated with evolution. In psychoanalysis, on the other hand, the third is the father, who appears between the dual-unit of mother and child with the role of separating them. From my ethnopsychoanalytic perspective, the placental imago is the precursor of the father and plays the role of protecting (by its biological "placental barrier") the dual-unit during prenatal life and allowing mother and baby to exchange substances for the well-being of both. In effect, we always need a third to let a dual relationship take place safely. The third guarantees the chance of "esperable uberty."

Now let's get back to multimedia psychotherapy. This new therapy is a process that was conceived in my mind under the sign of hope ("esperable" = desirable, something we wish for as it is useful, attractive, or necessary) to face the experience of mourning in its broader sense. Mourning is a process that is inherent to every meaningful passage in the life cycle, from the first human breath (death of the placenta and rebirth of the mythical ancestor, as experienced by mothers at delivery) to the last exhalation (death of the individual and regeneration of the group, as experienced by all group-individuals around the dying member of their community). It is a process that takes place in all ritual passages of the life cycle since such transformations inevitably imply a separation/individuation dynamic: exit from the initial state, transition through a neutral state, and access to the final state in the perspective of "the Eternal Ones of the Dream" (Róheim 1945b) that still live in our unconscious mind.

During this process, we always shape some equivalent of the discarded placenta to let ourselves find a new beginning and adopt a new psychosocial identity: it can be a "symbolic wound" (Bettelheim 1954), a tattoo, a concrete object associated with our memories (like today's tourist souvenirs, as proof of one's passage in a foreign country). In every case, it can be conceptualized as a "three-faced double," condensing the multiple points of view of the group-individual. The easy triad conceivable by the individual mind (subject, object, and intermediate object) is unable to tune in with the ambiguous syncytial three-faced double minds of the group-individual (the fetoplacental unity in the body of the pregnant woman within the group of mothers), who lives in our unconscious. And yet we need to resume an inner dialogue with it if we want to deal effectively with our anxiety about our own finitude.

Probably, the concrete making of the memory objects in multimedia psychotherapy is a process that must be worked through a team (patient, therapist, and multimedia artist, at least) if we hope to make it still another valid and effective version of a therapeutic process as old as humankind. And, probably, supervision too needs to find a new and different setting, if we want to meet the needs of the group-individual mind. As we will see in chapter 9, where a new supervision format will be introduced, we need the "three-faced double" of a group setting if we want to find a chance to reach some "esperable uberty," recreating a syncytial human environment within our contemporary individual mentality and culture.

POSTLUDE: THE MAN IN THE LABYRINTH

On the wall of my home in Rome, I have a coiled basket (by a Tohono O'odham artist) depicting a man in a labyrinth, a traditional subject in Native American paintings. I bought it at the Heard Museum gift shop as a "souvenir," out of my interest in the myth of the Cretan labyrinth. According to Kerényi, the labyrinth is the design and reflection (*Linienreflex*) of a mythological idea, that is, of a primal mental representation (1950). In fact, the labyrinth appears as a pattern in almost every culture and in infinite multiforms. It can be a dance (from the exotic Polynesian Maro to the classic Greek Gheranos), or a building (from the Labyrinthos in Crete to the Scandinavian Trojaburgen), or a graphic sign (from the spiral to the swastika).

From my perspective, the most profound meaning of the labyrinth has to do with its therapeutic power. According to ancient Greek tradition, the very fact of walking inside its architectural structure allows the patient to see the center from endless perspectives, thus gradually reaching full knowledge of the symbolic object standing there (usually a tree or a sacred stone). You cannot get lost in a Cretan labyrinth: you just follow a one-way path, reach the center, and then go back to the exit. By doing so, however, you see the sacred object in all its possible aspects . . . and you are healed—not because you have seen all the possible solutions but because you have finally come to experience that there are always multiple points of view from which you might find (or hope to find) new perspectives. This was the therapy for the group-individual, the syncytial prehistoric human being that lives atemporally in our unconscious mind. *Spes ultima dea* . . . Hope is the ultimate goddess.

NINE

Supervision in Multimedia Psychotherapy

This chapter tells the story of the "Clinic and Dreams Workshop," a new setting for supervision specifically designed with multimedia psychotherapy and its special features in mind. The evolution of the setting of supervision from its classical form (the dyadic situation of therapist and supervisor) to a new scenario, one in which the third brings uberty introducing a group setting, multimedia objects, and social dreaming into an ethnopsychoanalytic frame of reference, is a contemporary challenge! The goal of this change is to build a cultural environment where it is possible to integrate the individual with the group-individual points of view, which is what I am doing with my collaborators at SIPSI in Rome.

I will tell this story following a "narrative" pattern; in other words, I will follow the Ariadne's thread of one clinical case (Lucy), focusing on the three settings where I "met" her: the Balint-like group in psycho-oncology where I heard her therapist (Dr. Fazzi) talking about her, Dr. Fazzi's dyadic classic supervision with me, and the first Clinic and Dreams Workshop where her pictures (selected by Lucy and Dr. Fazzi in their multimedia sessions) were seen and elaborated by a large group of psychotherapy students at SIPSI.

I will divide this chapter into three parts. First of all, I will present the Balint-like groups in psycho-oncology and the other innovative settings I have developed with my collaborators for our CME programs at UCSC in Rome since 1993. Then I will discuss a few fragments from Lucy's psychotherapy, including her multimedia sessions and traditional individual supervision of Dr. Fazzi with me. Finally, I will quote large excerpts from the tape recording of the Clinic and Dreams Workshop where Lucy's pictures were shown and elaborated.

This approach clearly reveals the historical roots of multimedia psychotherapy (Part I) as well as the difference between classical supervision (Part II) and the new "Dreaming Team" supervision model (Part III) we are developing at our School of Psychotherapy in Rome, and whose most sophisticated setting is the Clinic and Dreams Workshop, which is what we really want to describe.

PART I: FROM BALINT-LIKE GROUPS TO THE CLINIC AND DREAMS WORKSHOP

When I began to develop courses in psycho-oncology at UCSC (Rome) with Dr. Poliseno (a group analyst and co-director of my School of Psychotherapy), we had several ideas in mind.

1. Participants should come from different backgrounds and cultural roots (medical doctors, psychologists, nurses, social workers, volunteers, students from every health-related course, etc.) in order to form an interdisciplinary group with members of different age, sex, and professional experience.
2. In the wards, they should meet with cancer patients and their relatives protected by a tutor, who can become the imaginary container of their unconscious anxieties.
3. In the classroom, classical lessons (ex cathedra) should be reduced to a minimum and/or completely replaced by group discussion of clinical cases in the setting of a Balint-like group where a psychoanalyst and a group analyst share the leadership.

The original psychoanalytic model of the Balint group was developed by Michael and Enid Balint (1957). It is still practiced in many countries since it allows a small group of medical doctors "to share experiences and rethink aspects of their relationships with patients" (Balint et al. 1993).

In our Balint-like groups, clinical experiences are discussed together with all kinds of health professionals (as well as students and volunteers) coming from very distant places (which in Italy means speaking different dialects and having dramatically different cultures and mentalities). The aim is to make them all familiar with working as an interdisciplinary team and to promote the concept that cancer patients and their relatives have to be understood within a common psychodynamic frame of reference.

This means that all health professionals have the opportunity, guided by psychoanalytically oriented supervisors (a psychoanalyst and a group analyst) to become aware of their unconscious emotional response to their patients. The space/time setting of the Balint-like group becomes the container of the patient's unconscious transference and of the health professional's unconscious countertransference, the safe place where all these emotions can be acted out, expressed, and elaborated rather than inhibited, or, even worse, acted out, repressed, and disavowed (Nesci et al. 2000).

However, after many years of guiding such groups in psycho-oncology, I noticed that sometimes, after long emotional discussions, the students were exhausted. Complete silence would reign in the classroom. When the supervisors did not break that silence, something would happen: a group participant would finally begin to talk, evoking a familiar song or describing an image or a scene from a movie. From this unusual (multimedia) "memory," the group was always able to recover and find a way out of its block.

From my perspective, this multimedia memory played the same role in the Balint-like group setting that a dream usually plays in psychoanalytic therapy. When patient and therapist feel exhausted, empty, or simply stuck, the memory of a dream suddenly comes to the surface, and the psychotherapeutic process starts up again. Hence my idea: why not screen a cancer movie at the end of our courses in psycho-oncology and then have participants share their dreams on the subsequent night? Why not combine the multimedia evocative power of cinema, the dream machine, with the power of dreams, the *via regia* of the unconscious (Freud 1900)?

There and then, around 2000, I conceived a new setting for group supervision: the Movies and Dreams Workshop, a new tool to help members of interdisciplinary oncologic teams to dream and reach some deeper insight into the unconscious dynamics within their own professional relationships with their cancer patients. In 2001, I tried my first experiment with a small group of my students in a summer course at UCLA during my stay in the Department of Psychiatry (with Professor Robert O. Pasnau at the NPI and Prof. Milton Miller at the Harbor-UCLA Medical Center). I showed the students a movie, collected their subsequent dreams, and worked them through in a group setting. The feedback was very positive: in fact, the students told me it had helped them to finally understand the concept of unconscious dynamics.

Back in Rome, with two psychoanalysts (Salomon Resnik and Igor Kadyrov, members of the scientific committee of IIPRTHP), I organized an international "Movies and Dreams Workshop" to test my idea in a large group setting (approximately 250 health professionals) at the "Giancarlo Brasca" conference room of the *Policlinico Universitario Agostino Gemelli*. On Friday night we showed the movie *Eternity and a Day* by Angelopoulos; then, on Saturday morning, we shared our dreams, constructing an associative chain by linking these dreams with scenes from the movie and/or clinical vignettes experienced personally and evoked by the participants.

The workshop was credited by the Italian Department of Health in the national program of Continuing Medical Education (CME). It received very positive feedback from all participants and was noticed by the Italian media as a new methodology to train all categories of health professionals on the psychological problems of cancer patients and their relatives and to prevent their risk of becoming victims of the well-known "burnout syndrome" (Maslach and Goldberg 1998). In 2002, the Movies and Dreams Workshop (based on the cancer movie *Marvin's Room*, directed by Jerry Zack) was conducted by Dominique Scarfone (training analyst of the Canadian Psychoanalytic Society), Tommaso A. Poliseno, and myself. The event was filmed by a prestigious Italian Company (RAI-SAT Cinema), which produced five episodes of a television series, conceived by Dr. Poliseno, whose copyright belongs to our international institute (IIPRTHP). In 2004, one episode of the same series (which I named "Double Dream") was presented at the Congress of the International Psychoanalytic Association (IPA) in New Orleans (Nesci and Poliseno 2004). The theme of that short film was the first trimester of pregnancy and prenatal life. Perhaps the seeds of multimedia psychotherapy were sown a long time before it was actually born . . .

Guided Social Dreaming and the Process of Supervision

Thomas Ogden (2005) describes the process of supervision as a form of "guided dreaming" where the supervisor helps the therapist to "dream up" the patient and create a "fiction" that helps therapist and supervisor to be in touch with the emotional experience taking place in both therapy and supervision. The goal is to enhance the capacity for associative thinking and ability to reach new insights in all participants (patient, therapist, and supervisor).

Referring back to our nine points problem, we might say that therapist and supervisor are the two virtual points that allow full coverage of the patient's issues. In other words, one (the patient) has to enter into a relationship with at least two different external viewers (not just a therapist but a supervisor as well) if he/she really wants to reach a deeper insight into himself or herself as a group-individual (a nine-point entity). Furthermore, in this new metaphor, we do not have a triad (patient, therapist, and supervisor) but rather a group (eleven points, or even thirty-three if we consider that therapist and supervisor were created out of prior eleven-point configurations since they both had been patients and supervisees in order to become what they are).

Supervision, and all trainings (and therapies), imply a group pattern (or patterns) if we acknowledge that, in the deepest strata of our unconscious mind, we are all the group-individual described by Briffault (1927). In fact, focusing here on supervision, we know quite well that group discussions of clinical cases and group supervisions are as old as individual therapy and supervision, not only in the history of psychoanalysis but in every medical profession. In hospital rounds, for example, we are all familiar with the scene of a group of younger people in white coats led by an older, more experienced "supervisor." Indeed, the presence of a group setting has always been considered an essential tool in the endeavor to practice first-class care.

Ogden's conception of supervision as a form of guided dreaming suggests new approaches and reflections when we consider my Movies and Dreams Workshop as a form of *guided* "social dreaming" (Lawrence 1991). In fact, the inventor of social dreaming, Gordon Lawrence, at the Tavistock Clinic in London, once produced a film to introduce a social dreaming whose aim was to help a particular organization solve its inner conflicts and enhance its potential. This is analogous to screening a cancer movie to promote "guided" social dreaming in a group of health professionals who care for cancer patients and their relatives.

When I first conceived the idea of my Movies and Dreams Workshop, I didn't even know that such a thing as social dreaming existed, so I was full of doubt and hesitation. Later on, I was told that what I was doing was not such an extraordinary "invention" after all but, as we say in Italy, more like the "discovery of hot water" (something obvious and already known). In a certain way, I felt relieved and ready to try new variations, such as "theatre and dreams," "puppet-show and dreams" (Nesci et al. 2008), and "clinic and dreams" (while "music and dreams" is another I have in mind to try in the future with Dr. Domenico Agresta, one of my collaborators, who is a musician with experience in music therapy).

In these special forms of guided social dreaming, as in Gordon Lawrence's classical social dreaming, the dreams are not interpreted as personal experiences but are shared as collective dreams that help everyone reach a deeper understanding of an apparently impossible problem or complex issue. In my Movies and Dreams Workshop, the theme is chosen by the supervisors/group leaders (for example, cancer, pregnancy, etc.) and is presented by a movie focused, directly or indirectly, on that issue or, in my Clinic and Dreams Workshop, on the presentation of a real case.

My workshops aim to uncover unconscious fantasies, emotions, and dynamics experienced by health professionals with their patients. The invention of multimedia psychotherapy immediately made me think that the best possible setting for supervision of my cure might be that of guided social dreaming in the form of the Clinic and Dreams Workshop. The memory objects of multimedia psychotherapy represent something very close to a movie, in fact. What's more, the workshop itself can be filmed and played back in the same group and/or reused as a movie to produce new dreams to be worked through by another group in a similar or different setting (Balint-like group, training group, etc.) over and over again. In this way, my guided social dreaming becomes a tool to open new doors, not to close the elaboration and pretend to establish a final conclusion or interpretation of a clinical story or experience, as in old-fashioned supervision.

PART II: LUCY'S STORY

by Marcella Fazzi, in collaboration with Domenico A. Nesci

When she asked for psychotherapy in 2006, Lucy was a fifty-year-old woman who had survived leukemia and a bone marrow transplant about ten years earlier. She had a few consultations with a colleague whose office is in the same building where I see my patients. During these preliminary consultations, my colleague felt uneasy as soon as she understood that Lucy had a psycho-oncologic problem; since I had always been working with cancer patients, she decided to refer Lucy to me. Moreover, she knew I enroll in the psycho-oncology courses of UCSC practically every year to continue my CME program as a licensed psychologist.

The first meeting with Lucy was awkward. My colleague told me that Lucy was obsessed with the feeling of "always being abandoned." To prevent this from recurring during the transition from one therapist to the other (from "hand to hand," so to speak), my colleague decided to work as an intermediary, negotiating the day and time of the first meeting, which had to take place on a Saturday since Lucy's reduced vision meant she needed to be accompanied to our office by her husband (who didn't work on Saturdays). Furthermore, my colleague reorganized her schedule at our office so that she could introduce the patient to me—and me to the patient, at the same time—in a "personalized" way so that Lucy would not feel like she was just being dropped off.

After this ritual "handshake," I found myself alone in my room with Lucy, enveloped by a dark atmosphere. Having known in advance about Lucy's serious visual problems, I had prepared the room by dimming the lights. Nonetheless, she kept her eyes covered with one hand (even though she was wearing sunglasses as well) and told me she would never look at me. In fact, it took three sessions before she began to look at me.

Here are some excerpts from my notebook:

Lucy is a very slim woman with a stooped posture. Her initial communications are focused on her own physical appearance: she thinks her way of dressing youthfully is inappropriate while her short hair makes her look like a "tomboy." The first sessions are full of hopelessness and self-depreciation ("It was all a mistake . . . I'm the person who makes it wrong.") and rage toward her illness (which she never names), her relatives, the health professionals who took care of her, and the bone marrow transplant. She says, "I'd been waiting for my transplant with high hopes and expectations, but now I don't trust it anymore." Although ten years have passed since she received her sister's bone marrow cells, Lucy still disavows its success. Every time the Hematology Center calls her on the phone, she expects to receive bad news, and when they say her exams are good, she always thinks they made a mistake or exchanged her tests with someone else's. She speaks of herself as a patient who will never be cured, a person whose life is marked only by medical checkups to monitor any minimal change in her bodily functions. She is exhausted. "This is not living . . . I just survive. What's the meaning of this life? Like in the song by *Vasco* [a well-known Italian singer-songwriter], this life has no meaning at all!"

At the beginning of her psychotherapy, Lucy's conversation revolved almost exclusively around her own body: her eyes ache, her skin is so thin that it is "transparent" and shows the capillary vessels, her right foot suffers from a painful neuropathy . . . I felt sorry for her and, more than once, I felt I might even cry. In fact, this issue of crying and tears kept me very busy during the first months of therapy. Because Lucy has an atrophy of the lacrimal ducts, her cry is a disquieting tearless one. I felt uneasy, vis-à-vis a person who had no tears yet seemed to cry the whole time during our initial sessions.

Unable to understand if she was really crying or not, I asked for help during a Balint-like group in the protective setting of the courses in psycho-oncology. The "supervision" offered by the Balint-like group (whose leaders were, and still are, Dr. Nesci and Dr. Poliseno, a psychoanalyst and a group analyst) helped me to understand that cancer patients feel like mutants as a result of all the bodily changes they experience from their illness and the iatrogenic effects of oncologic therapies. In the transference, this uncanny aspect of the patient can easily disorient and confuse the caregivers.

During the group sessions where I presented a clinical vignette about my patient, who was continuously weeping her tearless cries, Dr. Mariarosaria Squillacioti (a course tutor who had been working in hematology for a long time) associated with one of her patients and suggested I might go so far as to really cry Lucy's tears myself. Maybe her comment helped me to ask Dr. Nesci for individual supervision. The truth is I was unable to keep calm, reflect, and "hold" the uncanny aspect of Lucy's tearless cry until I shared my countertransference emotions and felt reassured by a "double container": classical supervision in individual sessions with Dr. Nesci and Balint-like group sessions in the psycho-oncology course, at the same time.

Lucy's life is also limited by other medical problems (osteoporosis, arthrosis), several phobias, and a paranoid belief that the external world is full of germs, bacteria, and viruses. She lives in terror of being touched by people (especially children) who might infect her with communicable diseases. She is afraid of telephone calls, which might bring bad news. She is constantly preoccupied with her lymphocyte counts and their relation to her own private theories that predict the outcome of her bone marrow aspiration.

As a result, Lucy spends her time isolated within the walls of her home, in the dark. She doesn't go out so as to prevent any possible contagion. She doesn't switch on the radio; she "watches" television but doesn't pay attention to what they say. She has renounced a number of domestic activities that she used to enjoy before her illness. She is convinced that if she makes something good or beautiful, for example, if she makes bread or pugs salt dough (a homemade play dough), her health will decline. My association, listening to her, is that renouncing these activities is like renouncing creativity. In the Bible, God created man by kneading mud, a mixture of soil, clay, and water.

According to Melanie Klein (1957), creativity is deeply envied at unconscious levels. Lucy, with her sight problems, starts me thinking about envy. Envy means to look at something or someone in a destructive way (from Latin *in* = against and *videre* = to look at). In my countertransference, I see Lucy as a woman who is blocked, trapped, frozen . . . From this point of view, it is interesting to me that her husband works for a firm that manufactures frozen foods.

I see her as a woman full of envy for all healthy people, including her own relatives, about whom she often says, "They're fine. They don't understand me; they're well; they don't care about me. They treat me like an object . . . Why did it happen to me? Why does it always happen to me? If only I could drive a car!"

Lucy's limited vision also makes it impossible for her to read. She tells me how much she used to enjoy reading. I think that Lucy badly needs to emerge from her dark prison, and I give her the telephone number of a nonprofit organization that distributes audio books to patients at no cost. Lucy claims she will contact them immediately, but she actually waits for a long time before ordering her first free audio book.

Supervision: Prelude

In the first supervision session, Dr. Nesci thought Lucy should take a drug and advised me to encourage the patient to get in touch with her general practitioner to have him prescribe a very low dose of levosulpiride, a medication Dr. Nesci uses for onco-hematologic patients since it is not myelotoxic and has proved very effective (Nesci et al. 1998). At first I was perplexed. Actually I already felt uncomfortable since I had given Lucy a way to contact the nonprofit organization dealing with free audio books, so I was afraid a second "prescription" might seem like I was intruding too actively into her life and could risk spoiling the process of establishing our therapeutic alliance.

The supervisor helped me to have a different perspective and conceive the professional figures on the scene of the cure/care as the plural components of a placental imago (a syncytial multidisciplinary team) that allows the mother/therapist and the fetus/patient to stay alive and not to reject each other so the patient can grow and develop: a "smart" filter of exchanges between the "blood" of the mother and the "blood" (emotions) of the prenatal baby. From this perspective I felt relieved, after the first moment of disorientation, when Dr. Nesci explained his ethnopsychoanalytic view of psychotherapy as a "rite of passage," an experience of death/rebirth in which the only object that should be left over, the only waste to be sacrificed, is not a human being (the patient or the therapist, the mother or the child) but an inanimate object: the afterbirth after the cutting of the umbilical cord (a dead fetish, an ideological rule, an element of our setting that is no longer justified by its vital function in the therapeutic scene).

In other words, all these atypical helpers around and in the middle of the psychotherapeutic relationship between patient and therapist (the nonprofit organization of the audio books, the therapist's supervisor, the patient's general practitioner, the psychiatric consultant, the drug, and so on) give shape to (and become) a placental setting (a cultural group setting) that protects the relationship (as a safe container = amniotic sac with amniotic fluid) and filters good and evil in the initial exchanges (interactions) between patient and therapist. Providing the patient with what he/she needs during this initial symbiotic stage is the only way to let him/her become implanted into the space/time coordinates of psychotherapy and survive long enough to develop, metaphorically, from prenatal dual-unity (Róheim 1945a) to "separated" mother, baby, and afterbirth (Nesci 1999). Once this stage is completed, a more mature therapeutic alliance is possible, where patient and therapist can reduce acting (repeating) and begin to remember and work through, as theorized by Freud (1914), in a "postnatal" adult scenario.

These discussions during supervision encouraged me to go on adjusting to Lucy (as I had instinctively done, for example, by darkening my room) and constructing a personalized setting (as I had been doing from the very beginning since in the School of Psychotherapy we are always taught to do so), tailored as a custom-made dress for her, a common space for the two of us. Within this placental setting, all external helpers proved useful for building a therapeutic alliance: the first audio book arrived for our first therapeutic "vacation," as did the drug (levosulpiride, as suggested by the supervisor), which she began to take at the same time. It was as if she were taking both the therapist and the supervisor with her during our first separation for the summer holidays.

But let's back up a little. Lucy was puzzled in the session when I suggested that she contact her family doctor and take a drug, just as I had been during my supervision session. Then, in her next session, she told me two dreams. In the first, Lucy's son was a drug addict. She cried out loudly, "How is it possible that after so many years—my son is thirty-three now—I'm still afraid of these kinds of things?"

In the second dream, Lucy is with a friend. "I knew she was dead." They go together up a corridor in the dark and see a window and the sky at the end of the climb. In the dream, Lucy was scared. "Did you come and pick me up?" Then, suddenly, her friend disappears, but she leaves her hand and arm attached to Lucy. "I remember her hand quite well . . . however, also my friend's arm remained attached to me . . . I thought I had to give her a hand to climb up the sky and reach Heaven . . . I paid the church to say a mass for her . . . They say dead people need prayers to be able to go to Heaven, and she was very religious." "So they say," I comment. "Or," Lucy adds [and here she uses the ambiguity of Italian to make a pun that covers up the identity of the person she is talking about], "someone [the therapist or the dead friend? We will never know] will help me along the upward trail I still have to climb."

At the end of the session, she shakes my hand, which she had never done before. I let her do it, but I felt bad. After the session, I still felt bad. I was happy I would soon be shaking hands with my supervisor (since his roots are from southern Italy, he shakes hands twice, at the beginning and at the end of each supervision session) and "transfer" onto someone else, concretely, the oneiric hand-and-arm of Lucy's dead friend.

In our supervision session, Dr. Nesci and I talked about the "placental setting" of psychotherapy with my onco-hematologic patient. In this metaphor by Dr. Nesci, Lucy was an unborn baby who required not only a placental therapist (me) but also a broad external environment (classical individual supervision, a Balint-like group in the course of psycho-oncology, "Dreaming Team Clinical Seminars" at our Specialization School of Psychotherapy where we all associate on the clinical case rather than try to interpret it), playing the functions of body-of-the-mother/ecosystem, where I could imagine the real elaboration of such death anxieties that I had absorbed during the sessions could finally take place, safely. Lucy and I (as well as all our placental helpers) were unconsciously located within a prenatal scenario.

From this perspective, Lucy is repeating (in her transference with me) her traumatic bone-marrow transplant; she is reexperiencing the story of receiving good and evil (life/blood stem cells, as well as poison/chemotherapy) from an ambivalent donor (her sister and the medical team, combined into a hybrid syncytial entity) and is playing dead in order to be spared by Death. There are in fact two risks with transplants: graft versus host disease, when the donor's stem cells fight against the organism that received the transplant, and rejection of the donor's cells. In either case, the patient can die.

That is why Lucy is so afraid of emotions, feelings, light, warmth . . . in effect, of life. Life can bring death; affects can bring death (her dead friend in the dream), and affection (for her son, in the dream, or for her therapist in transference) can bring morbid dependency (drug addiction). Lucy constantly monitors her own body looking for Death and lives in a sort of clandestine way to look like Life-in-Death, the other immortal character in Coleridge's "Rime of the Ancient Mariner" (1798).

It took one more year of psychotherapy to learn from Lucy that these countertransference feelings were appropriate. In a whisper, she told me something she would never repeat: ten years before, the doctors had told her that she no longer had cancer. It was like a secret, something she should never know . . . To prevent death, she lives in the dark, she hears confused sounds (like a fetus in the womb) from the TV but pays no attention to it. She lives like dreaming into a corridor; she plays dead as animals do to defend themselves from dangerous predators. She is afraid of coming to life . . .

Interlude: Writing a Paper within a Network

We wrote a paper on Lucy. Maybe we were just unconsciously trying to put death somewhere into a safe place. Our paper focused on supervision as a tool to uncover and work through the unconscious resistances of psychotherapists to approaching cancer patients (Fazzi and Nesci 2008). It was published by a scientific Italian online journal www.psychomedia.it/psic-onco/index.html, in a column called "Lavoro scritto in rete," which means literally "paper written within a network." These are papers conceived specifically through the facilitating role played by the setting of the Balint-like groups of our psycho-oncology courses, where difficult clinical cases are discussed among health professionals with different backgrounds and levels of experience. Thus the final paper is the outcome of a group process whose facilitating role is acknowledged by the "recognized" authors (those who presented the clinical vignette and wrote the text).

The motif of *thanatosis* (Miyatake et al. 2004) was not new in our courses in psycho-oncology. Actually, in a class in 2006, three students (clown doctors) had performed the famous bagatelle, *Pulcinella, Teresina, e la Morte,* using a small portable puppet theatre. In this comic piece, Punch plays possum as soon as Death appears on the stage (Baldazzi, Suppi, and Cicchetti 2006). In fact, *thanatosis* seems to be an adaptive mechanism that different species (including humans) are able to use. But what exactly happens if a cancer patient recurs to it? What kind of transference might affect his/her relatives and friends? What kind of countertransference might be experienced by the psychotherapist? Maybe it is not without unconscious meanings (and resistances) if so many schools of psychotherapy do not include any specific training in psycho-oncology in their curriculum, even today. Nobody wants to shake hands with Life-in-Death.

Supervision: Postlude

At a certain point during Lucy's therapy, her husband's father fell ill and died. Lucy experienced these events as a repetition of her own father's illness and death, and she began talking about it. It came out that he had died of liver cancer many years before. Lucy told her therapist she had to take care of him during his illness, whereas her sister didn't want to see him at all to protect herself from emotional distress. Within a year of his death, Lucy developed leukemia.

Believing that Lucy had failed to work through the oncologic mourning for her father, I offered her the opportunity to try multimedia psychotherapy, which she accepted. The next session, she came with a series of pictures that were generally very poor, technically speaking. The first was an ID photo of her father as a young man. There were no childhood pictures. Instead, she brought pictures of her own engagement, marriage, honeymoon, life in her small native town near Rome, her father hunting, her father entering the church with her on the day of her marriage, her children, and a large color photo of herself with her husband . . . and that was all.

Although she had been clearly told to bring photos for a strip of life of her dead father, the sequence only represented him as an adult and her own life as a child, a young woman, and a mother, stopping before her father's illness and death and her own ordeal. I asked her for more. So a second series of pictures arrived, portraying Lucy's father at his hobbies (hunting, playing squeeze box, making jokes on the beach, enjoying a little house in the countryside) and the photo they put on his tomb (the *ricordino*).

Lucy didn't discuss the pictures anymore in the following sessions, however. They passed from the hands of my patient through my own hands (as her therapist) into the hands of the supervisor . . . and there they remained. Dr. Nesci still has them in his office in a closed desk drawer. She still hasn't asked me to give them back. A soundtrack was discussed, but not chosen, making it useless to give the pictures to the multimedia artist since his methodology is to begin with the music and then arrange and edit the pictures accordingly.

In the meantime, Lucy's father-in-law died and Lucy's son planned his wedding. In Italy, a wedding is a *big* event. Lucy worked on her image to make herself beautiful for the photographer. My fantasy is that Lucy celebrated the mourning of herself as a healthy young woman in the first photographic series and the mourning of her father in the second. Perhaps she is unconsciously planning a third series associated with her rebirth at her son's wedding as a healthy survivor. When I discussed this in supervision with Dr. Nesci, he said that his fantasy is that the third series will be taken to a therapist in the future, when Lucy's son becomes the father of a boy named after his grandfather . . . so that the circle of life will close itself in rebirth, following the pattern of syncytial cultures. In Dr. Nesci's mind, only then will Lucy complete the choice of the music, ask me to entrust the whole thing to the artist, and complete her multimedia psychotherapy with the production of the memory object that can "establish the terms" of her syncytial mourning.

At the moment, Lucy is not interested in remembering and dangerously mourning the loss of her father to cancer; something might still remain "attached" to her. She is still acting like one of Briffault's "group-individuals" (1927). She prefers to have entrusted a part of herself (the pictures of her previous life with her father) to her placental leader (the therapist) and its safe container (the body-of-the-mother/supervisor/Balint-like group/Dreaming Team Clinical Seminars) in order to feel protected from the risk of death if she remains "attached" to her dead father in syncytial mourning. For now, she cannot work it through; she can only deposit it.

Therapist and supervisor look at the pictures from the two series on the supervisor's computer, whose orientation is changed to let them observe the scanned images together. The therapist comments on each one, pausing on the hunting picture and reading from her notes what the patient said during the multimedia session. As a girl, Lucy used to help her father make his own bullets for hunting. The supervisor makes a lapse, however, saying "husband" instead of "father," while looking at the picture of Lucy's father with her at her wedding. Therapist and supervisor laugh at the closeness between the two words (and at the closeness between the two of them looking at the pictures on the monitor screen) and conclude there is an opening here, rather than a closure/termination. The supervisor's Freudian slip of the tongue reveals some Oedipal layers coming to the surface that require more analytic work in the future. "It's a long way to Tipperary . . ." Therapist and supervisor had met to "close" their work on Lucy's case and to terminate her multimedia psychotherapy. Instead, they have become aware that it is a work in progress. Lucy's therapy cannot be ended here. She is still "too" close to her therapist, as the supervisor's lapse and acting out reveal.

From this "conclusion," Dr. Nesci offers a deeper interpretation: "Mourning, in multimedia psychotherapy, is a pre-text. Life is a series of passages, of mourning experiences. We exit A, we live a transition into NOT-A/NOT-B, then we reach B, but we will soon have to abandon the new position too, and move toward C, D, and so on . . . Multimedia psychotherapy, defined as a work in progress, could be a pattern for every psychotherapeutic situation. A therapist might always wish to come to conclusions, to 'terminate,' to fix and freeze the patient in a determined position . . . and the patient, as every living being, will always go on changing (developing, progressing, or regressing) and reopening the game . . . The memory object of multimedia psychotherapy is a placental symbol, the baton to be handed on, the changeover, the recyclable discarded matter of an interminable process (Freud 1937) that will go on even after the agreed-upon end of therapy . . . Why don't we plan a clinic and dreams workshop for next Saturday presenting Lucy's case and her scanned pictures so that our colleagues at school can see them, go to sleep, and then dream about her and her therapy? Why don't we ask Professor Scafoglio, our anthropologist, to join us?"

Thus our individual supervision session ended with this move toward a new supervision setting created for Lucy's case in multimedia psychotherapy.

PART III: THE CLINIC AND DREAMS WORKSHOP

by Domenico A. Nesci, in collaboration with Marcella Fazzi, Tommaso A. Poliseno, Domenico Scafoglio, Domenico Agresta, Chiara Maria Barbato, Grazia Cassatella, Stefano Daprile, Marina Delle Cave, Miguel Del Pozo, Vincenzo Florio, Cristina Foti, MariaChiara Marra, Monica Medici, and Valentina Scopone

On October 30, 2010, on a Saturday night, a special Dreaming Team Clinical Seminar took place at our School of Psychotherapy. The Dreaming Team approach aims at creating a cultural and emotional environment, a setting, where the presenter introduces a clinical case not to discuss it but to receive free associations from all other participants in order to be helped in the treatment. In this instance, students from all courses (first, second, third and fourth year) met to listen to Dr. Fazzi's presentation of Lucy's case and to see the pictures the patient had given her therapist during the multimedia sessions. As always, the clinical seminar was conducted by me (a psychoanalyst) and Dr. Poliseno (a group analyst), the school's co-directors.

Dr. Fazzi's presentation focused on the two dreams she had discussed in her individual supervision with me, the dream about Lucy's son being a drug addict, and the dream about the dead hand and arm. Then the pictures were projected on a screen and commented on in the school's associative atmosphere. Finally everyone went to sleep, looking forward to the next morning's guided social dreaming, the first experiment in the newly created Clinic and Dreams Workshop. The day after, Professor Scafoglio (a Neapolitan anthropologist from the University of Salerno and the greatest living expert on *Pulcinella*) arrived to join me and Dr. Poliseno in leading the workshop, a role he had played several times in previous Movies and Dreams Workshops at the end of the UCSC courses in psycho-oncology (that the students of our School of Psychotherapy take regularly as part of their curriculum).

The atmosphere was intimate and familiar, since this time we were working in the school's "Maria Augusta Foti" multimedia room, a place designed to facilitate a warm group experience. Most of the people had been at the Saturday night presentation, but Prof. Scafoglio and a few students had been unable to attend the event or see the pictures. So there was a subgroup within the group formed by people who were "new" to the whole thing or just "blind" to it. The workshop lasted about three hours. I will try to give an idea of what really went on, translating some excerpts from the transcripts by Dr. Grazia Cassatella. All italicized parts in parenthesis (. . .) belong to the text of the transcription, while all parts in brackets [. . .] were written by me to clarify what was going on by adding information or comments.

Excerpts from the Transcripts

Dr. Nesci: Welcome, Professor Scafoglio. Your presence as the third leader in this experimental workshop is very important. For us, as everybody in this room knows, anthropology and psychoanalysis should always be integrated when one is serious about understanding human experience. Yesterday evening, we discussed Lucy's clinical case and saw her pictures, the photos she brought her therapist in their multimedia sessions; this morning we're going to share the dreams we had during the night and freely associate. Let's try and see if this new Clinic and Dreams Workshop will be able to help Lucy's therapist, Marcella [Dr. Fazzi], and myself, her supervisor, to feel more at ease, more at home, in the clinical scenario.

Dr. Cristina Foti: I'd like to tell you the experience I had last night. I dreamt I was at a beauty parlor where I had to do a two-hour treatment. The treatment was going to last longer, so I left the shop and then I woke up. It was 4:00 A.M. This is the time I usually wake up every day. However, this time I noticed I was in the dark and I thought, "This is Lucy's dark." I associated with the movie *Buried*, where a man is kidnapped in Iraq and buried alive in a coffin with a lighter, a cell phone, and a knife. Then I associated the movie with a real personal experience.

Last year, going to visit a dead relative with my mother in Prima Porta Cemetery [Prima Porta = First Door], I entered one of these "homes" [the dreamer is using the word "home" although she is clearly speaking of a funeral chapel] where there are these gravestones inside, and . . . (*the dreamer changes her tone of voice*) I become afraid and begin trembling. I heard some moaning . . . "Mm . . . mm . . . mm . . ." "Well," I thought, "maybe it's an old creaky ladder." Then I went out and saw my mother who asked me, "Did you hear anything inside?" "What?" I replied, and she said, "I heard some scratching by a gravestone." So we went back inside . . . This scene is taking place early in the morning . . .

Even today I feel uneasy telling this story . . . Actually in a series of gravestones there was one tomb whose marble was still missing and you could hear some moaning . . . some scratching sounds . . . "This must be a joke!" I said to my mother, and we went out looking for someone. We were alone, completely alone, and we could hear this uncanny moaning. [. . .] So we began to make absurd conjectures about the mafia and the people they make disappear. We even thought about calling the police. [. . .] We were scared . . .

So all this came back to mind this morning and I couldn't sleep anymore. It was really bad. I had to share this with you. (*Two minutes of complete silence*)

Dr. Marcella Fazzi: Last night I dreamt about a coffeemaker. Actually, I'm a little confused. I don't know if it was one coffeemaker in three different moments, or three coffeemakers from different perspectives. One machine was very dirty and clearly not in use; another one was clean, very clean but not new. It looked like a Napoletana, as we call the Italian coffeemaker, which had been disinfected and washed with water vapor. The last one was in use, but a little dirty. I couldn't understand if I was looking at three coffeemakers put on the same plane, or at one coffeemaker in three different ways.

My association went immediately to something Lucy had told me. Once, maybe after one or more years of our therapy, she whispered to me, as if she were revealing a secret, that she had tasted some coffee. Actually she had stopped drinking coffee many years before since she was afraid it was unhealthy. "I sipped a spoonful of coffee from my husband's cup!" After that, she gradually changed her habits. At times she even talked about huge stocks of coffee she had bought. My association here goes to the possibility to feel excitement and to the stimulating power of coffee. By the way, this morning when Dr. Poliseno said that Professor Scafoglio was coming, I immediately thought, "I had a Neapolitan dream!" since the most famous Italian coffee is made in Naples. (*Everybody laughs*.)

Actually I dreamt the coffeemaker, the Napoletana! But Cristina's story reminds me of something about Lucy. When Lucy was encouraged to take a drug, she took such a small dose that I joked with her, saying she had improved thanks to a "cat's therapy." She felt better, more lively, thanks to a cat's cure.

Dr. Nesci: My association, as soon as Cristina shared her dream with us, recalled the movie *Buried*, and told her story, was that the mother and daughter at the cemetery were you [Dr. Marcella Fazzi] and me, therapist and supervisor, feeling this uncanny emotion regarding someone who is buried alive: the patient. Actually my first association, listening to the story, was about a cat somewhere in the funerary chapel. Often cats, or animals, in a dream represent a child or something lively. My feeling was that Lucy had buried alive her own vitality inside herself and that we were also scared to death, on the clinical scene, finding ourselves all alone in such an uncanny situation. (*Everybody laughs, including Dr. Nesci.*)

Dr. Marcella Fazzi: Let's go find someone. Let's look for someone!

Dr. Nesci: Let's call the police, the Carabinieri! Will they think we're crazy? (*A short silence*)

Dr. Nesci: My espresso was very good this morning. I had a cup from Kona on Hawaii's Big Island. It's hard to get Kona coffee in Rome. It can be transported easily from Hawaii to the U.S., but then you need someone to bring it, carefully hidden, because if you mail it from the States, the Italian custom officers seize it!

Dr. Stefano Daprile: Cool! So, we're talking about the police here! (*Everybody laughs.*)

Dr. Chiara Maria Barbato: Listening to Cristina, I was reminded of a book I'm reading by Jorge Amado, called *Tereza Batista: Home from the Wars* . I'm up to the point where there is an epidemic and every field was turning into a graveyard to bury the dead . . . and dying people as well since they were going to die anyway. Then I associated with horror stories told to me and a group of other children at my parents' little town in southern Italy during our summer vacations. The teller pretended the stories were true. The scariest one I remember was about a little girl who died in an epidemic. (By the way, the father and the grandfather of the woman who told the stories were both carpenters.) A small coffin was prepared for the little girl. For three days after they buried her, the whole town was haunted by a noise that kept everyone from sleeping. At last the carpenter went to check on the little coffin. He opened it and found the girl's hands full of wooden splinters. Maybe they had buried her alive . . . And here the dream stops! [This is a lapse; she is telling a story, not a dream!] Terrible . . .

Dr. Nesci: This is not a dream or a story but a psychical reality in many cancer stories. We often see when a person is diagnosed with an oncologic disease, all the people around him or her consider the patient already dead. That's why they bury the person alive, metaphorically.

I have two associations. The first goes back to coffee. Roasted coffee beans are dark . . . [like Lucy's darkness]. When you make coffee, its aroma gives flavor to the atmosphere and fills the whole kitchen with its fragrance, as if something dead had been revived and brought back to life. My second association has to do with the psychoanalytic interpretation of *das unheimliche* [Freud 1919], where the universal fear of being buried alive is only a transformation of another fantasy, of the unconscious wish to go back into the womb of Mother Earth to become a fetus again and start a new life cycle.

Prof. Scafoglio: I also have two associations. One is with the ritual of cremation, which I think is becoming more frequent in Italy precisely because so many old people are consciously afraid, not just unconsciously, of being buried alive. My second association has to do with the anthropological meanings of the cat. The domestic cat is a phallic animal (tail raising, rubbing itself against women's legs, etc.), but it is also a demonic beast, which implies a further association with death. Freely associating with the dream of the three coffeemakers, I might spend a few words on the ritual of *consolo* (consoling), which traditionally involves bringing coffee (and/or other beverages and food) to the relatives of a deceased person after a death in the family.

Dr. Poliseno: Listening to Cristina's story, which I also, like Domenico, consider an association to Lucy's problem [i.e., defensively experiencing herself as a dead-and-alive person], I interpreted the mysterious noises at the cemetery as the sound of the uncanny transformations of a corpse . . . an uncanny fantasy indeed! Then Chiara told another horror story and following this leitmotif, I remembered my own childhood.

We had a neighbor who used to tell stories to children, too, at night. Fears can shock and freeze us, it's true, but they can also have a cathartic effect and help us think the unthinkable. So, following this unusual path, I came to one of our Movies and Dreams Workshops, the workshop we did last year, but I don't remember the movie title . . .

Dr. Nesci: *The Bucket List.*

Dr. Poliseno: Yes, *The Bucket List*, which was released in Italy as *Non è mai troppo tardi* ["It's never too late"]. One of the most exhilarating moments in the movie is when Morgan Freeman, who plays the part of a poor but cultured mechanic, reveals that Jack Nicholson's most expensive favorite coffee had its unique flavor only because monkeys used to shit on the coffee beans . . . and this gave the beans their special taste! Eating shit . . . (*Everybody laughs.*)

As Professor Scafoglio was suggesting, we have to work through our "shit" [cancer, death, and so on] a lot, culturally, if we want to take it in and survive!

Dr. Nesci: Instead of "eating shit," let me say that the story of *The Bucket List* would rather suggest the metaphor of making and drinking "shit coffee," which is a more complex process (you need the monkeys, their shit, coffee beans, roasting, the coffeemaker . . . and art!) Actually, associating with Scafoglio's remarks on cremation, let me remind you of a few details from the movie's plot. Jack Nicholson was the extremely rich owner of a clinic where the two cancer patients had to share a room. They became friends and decided to be incinerated after death and buried at the top of the Himalayas. In the last scene, we see Nicholson's loyal secretary bringing his ashes (after incineration) to the top of the Himalayas and putting them close to those of Morgan Freeman (who had died long before him). Rather than being in urns, the ashes are contained in two coffee cans of Morgan Freeman's favorite brand, the cheapest and most popular, not the exclusive "shit coffee beans" the rich man used to drink . . .

Dr. Domenico Agresta: Let me go back to Professor Scafoglio's *consolo* and tell one more story about coffee . . . In Abruzzo, we have this tradition of bringing coffee when somebody dies. We call it *lu conz* in our dialect. Some years ago, when the father of one of my cousins died of cancer, a terrible mistake was made. My relatives brought the coffee before my uncle had actually died. The whole family felt insulted and a serious conflict began. I was in the town square, the place where social life usually converges, and my aunt came and told me (and another family member with me) to come back home since something serious had occurred. That serious offense was the premature gift of coffee!

I'd also like to share a curious dream I had a few days ago. Actually something similar to what appeared in the dream had taken place in reality, as I told Dr. Nesci a few days ago, before I had this dream. [Dr. Agresta visited the home of a possessed woman in his little town in Abruzzo and was able to convince her that her possession was over and she should swear to God she would go back to her psychiatrist, take her medications, and do psychotherapy to prevent this possession from occurring again.] In my dream, I was summoned to the home of my aunt who was possessed by the devil. The situation was grotesque but not scary. The grotesque part was that all the people around the possessed woman (probably her relatives, aunts, and grandmothers), the relatives of this girl lying on a stone couch (a meaningful detail), all looked alike, identical to the woman on the book cover of the Italian edition of van Gennep's *The Rites of Passage*. [Actually the book cover shows a woman and a girl, which might be associated with the two different expressions, "woman" and "girl," used by Dr. Agresta talking about his aunt in the dream.] They were all the same, while my aunt was the only normal person. In the dream I told her this (and another person did, too). I said, "Don't worry, you're the most normal person here" and she was liberated from her situation. All the other women were dressed in black, all the same, with this apparently happy smile . . . ambivalent figures . . . and yet, strangely, the dream was full of vitality. I felt alive and energized when I woke up . . .

Dr. Marcella Fazzi: I'd like to say something connected to what Mimmo [Dr. Agresta] is saying here. However, first let me say something else . . . When I first met Lucy, I felt very uneasy. That's why I asked Dr. Nesci for supervision. We explained this uncanny effect as a transference of her oncologic experiences and yet I'd like to ask Mimmo, "Didn't you feel afraid with your real possessed patient?" I'm not talking here of the dream, but of the real experience Mimmo had with a real possessed woman, before having the dream. When I asked him this question, he answered spontaneously, "No, not at all! In my little town, people are used to it."

Dr. Poliseno: People are used to it? Is it a habit to be possessed? (*Everybody laughs.*)

Dr. Marcella Fazzi: I was really surprised, too! But now, maybe thanks to the presence of Professor Scafoglio, who wrote a book on this topic and presented it at our School of Psychotherapy, I feel I'm beginning to enter deeper into the cultural dimension of clinical situations. This stone couch of the dream makes me think of the analytic couch, and then of the benches in the squares of all little towns. Sitting there, you take in a lot of local culture; you observe the environment, learn the mentality of the place, get to know the people and their life styles . . .

Dr. Domenico Agresta: At the end of the home visit, the exorcized woman got up from her bed, threw everything away, all her crosses and holy water, and then said, "Let's go out and have a coffee, Doc!" and she bought me an *espresso* at the bar . . . which was very good, by the way!

Prof. Scafoglio: I'm afraid if I delve into this topic of possession, we'll go beyond the scope of our work . . . But, since I know you practice associative thinking, I'll dare to digress and say just one thing that is commonplace in anthropology. In the situation we call "possession," the person believes the state has a sacred origin. The devil (or a lost soul, but discussing this distinction would make my digression too long) has taken possession of the person's body and it is the priest, not the therapist, who is the socially recognized figure who can cure the patient by expelling the devil, in the name of God. Where faith in God (or the sacred) has been lost, we have the therapist who takes this task upon his or her hands.

Dr. Marcella Fazzi: Yesterday, when I presented the case of Lucy here, I recounted her dream of the dead hand and arm. I could never be Lucy's therapist all alone. I consider her as "our" patient, thanks to my supervision with Dr. Nesci. The reason is that, even if I don't consider myself a superstitious person, I could never be the only therapist in this clinical scenario. Let me try to explain this better with a digression.

When I play cards with a group of friends, we always want a certain Charles to play because we believe he's a really unlucky person. He tries to defend himself saying, "No, I don't want to play since I always lose!" And we always insist saying, "No, no, you must play! Otherwise we don't know where the shit will be going!" Do you know what I mean?

So this gives me a new idea . . . Maybe Lucy's problem is that if she is the one with cancer, then all her relatives can relax because everybody knows where the shit is. On the other hand, if she or her relatives acknowledge that she doesn't have cancer anymore, then the uneasy question might lurk behind the scenes, "Where will cancer go now?" Contagion anxiety is the deepest agony in this cancer story . . . this uncanny "shit." Who is going to have it?

Prof. Scafoglio: When one is a victim of the evil eye, it is necessary to look for an *occhiarola* [*occhio* = eye] and it is she who will undo the spell. The ritual calls for dipping and dissolving the evil in a washbowl full of water. At the end, the water is thrown out the window. In this way, the evil that has been expelled will be taken into a passerby . . . It goes without saying that some cultures have been able to evolve and conceive the idea that water with "the whammy" should be thrown into the sea to prevent this from happening. But I am wandering now onto something else . . . How come there is no trace in your dreams of the relationship [contagion anxiety] between death and the insurgence of a disease in a relative of the deceased person?

Dr. Miguel Del Pozo: Let me take my cue from Professor Scafoglio. Last night, around 4:15 A.M., I woke in the heart of darkness . . . I had to make a great effort to switch on the light, find a pen, and write my dream. I wanted to repress it, but I was unable to forget it. I wrote it down for our workshop, but I don't need to look at my notes since I still remember it very well. It's an uncanny dream. I feel deep emotions, even now, retelling it. There's a couple, a man and a woman, in my dream. The man is very handsome, and the two are dancing in a courtyard. The setting is a nineteenth-century historical atmosphere. Suddenly there is something wrong with the young woman. At first, the young man seems not to pay attention to her condition. Then he takes her in his own arms and brings her somewhere. I think he is bringing her to a place where she can be cured. The place is a nun's convent as well as a hospital. I arrive at this hospital. It's me now. The doctor looks like a cartoon character, a strange figure . . . The girl is in a sort of liminal state of consciousness. She lies on the operating table in a sort of anesthesia or deathlike condition; she looks dead. The doctor tells me there is nothing to do and that it is necessary to remove everything: a radical hysterectomy. I look at this woman . . . now she is my wife . . . and (thinking about zombies that leave their arms attached to the body of someone else, as in Lucy's dream), I realize that her legs are missing. That's it . . . I dream this uncanny mutilation . . . I get closer to my wife, who is reawakening. I put my hand under her head, and I notice that her legs are there but they look like the legs of a child; in fact her whole body looks like the body of a child. It is as if she had awakened from her anesthesia or liminal death state. I have a strange feeling, the feeling I know everything (while before I thought I knew nothing about what was going on). And that was a really uncanny feeling! And then I awoke.

Associating with the issue of spells, when someone in my wife's village performs these rituals, they take what is negative upon themselves and then work it through and dispose of the evil by yawning repeatedly. The person can be present or far away, somewhere else, it doesn't matter . . .

Prof. Scafoglio: That's quite interesting. Ernesto de Martino, the most important Italian anthropologist between the 50s and the 70s, maintains that the *sfascinatrice* (the woman who can remove the evil eye and the negative spells) yawns while placing her hands on the "fascinated" person. While his interpretation is that this is a psychosomatic expression of the deep emotional involvement of the "*sfascinatrice*," I personally think it has to do with ancient shamanic practices according to which the shaman was able to absorb evil from the person by laying his hands on, taking in the patient's negativity, and then expelling it by yawning and breathing it out.

Dr. Nesci: Yawning as well as laughing are normal means to reduce respiratory "dead space" and give us spirit, vital breath, oxygenated air . . .

Dr. Marina Delle Cave: In the area of Cilento Natural Park in southern Italy, I heard that mothers help their babies suffering from a bellyache by chewing a bit of bread, softening it with their saliva, and then feeding it to their children. I think we are working through, here, the theme of the capacity to contain negativity and elaborate it. Once again cats come to mind. There's a story on this theme in *Cinderella Cat,* which was the nickname for Cinderella in the Italian version by Giambattista Basile. Roberto de Simone turned the tale into an opera in 1976, writing the musical score and the libretto. The Cinderella cat is a woman and she has the power to cure.

Dr. Marcella Fazzi: I'd say that pity is made edible through the woman . . . Listening to Marina [Dr. Delle Cave], I made a few associations. My office is over a baker's shop. As I said yesterday, Lucy benefited from psychotherapy because it allowed her to get out of the house, go to the town square, and buy food. The first thing she bought was bread from the bakery. The whole family benefited from this change. "Finally we can eat fresh bread!" they all exclaimed.

My associative path then brings me to the "bread of forgiveness" in the famous historical novel *The Betrothed* by Alessandro Manzoni. This was the bread that the Franciscan friar accepts as a sign that the relatives of the man he has killed before his conversion (and that he visits to ask to be forgiven) have truly pardoned him since they understand that he is sincerely repentant for the murder. Usually Lucy comes to my office with her bread in the bag and leaves the bag in the waiting room outside the therapy room. Even though she is paranoid, she leaves her bread outside.

My last association (perhaps an interpretation) is that she asks her own relatives to pardon her because she didn't die of cancer. Cancer survivors might feel responsible for the affective disinvestment of those around them in anticipation of their death . . . and such expectations might be disappointed, which implies, perhaps, a need to be forgiven . . .

Dr. Nesci: Let me go back to Marina's story and food rituals. There's an interesting ritual I experienced in the Fiji Islands recently, the Kava (or Yaqona) ritual. The root of the *Piper methysticum* is dried, aged, pounded to become a powder, and dissolved in water so that all the community members can drink it from the same coconut cup, ritually, while telling stories. In ancient times, this ritual was a serious business. The children had to extract the whole roots from the earth with their delicate little hands, wash them in their mouths with their own saliva, and put the roots in the sun to let them dry . . . Here I'm thinking about our group elaboration, our group supervision, our "guided" social dreaming where we are the children that chew these tasty roots from our patients (their transference communications), let them dry, mature, even age into ourselves safely . . . and then we analyze them by pounding and dissolving them with fresh water (the flow of free associations) so that everyone can drink, digest, and feel better tasting the flavor of life . . .

Prof. Scafoglio: Let me add that children in all cultures are believed to have special powers. Even today, the lotto draw is performed by a child . . . Associating with the motifs of women and bread, let me quote from Corrado Alvaro, who wrote that southern women look at men as if they are actually seeing some bread. I never understood what he meant by that, but now I associate his words with the role of women as those who distribute, give out, deliver . . .

Dr. Poliseno: Thinking about Lucy's bread in the waiting room . . . out of the "tomb," out of the dark room where it waits to be integrated, at last, when the need to protect it from the deadly contagion will be less urgent and extreme . . . with the passing of time and the progress of therapy . . . I feel something important has been discovered here. We began with Lucy's uncanny feeling of being a zombie and gradually understood that this identity was necessary. To safeguard her relatives, she had to freeze herself, her own life, everything. Once again we're in a tomb, a claustrophobic space . . . we're buried alive in our countertransference. Claustrophobia has to do not only with an inner need to bury ourselves alive, it also deals with an external mechanism that prevents us from wishing to live and enjoy life. In the theatre, before going on stage, the actors yawn and laugh to prepare themselves and reduce the dead respiratory space. To impersonate a character, we need to get rid of deadly objects and feel ourselves more alive.

Dr. Miguel Del Pozo: Associating on bread and women . . . in my homeland, when a man gets engaged with a woman and you want to wish him to get married, stay with her their whole life, and be happy, you are supposed to say, "Eat the bread, too!" This means, don't eat the meat or the cheese or whatever you find inside the bread immediately. Take your time eating bread and butter (or whatever) so that the whole thing will last longer. Don't eat the meat alone, just the content, the object of your desire. Take all of it and make it last as long as you can . . .

Dr. MariaChiara Marra: Last night I had a dream that I think is connected with Marcella's patient. The dream reminds me of the movie *The Chronicles of Narnia: The Voyage of the Dawn Treader*. In the movie there is a White Witch, a character reminiscent of the Snow Queen in Andersen's famous tale. The White Witch seized Narnia and changed everything into a frozen sea. I dreamt the children of the movie . . . maybe there were more children in my dream . . . and they were traveling on a multistory bus. They were hiding; otherwise the Witch would freeze them, too! When I awoke, I thought my dream had to do with Lucy's need to go underground, to disavow her own healing in order to defeat this ice, this cold darkness, where she had hidden herself. This fact of invisibility really impressed me! In my dream (and here I see the intrusion of the latest

Harry Potter movie I saw recently), the children wore blankets to be invisible and made a detour to take her from behind and defeat her unseen.

Dr. Marcella Fazzi: That makes me think about Lucy's pictures. Doctor Nesci didn't show them to Professor Scafoglio. He didn't bring them again this morning. It seems there is someone here too who cannot see! Which brings me back to my first session with Lucy. "I will never look at you!" As if she had already assigned to the therapist the role of being unseen . . . or to herself to remain hidden . . .

Dr. Domenico Agresta: I was thinking about yesterday's clinical seminar and our association during Lucy's case presentation with the movie *The Others*, where the characters are both seen and unseen . . . During the discussion last night, our idea was that looking at the pictures would mean death for the patient, so keeping the photographs unseen would be a way to keep her alive . . . [In the movie, there is a book with pictures of deceased people, taken immediately after their death, which was not uncommon in the nineteenth century, while a book of old pictures from southern Italy, including photographs of dead people, was brought by Dr. MariaChiara Marra and circulated among the participants before the workshop began.] Yesterday, Marcella showed us that some changes occurred in the patient's behavior slowly . . . She gradually increased the light in the room. Did Lucy realize it? Did she notice but refuse to acknowledge it? There are complex vicissitudes indeed taking place during psychotherapy . . .

Dr. Marcella Fazzi: The patient did notice the changes. One day, for example, she realized the room was darker and said, "How dark it is today!" One light bulb had actually burnt out . . . (*Everybody laughs.*) Usually Lucy notices changes (inner and outer) but doesn't talk about them unless they are regressive changes, as in the case of the blown light bulb. Now she is beginning to notice and verbalize some progressive changes . . . She told me this story: Her son was going with his future bride to visit some friends and invite them to the wedding. Among them was a woman who had just undergone breast surgery for aesthetic reasons. The woman insisted that Lucy's son touch her new breasts and verify how firm they were! He and his fiancée were perplexed and embarrassed. "My son turned as red as a beetroot and my husband, who usually says nothing, commented that it must have been really terrible. Then he added that he also found himself in such a situation once at his office, where a woman colleague had similar surgery and obliged him to touch her breasts as well!" Then Lucy confessed, "I didn't sleep the whole night . . . Then, this morning, I thought, 'Don't you see that if you're jealous, it means you're not dead?'"

Dr. Poliseno: To see we are alive must be a real problem! A huge one! (*Everybody laughs.*) I say this associating with the absence of the pictures here to look at today, and with the sequence Lucy followed when she brought them to the therapist—a fact that was mostly left in the background yesterday. The patient brought a first series of pictures she had selected, a process which implied anxiety. The second series was requested by the therapist in an excess of enthusiasm which might have scared Lucy. In fact, the following apparent abandonment of the pictures in the supervisor's office seems to signal the need for great caution when dealing with this patient.

I imagine, when working with Lucy, one feels the risk of spoiling or ruining any progress every time it seems that something good is slowly coming out of the therapy. I think our group's working through is really wonderful since it shows how the therapist should be and act in the clinical setting, the attention she has to pay to the emotional temperature, to the climate of the contact with her patient. Lucy's therapy takes place on the preverbal level. Not just symbolic but concrete elements need to be integrated in the narrative of psychotherapy as well as in her own identity. As a group analyst, I can also see these dynamics in another meaningful detail. Today we have chosen not to have our traditional coffee break. Once again, an act of cautiousness . . . who can really know what we would be drinking at the coffee bar? (*Everybody laughs*.) The patient herself takes only a little sip, her own personal dose of coffee. I think this has to do with the idea that in a coffee break, we might disperse our energies, which are limited and shouldn't be wasted. At the same time, I think we're afraid we risk missing our target if we move away and leave our work unfinished . . . I'm afraid it could have happened . . .

Dr. Nesci: Let's make an agreement. We *do* take a break and you promise to come back after the pause . . . (*Everybody laughs*.) It's 12:15 P.M. now. What should we do? (*Many voices in the background speaking at the same time*) What about fifteen minutes?

Dr. Poliseno: Why don't we just pause to have a rest and then come back and make conclusions and close at fifteen or twenty minutes to one? So we can go to the bathroom, smoke a cigarette, and enjoy a real break . . . and we can make some very short concluding remarks when we come back?

Dr. Nesci: So, do we have time to buy a *coffee* for Professor Scafoglio? (*Everybody laughs*.)

Dr. Marcella Fazzi: A safe coffee, of course . . .

COFFEE BREAK

Dr. Monica Medici: I thought my dream was so banal I was ashamed to tell it . . . However, during coffee break, a colleague encouraged me to. I dreamt I was . . . I don't remember exactly where . . . maybe at a market. There was a person with me who was saying, "These clams are wonderful!" Actually the clams were bigger than usual, so I considered buying them. I got the urge to eat pasta and clams. I thought it would take too much time, though, since it's quite complicated to get the clams ready for cooking; you know, you have to leave them in water for a long time to get cleaned, filtered, and purified.

Dr. Valentina Scopone: I was wondering whether it wouldn't be easier to buy frozen food and get the same result, although not exactly the same, of course . . .

Dr. Monica Medici: Cleaning clams implies expelling and removing something bad, the sand and debris. I associate with the movie *The Green Mile,* where the main character has the power to take all negativity into himself and then discard it outside.

Dr. MariaChiara Marra: In *The Green Mile,* the good character (who is sentenced to death anyway) had the power to absorb evil from other people into himself and then expel it through his mouth, not by yawning but by taking a deep breath. Some black things would come out from his mouth . . .

Dr. Domenico Agresta: Black as coffee beans . . .

Dr. Vincenzo Florio: The movie's main character was a black man named Coffey. He used to introduce himself saying, "My name is Coffey, like the drink!"

Dr. Valentina Scopone: This theme of clams, the fact that someone might clean them for you, making everything easier (like with frozen food), leads me to another thread of associations . . . For about two weeks, I've been fascinated by *Six Feet Under*, an American television series about a family who owns a funeral home. Someone dies in every episode, and there is the problem of mourning and trying to come to terms with the meanings of death and life. So, for about two weeks, I've been elaborating this issue of being buried alive. The other night, with a friend of mine who is a bit down in this period, we were fantasizing that we should be able to go into hibernation, like some animals, and spend time in a cave, curled up in a sort of fetal position . . . and the rest of the world, too. The whole world should go into hibernation so that we wouldn't have guilt feelings or worries about what we should do or say since all humankind is asleep. And when spring comes back with its flowers, we would blossom again, too! A period of rest . . . a pause . . .

Dr. Nesci: You're talking about psychotherapy . . . the suspended time of every session . . . the miracle of the psychoanalytic setting where this seems to come true, every time . . .

Dr. Miguel Del Pozo: I was thinking about the meaning of our being here today. We're here in order to clear our minds of the malignant intrusive elements that remain attached to us during our contact with our patients . . . I was reflecting on repetition. We often need to read a book, go to the movies, go to the theatre and contact those more fragile parts of ourselves, the more emotional, warmer parts that need to be cured and cared for, by cleansing ourselves within the flow of life where we always need to find ourselves.

There are some traumatic experiences that cannot be worked through. Period. And yet, they can be elaborated through repetition. In other words, what we need is to put our hands into this impossible work, over and over again, so that we feel more alive, which is exactly what happens in a group setting like this. We need this experience, and we'll always need it as long as we are seeing patients. We need this work of reclaiming, redeveloping, clearing up . . . And I was also reflecting on psychoanalysis. In this regard, Freud was right when he wrote about analysis as interminable. In the same sense, our analytic endeavor is interminable.

Dr. Domenico Agresta: I'm thinking about time in cancer patients . . . Time flows differently . . . and we find ourselves in this uneasy situation where we have to adjust and attune the timing of therapy to the cancer patient's subjective time. Cancer time is a suspended time, too, although in an objective way [the permanent risk of a relapse]. I was also thinking about how we managed our time here, in our group setting. We took all the time we needed for a pause . . . an indefinite coffee break but a definite end time for the workshop. It seems like a good choice: the coffee we had seems to have recharged us!

Dr. Nesci: [to Prof. Scafoglio] A final remark?

Prof. Scafoglio: I've really enjoyed working with all of you. I love this way of working. We anthropologists also do group work, but what you do here is much freer, more associative, unrestrained by academic considerations. I consider your workshop very effective and innovative. Let me offer a final remark on the theme of repetition. I agree with what was said here. We have a need for repetition. Continuous exposure to change, novelty, news can be a problem; it can even be dangerous, at times.

I associate with poetry. Poetry is one of the things that structure our life. In poetry, we move along between change and repetition. A poem is a continuous series of lines, where each line refers to the next one and to the previous one, at the same time . . . We need monotony; we need confirmation, validation, acknowledgment . . . If we receive it, then we can appreciate some change, too. Only in this way can we open ourselves to the moment of innovation.

Afterthoughts

From the very beginning, the dreams and associations in the workshop help therapist and supervisor to acknowledge some of the patient's meaningful unconscious fantasies: Lucy "sees" herself as a three-faced Janus, a person who has been buried alive, a person who should play possum and pretend to be dead in order to survive, a person who might change and start living again. Lucy is the three coffeemakers or the one Napoletana seen from three different points of view in her therapist's dream.

From my perspective, I would say that

1. Lucy (in her "buried alive" aspect) has been partially replaced by her pictures (her double) and relocated, as an object in hibernation, into the locked drawer of the supervisor's desk; in this way she feels better thanks to this concrete projection/displacement acted out in multimedia psychotherapy.
2. Lucy (in her "play possum" aspect) has been partially projected into her therapist, who is very careful not to overly excite her and, eventually, puts the process of multimedia psychotherapy in "pause mode" until she expresses a clear wish to complete it. Once again, she feels better thanks to these unconscious transference/countertransference dynamics.
3. Lucy (in her wish to start living again, not just surviving) has been able to make small changes in her life, including going out, buying fresh bread, drinking coffee again, feeling jealous, and so on. At the same time, via transference triangulation, she has been able to induce her therapist's supervisor to make setting variations and to conceive a Clinic and Dreams Workshop to let her be at the center (through the mediation of her pictures and the narrative by her therapist) of a partially "syncytial environment" where her syncytial mourning might finally begin to be elaborated. In this way, the three-faced Janus-like aspects of the patient are integrated in the workshop. The path of the participants parallels Lucy's path in her working through of her individual and group-individual anxieties, needs, and wishes.

In the workshop, everyone is surprised that there is more than they expected. "The treatment was going to last longer" in the first dream, or the "wonderful clams . . . bigger than usual" in the last dream. At the beginning, the group speaks through Dr. Foti, expressing its resistance: "I dreamt I was at a beauty parlor where I had to do a two-hour treatment. The treatment was going to last longer, so I left the shop and then I woke up." Multimedia psychotherapy is devaluated as a cosmetic treatment and rejected (awakening = emerging from free-floating attention).

At the end, instead, after the coffee break, the group speaks through Dr. Medici, who reveals her dream and confesses, "I considered buying those clams. I got the urge to eat pasta and clams." Multimedia psychotherapy is now seen as something valuable and nourishing. Here the participants come in to help with a collective attempt to integrate two (apparently) opposite perspectives on how to prepare this tasty clam recipe: by using fresh food (which implies a long time to let the clams get rid of their debris) or frozen food (which implies a lot of teamwork done by other people in other space/time coordinates, not just in the patient/therapist dual relationship but also in the artist's work and in the Clinic and Dreams Workshop).

In this group metaphor, multimedia psychotherapy is both fresh and frozen food. We produce it when it is needed, in fresh sessions, but we use frozen objects (old pictures and music, the best "cultural" products) and "store" them somewhere so we can reuse them, bringing them back to life (like coffee, when we make it from roasted beans) any time we need them again. I think this is the interesting path followed by the workshop: integrating two apparently opposite perspectives, two worldviews (fresh versus frozen food) that find a new synthesis in the poetic expressions of Dr. Scopone when she fantasizes the whole world going into hibernation and then coming back to new life in spring.

We need change; we need repetition. This is another way to convey the same deep meaning. We can accept some change (new life in spring) if we had enough lack of change in winter (hibernation). Multimedia psychotherapy offers us both: change and repetition, teamwork (the group-individuals points of view in the work of the artist), and individual work (in the dyadic therapeutic relationship).

We have reached the end of the workshop here, with Dr. Del Pozo's comments on our "interminable" need as therapists to work through our countertransference, to always go on analyzing ourselves, and with Professor Scafoglio's conclusion on poetry and the human need to blend repetition and change since we are unable to tolerate too much transformation in our life.

My association here is with a game called "Chain of Words." The pattern is easy: you make a series of words where the first is connected to the second by the fact that the last syllable of the first word becomes the first syllable of the second; then you take the last syllable of the second word and use it as the first syllable of the third word, and so on. The last word has to have the initial syllable of the first word as its last syllable, so that you close the chain.

Of course this is just the pattern of the game. The game itself, as always happens in classical enigmatography, is a poem. Every word is described in one or two lines, a short riddle where you have an apparent and a real (hidden) meaning. Thus, in the poetic lines, every word of the chain becomes an allegoric double. Like the apparent and real (hidden) meanings in a "Chain of Words" game, pictures in multimedia psychotherapy flow one after the other while the soundtrack unifies them into a whole, thanks to the cinematographic editing of the artist.

The lively form of psychotherapy we try to practice here in our school in Rome requires a lot of time and effort by the therapists but significantly reduces the time and effort required of the patients. Patients need to attend fewer sessions while we, the therapists, need to devote more of our time: we have to pause until "clams" are cleaned, filtered, and purified in fresh vital water by attending Balint-like groups, Dreaming Team Seminars, and Clinic and Dreams Workshops. In this way we can pay attention to our countertransference and work it through, continuously.

We can try to adjust the setting of psychotherapy to our patients' time, which might include respecting their need for frozen fast food and/or for fresh food as well. If we succeed in this challenging endeavor, if we blend multimedia sessions with classical psychodynamic psychotherapy, there will be more flavor at the end!

The same applies to supervision. If we blend classical dyadic sessions with our Dreaming Team Seminars (where the therapist presents a clinical case or vignette asking for the group of colleagues and supervisors to associate on it rather than discuss/analyze/interpret it) or with our Clinic and Dreams Workshops (with the contribution of guided social dreaming, where participants' dreams are induced by a case presentation and subsequent associative elaboration in a group setting), supervision works much better, too.

TEN

Looking at Multimedia Psychotherapy from Different Perspectives

Up to this point we have explored multimedia psychotherapy from an ethnopsychoanalytic perspective, considering it as a personalized mourning ritual conceived to repair, through the construction of concrete doubles/memory-objects, the traumatic aspects of actual loss as well as the repressed mental pain associated with human passages in the life cycle. This study allowed us to discover interesting analogies with the construction of screen memories that takes place physiologically in childhood to work through any traumatic event. At this point we are ready to further explore my new technique from the point of view of Dr. Wright, a psychoanalyst who was able to blend psychoanalytic and phenomenological ideas (Sartre 1957) in a most creative way. If we look at the process of making the "strip of life" and the "psychodynamic montage" from his original approach (Wright 1991), we can reach a deeper understanding of what the patient, the therapist, and the artist are doing in the different phases of multimedia psychotherapy.

THE PHASES OF MULTIMEDIA PSYCHOTHERAPY

According to Kenneth Wright, a British psychoanalyst who studied vision and separation between mother and baby, there is a twofold aspect in their face-to-face relationship. On the one side the mother looks at her baby in such a way that the baby is able to build his/her own Self thanks to the "true reflections" he/she can see in her face. If we have a "good enough mother," this process develops normally. On the other, this process might be hindered; "the fixed face of the unresponsive mother could equally be experienced as a reflection, but a distorting one, giving a false feedback of deadness," (Wright 1991). According to this author we "come to discover our own faces [. . .] in the eyes and faces of those who regard us, as a kind of emotional reflection." (14)

In his words,

> we come to see our own self [. . .] through the eyes and looks of others . . . [. . .] The self that is offered by this Other arises at the interface between this self and the Other . . . [. . .] This mediation or reflection is thus exposed to all the risks of distortion and misrepresentation that interpersonal perception and communication are heir to. I think it is becoming clear that I am using the term *self* in two distinct ways. On the one hand, I am talking about the *self-as-subject,* the experiencing self who exists prior to this encounter with the Other's view. On the other, I am talking of the *self-as-object,* that starkly visual and externally formed image of the self which is constituted by that view. [. . .] Does the objective self in some way integrate with or modify the subjective self? Is the objective self repudiated? Or is there a capitulation of the subjective self, a sliding of the subjective self behind the objective form which has been offered? These questions [. . .] will bring up the relation between different sense modalities in experience, in particular, between the *distance* modality of *vision* and the more *proprio*ceptive modalities of *touch and visceral sensation.* (24–25)

These illuminating perspectives by Dr. Wright, can help us understand the two initial phases in the process of the construction of the memory objects in multimedia psychotherapy. The first is the visual phase during which emphasis is on distance between the subject (the patient) and his/her dead love object (or a traumatic passage in the life cycle), a distance we want to increase with the negative aspects and reduce with the positive aspects. This first phase is protective against persecutory anxieties and deals with the affective ambivalence toward the lost love object. This aspect has to do with the times when the subject experienced the love object's gaze as a negative one, a gaze that made him/her feel not only as a *self-as-object* but as a negative Self!

In fact, the rationale for the multimedia artist's work on the pictures selected by patient and therapist during their sessions is to "cure" (shape) our memories with a "reparative feedback of aliveness" in order to replace a "false feedback of deadness" from which inevitably we all suffered, more or less, during our individual development. From this perspective it is very important to reflect on the choice (and the editing) of those pictures where the relationship between the patient and his/her lost love object is portrayed. This choice is worked through during the sessions, by patient and therapist together. For example, in the case of Elisabetta's "memory object," the pictures that documented the presence of "a good enough mother" in a good "holding" attitude with her little daughter were instrumental in reinforcing the memory of a good relationship between subject and lost love object. Looking at them, Elisabetta was able to reinforce all her past experiences of building a true Self thanks to the "true reflections" from her mother's face precisely because the training group was there to help her to acknowledge that she was crying and that her mother was smiling in a "good enough" mother-child relationship.

In multimedia psychotherapy, patient and therapist are engaged in the task of rescuing what was good in the relationship with the lost love object and trying to reshape the relationship itself for the better. They work through a series of triangulations: with the concrete materials (pictures and music) brought by the patient, with the editing done by the multimedia artist, with supervision (in all possible settings), with the placement of the "memory object" in the virtual space/time dimensions of the web, and/or with the feedback that comes from relatives and friends who watch the psychodynamic montage.

The theme of mediation and the need for triangulations were present from the very beginning in the story of multimedia psychotherapy. Let me quote again some excerpts from my first session with Serena (Nesci 2009).

> "There is a third dimension . . . not dead nor alive . . . and it is less painful . . ." I associated the patient's third dimension with the Internet and told her about my idea [of multimedia psychotherapy] . . . She responded spontaneously, with enthusiasm, and told me a dream she had had. "I dreamt about my father. He was a little angry at me. We were at home, my home or his home, I can't say, and I was chatting with my mother. Someone else was there too . . . I don't remember who . . . I was chatting with him also, astonished; is he dead or alive? Even in my dream I was unable to locate my father somewhere, among the dead or the living ones." (213)

Mourning takes place in a third dimension (the cultural dimension of transitional phenomena described by Winnicott), through a third person (the neutral therapist, from Latin *nec uter*, which means, literally, "neither I nor you"), and by a third inanimate object (the memory object). Without being aware of it (or probably without knowing it at all), Winnicott constructed his idea of the transitional object (and transitional phenomena) on the blueprint of Róheim's "intermediate object." In fact, Winnicott (1951) writes: "The transitional object is [. . .] the thing created by the infant and at the same time provided by the environment. [. . .] Gradually [. . .] the transitional phenomena [. . .] become diffused [. . .] over the whole intermediate territory between 'inner psychic reality' and 'the external world as perceived by two persons in common', that is to say, over the whole cultural field" (95).

Without access to this third dimension/person/object, mourning takes place in a paranoid (persecutory) dyadic scenario, since only two options are possible (life and death, subject and object) and neither transitional object nor intermediate territory can be perceived/conceptualized between them.

> In Serena's dream, for example, her father "was a little angry at me [. . .] He was gloomy and said to me: 'Let's stop suffering . . . I am too close to you and too far from my place . . . If you want to help me, pray . . . Let me go!'" It is interesting that the slightly persecutory aspect of her father ("he was a little angry at me") was able to emerge, with the memory of the dream, only after I had offered a ritual place for him to be "located" (on the Internet). Perhaps, in her dream (and in her transference) I was the unknown person who could mediate between her dead father, on one side, and her mother and herself, on the other side, the side of living beings. Maybe the Internet could serve the function of Serena's "third dimension" [Winnicott's intermediate territory of transitional phenomena] where some of this "suffering" could be imagined and eventually confined "between heaven and earth." (Nesci 2009, 213–14)

The presence of a mediator, the mental representation of a "third dimension" (concretely realized and psychodynamically evoked, at the same time, by the multimedia artist) where conflictual entities might be identified and eventually worked through, by patient and therapist, is extremely important to prevent the catastrophic consequences of syncytial mourning, as expressed by the Warramunga funerary rituals. In the Aboriginal rituals, in fact, there was no way to make any mediation: on the one side there was the group violence of the living beings against the dying one; on the other, there was the self-destructive behavior of the group-individuals who cut and wounded themselves as if they were all going to die together in order not to separate themselves from the "terminal" group member. They were all objectifying and aggressively attacking, at the same time, in fusion and confusion, the whole social body, the dying group member, and themselves.

If "separation sin" (Róheim 1945a) is intolerable, if there is no way to conceive triangulations, better to kill the dying human being, better to cut themselves and bleed, better to destroy the whole village, after his/her individual death, and restore the covenant of the symbiotic syncytial group rebuilding the village in some other place. In prehistoric times, the outcome was tragically destructive: the dying person died of the wounds inflicted by the community, and the group destroyed the whole village trying to find a new beginning as an ideal, eternal, evil, free syncytial group, somewhere else.

Our contemporary therapeutic and funerary rituals try to prevent this tragedy. In contemporary medicine we try to rescue our patients from disease or at least free them from pain, and we seriously reflect from a bioethical perspective on the viability of our "heroic treatments" before proposing them to our patients, since we are afraid of unconsciously re-acting out, regressively, the Warramunga ritual. In today's mourning rituals, we still try to go back to cyclical time or, at least, we try to save good memories of our beloved dead love objects (in real cemeteries and/or virtual cemeteries, as well as by establishing charitable institutions in their names) instead of destroying everything. We make creative triangulations, we produce creative doubles under "the sign of three . . ."

An example that immediately comes to mind is the foundation of Stanford University in honor of the death of the founders' only child. Actually, an impressive photographic book was published on this extraordinary university and its historical roots from the creative mourning of Jane and Leland Stanford, faced with the death of their sixteen-year-old son (Davis and Nilan 1989). Instead of destroying and self-destructing, they built a place where other young people might find their way in life. Even so, even back then in 1891, saving photographic memories of their son's life was extremely important to help them work through their mourning process and repair their wounds.

The second phase of multimedia psychotherapy, the choice of a soundtrack, has to do with what Kenneth Wright calls "touch and visceral sensation." The video where the still images are animated by the artist and move at the rhythm and sound of a song or a music, has more than just the magic power of cinema, of motion pictures . . . Music is sound, sound waves that concretely touch our tympanic membranes and are transformed into sensorial perceptions. Once again we find ourselves in the magic scenario of touchable transitional objects and illusion (Winnicott 1951): "Perhaps some soft object or type of object has been found and used by the infant [. . .] The parents get to know its value and carry it around when travelling" (91).

The movements created by the artist through multiform techniques (movements within each photo, movements to make transitions from one photo to the next, as well as all of a variety of possible changes to the original scanned images inspired by the artist's conscious and unconscious interactions with the objects delivered by the therapist's patient) turn a sequence of still photos (the strip of life) into a lively sequence of the circle of life of the patient's dead love object (the psychodynamic montage), thanks to the music. Here is the role of the artist: to move the pictures at the rhythm of the music so that we have the illusion of aliveness.

While the strip of life had provided a series of conscious "screen memories," the video brings them alive and transmits a powerful illusion of vitality of these "new" remembrances that cover up (as a dream sequence dreamt again by the artist, a sort of auxiliary Ego for the patient) the deadly reality of the irremediable loss of the love object. The magic touch of the artist synchronizes the warm musical memory of lively loving symbiosis with the frozen visual memory of the dead love object and even with the petrifying gaze of the hateful moments of the ambivalent relationship between subject and object. The psychodynamic montage creates a live, animated screen memory of the continuous passages of life experienced during the circle of life, along with the vicissitudes of their past relationship. We are left with the reparative feeling that everything happened as it was supposed to—not too soon, not too late, at the right time, in the right place, and in the right way. In this process, the multimedia artist plays the role of a professional auxiliary Ego for the therapist as well . . . If it is true that a picture is worth a thousand words, a video is worth even more. Here the multimedia artist is truly helping the therapist to help the patient.

Integrating "the *distance* modality of *vision* and the more *proprio*ceptive modalities of *touch and visceral sensation*" is like repeating a "passage" of human development. Eugenio Gaddini, the Italian psychoanalyst who translated Winnicott into Italian, with the help of his wife, Renata, used to say, in his ongoing clinical seminar at the Rome Institute of Psychoanalysis, that a child suffers both "dis-integration" and "integration anxieties" (1953–1985) in the course of development. Providing the patient a harmonious memory object of his/her lost love object can be not only a powerful reparative experience but an integrative experience as well. The mourner is offered an opportunity to repeat some critical "passages" of his/her own development. The dark side of separation is worked through . . . Or, at least, patient and therapist together watch a possible way to work it through, thanks to the third's artistic construction or "interpretation."

The third phase of multimedia psychotherapy takes place outside the analytic room. It belongs to another room, to another atmosphere, to another specialist: the multimedia artist. Scanning the pictures, adjusting them to the soundtrack, adding transitions, special effects, and movements within each picture . . . this is the work of the artist. Then therapist and artist discuss the outcome before presenting it to the patient. This phase is important not only in the therapeutic relationship but also to build a professional relationship between therapist and multimedia artist.

The fourth phase takes place during the screening session, when the therapist gets the first feedback from the patient. It is a very important ritual passage because this is the session in which patient and therapist decide if any changes must be made. Then follows still another phase: elaboration by the patient at his/her own pace.

An interesting aspect of multimedia psychotherapy is the opportunity to return over and over again to observe and/or discuss the memory objects with the therapist, and this suggests still another possibility. Since the memory objects are concrete, though virtual, one might consider that the same object could be reanalyzed by another therapist in another therapeutic relationship. This might be very important in particular cases, such as the death of the therapist. Having had experience with patients whose therapists had died, I have no doubt that mourning the previous therapist might have been much easier if something virtual and concrete had been available.

Even without considering this unfortunate case, multimedia psychotherapy allows for another interesting possibility: to construct a memory object for the process of psychotherapy itself. The patient could assemble a series of pictures that synthesize the main events of the period of therapy and make them the concrete/virtual memory object that can be played back (to the rhythm of its soundtrack) whenever memory alone is not enough, when some "magic" help, something moving and touchable, replaying the functions of Winnicott's transitional object (1951) is needed to go on in the endless process of analysis, terminable and interminable.

FURTHER REFLECTIONS . . .

I would like to discuss another psychoanalytic perspective that can help us reach a deeper understanding of multimedia psychotherapy: the analysis of the unconscious dynamics of mourning as explored by Calvin Settlage (2001) in a book written by a group of authors (Akhtar 2001) bound together by the ideas of Margaret Mahler, a psychoanalyst who studied human symbiosis and the vicissitudes of the process of separation-individuation between mother and child (1961, 1966). According to Mahler, the first expressions of sadness and grief in the child are precursors of the adult expressions of mourning (Mahler et al. 1975).

> Following in her footsteps, Calvin Settlage emphasizes that "the developmental letting go of the mother is correlated with the establishment of an intrapsychic image. [. . .] The defensive objective of the imaging is to contain the separation anxiety. The imaging also serves internalization and representation of the mother in the child's internal world. The process of psychic representation associated with relinquishment in development is very similar to the process of psychic representation associated with mourning. Developmental relinquishment would appear to be the prototype for mourning. If, however, separation-individuation is arrested and the mother is not relinquished, the prototype for mourning is not developed. This impairs the capacity for mourning." (Settlage 2001, 66–67)

In Settlage's clinical experiences, images and sounds are valued objects that play an important role in psychotherapy. In his work on the "defenses evoked by early childhood loss," Dr. Settlage tells the story of the vicissitudes of his patients when he moved from one place to another very distant one in America. Their experiences dramatically exemplify the differences "between the *distance* modality of *vision* and the more *proprio*ceptive modalities of *touch and visceral sensation*" as theorized by Wright.

I shall present brief excerpts here from two of Dr. Settlage's clinical cases since they allow us to reach a deeper understanding of the importance of the interactive, perceptual (visual and auditory) play between patient and therapist. To be explicit, what I am suggesting is that patients and therapists had engaged in multimedia activities during their sessions (consciously or unconsciously, voluntarily or involuntarily) in this Technological Age, even before the birth of multimedia psychotherapy.

> Ira was referred for treatment at age 3½ because of severe separation anxiety present since age 2. [. . .] Ira was 12 when I moved. [. . .] The separation anxiety had greatly eased. [. . .] Because his separation anxiety was not fully alleviated, I referred him to further treatment. [. . .] I talked with Ira several times by telephone. Our talks were friendly but they did not take the character of treatment sessions. I subsequently met with him in the living room of my hotel suite during several of my return visits. [. . .] I learnt from his mother about his experience in the realm of loss during the several months following my departure. He became absorbed with the news of a mass suicide by members of a cult . . . He had thoughts about death and reincarnation. He also had a dream in which he was going to commit suicide. [. . .] The first return visit began as a warm reunion. Because I had experienced expressions of anger about my leaving from other patients, I soon asked him whether he was angry at me for going away. He said, "No." During the remainder of the time, though, he assiduously played and expressed angry aggression in "who is going to kill whom" games on the hotel television set. I felt that his exclusive absorption with the games reversed our positions at the time of my leaving. He now was abandoning me. (Settlage 2001, 68–70)

In the next sessions, the patient made drawings, which allowed the therapist to understand what was going on in his mind and helped him to work through the patient's repressed anger. Here once again, we have images that help the patient to master persecutory anxieties. (Ira drew a clown with a damaged head, a machine gun, and a pilot parachuting himself from the airplane and mocking his passengers doomed to their death.) As in Wright's perspective, "the *distance* modality of *vision*" is at work, here.

Another case followed by Dr. Settlage confronts us with the more "*proprio*ceptive modalities of *touch and visceral sensation*" (Wright 1991), since patient and therapist agreed to continue psychotherapy by telephone. The phone sessions took place at 7:00 A.M. (patient's time) and this detail allowed for the repetition of old traumatic experiences within the protected space/time limits of the sessions: the patient (as a child) trying to fall asleep with the reassuring presence of her mother (whose role was played by the analyst, in the transference) at her bedside, while her mother was unable to stay in touch with her emotionally until she actually fell asleep. For this reason, the patient suffered from insomnia, among other symptoms. In therapy, the analyst was able, metaphorically, to wait until patient would fall asleep, to remain available, not to withdraw emotionally from her because of his own separation anxieties. In other words, Dr. Settlage was "aware of her impaired object and self constancy and [. . .] that these psychic structures" could "be strengthened through developmental interaction with the analyst." So when the patient (Ilana) presented the analyst with a gift (a bowl) full of symbolic meanings, he accepted it and gave her "a pottery bud vase" from his office desk (not only something she could touch but also a container) at the end of their last face-to-face session.

This is interesting since it reminds us of the role played by inanimate concrete objects in therapy (Akhtar 2003), especially when they belong to the analytic setting, like Dr. Settlage's bud vase. According to Dr. Akhtar (2007), patients who suffered from "dislocation" are specifically sensitive to the inanimate, concrete objects present in the setting of therapy and unconsciously make use of them in different ways. This is an important point from the perspective of multimedia psychotherapy, since the "memory objects" we build always have to do with taking care of something that went wrong in a "passage" of life: a metaphorical "dislocation . . ."

Let's go back to Ilana's case:

> Ilana [. . .] was referred to me at age 28. [. . .] Her presenting problem was severe, life-long separation anxiety. [. . .] Our geographic separation took place after two and a half years of analysis. [. . .] After some months of work, Ilana revealed that she usually talked to me while still in bed. [. . .] In the next session, I asked Ilana what she thought about falling asleep. She replied, "Separation." [. . .] Some months later, the infantile sleep transference appeared in another session. Ilana said she was lying in bed in a fetal position. It felt like being in a cocoon. The word *cocoon* reminded me that the word *develop* means to unfold and no longer be enveloped, like a chick emerging through the eggshell. I thought that her imagery could be an unconscious expression of her need and wish to resume development or perhaps to begin her life anew. [. . .] She had an image of me in a lounge chair [. . .] like a parent lying next to a child at the child's bedtime. [. . .] In the next session she said, "I'm still waking up. Get me a pacifier." She talked about how nice it was to fall asleep with me there on the phone at the other end of the line. I said that maybe the phone connection means that we are not separated. She said that being connected by the telephone line is like being connected by an infinitely elastic umbilical cord. (Settlage 2001, 72–76)

What do these clinical experiences add to our understanding of multimedia psychotherapy? A lot. Here we have two patients suffering from separation anxiety who are exposed to separation from their analyst—a major trauma, indeed, not only for the patients but for the therapist as well. How do they deal with it? Once again, patients and therapists recur to multimedia techniques.

In Ira's case we have the use of a video game. The video game is a virtual setting where, by identifying with the character of the game, the player (patient) can repeatedly work through traumatic scenes with the privilege of having many "lives" to live out the difficult "passages" of life over and over again. Playing the video game while being watched by the analyst is therapeutic, since it is as if the patient/child would be protected at a safe distance by the reassuring parent/caregiver while experiencing the challenges of life with all its dangerous trials of separation-individuation to pass from one "state" (A, B, C . . .) to the next, tolerating the NOT-X NOT-Y liminal states, in a virtual setting. In fact, video games are always organized in levels (developmental stages?) that the player has to overcome, one after the other, to succeed.

In Ilana's case we have the use of the telephone. The phone allows an intimate dialogue that annuls space and time limits, restoring the symbiotic relationship at a more developed level, the level of oral communication. Ilana feels as if she were into the womb/analyst but is able to feel it, understand it, and acknowledge it as an adult rather than as a helpless child. She is repaired in the dialogue, a dialogue that is made possible by the psychodynamic use of the medium (the telephone) by the expert therapist.

In multimedia psychotherapy, as in the case of a video game, the psychodynamic montage helps the patient to work through all passages of the life circle of the lost love object as harmoniously as possible. What's more, the video can be played over and over again, just like any movie, where our favorite actors (the "stars") are always the same, regardless of time and space limits, as in the syncytial cultural frame of the Eternal Ones of the Dream studied by Géza Róheim (1945b).

In our Technological Age, the virtual realm of the web and the new hardware and software are making fantasies and wishes realizable (for example, talking with and looking at our beloved ones even if they are in another distant country), which might be used to help our fragility, not just to destroy us by nurturing our pathologic dependence.

Transitional Objects?

In Freud's terms, when working with a patient on his/her lost "love object" in the strip of life we make a "construction," rather than an "interpretation." In other words, we actively make something that "lies between what happened and what was remembered" (as Peter Blos wrote in his poem, *Unicorn Park*).

The whole process appears even more complex if we reflect on the medium we are going to use, on the "container" of these images (a classical photo album, a digital device—and what kind of digital device—or something unique and original to be posted, or not to be posted, on the web). Once again we find ourselves, as therapist, constructing infinite possible "concrete" memory objects with our patients in multimedia psychotherapy. What are these objects? Inanimate "doubles"? Virtual screen memories? Don't they also look like transitional objects? Couldn't they be abandoned, some time in the future, once it is not necessary to look at them or even think about them (as concrete memory objects) anymore?

ELEVEN

New Horizons in Multimedia Psychotherapy

"Why only death? Why only mourning? Why not something more lively? Why not give images and sounds to what is usually invisible and hardly audible like the fetal heart beat?"

One of us, the artist, was wondering about new horizons in multimedia psychotherapy: making memory objects on the nine month period of our life from conception to delivery. Why not produce "memory objects" for a future mind? Why not document what is taking place during our prenatal life to fill the gap that we are destined to experience since our mind was not fully developed at that time, and we were confined in the womb?

My son was thinking for the fetus . . . The artist's perspective did not focus on illness and therapy, but on our well-being, on quality of life, on preventive medicine and health psychology.

This new idea materialized after my wife (Dr. Averna, a gynecologist trained in obstetrical ultrasound scanning) talked about it to one of her pregnant patients. We had come full circle, with our son (conceived during our research on prenatal life) conceiving a new study to offer "memory objects" to future children/teenagers/adults . . .

MEMORY OBJECTS FOR THE FUTURE

Giulia is the name we have given to the first woman who produced with us a "memory object for the future" dedicated to her baby. She was a special patient for many reasons, one being the fact that she lived in a town that was a one-and-a-half-hour drive from Rome. Patient and doctor agreed that, in case of pregnancy, she would have a local specialist in

Ob. Gyn. take care of her and be present at delivery. So, when Giulia got pregnant, Dr. Averna's role would be limited to obstetrical counseling on the phone complemented by our "memory object for the future" single-case pilot study.

The idea was to collect pictures from her pregnancy and perinatal period in order to let the future child "see" his/her parents' life and enjoy a "screen memory" actively produced by our team's multimedia artist after the "picture sessions" and the "music session," which, in this case, were planned to take place in videoconference after the baby was born. These Internet sessions, with both Giulia and her husband, were scheduled for during the night, while I would be on another computer, in Rome, a hundred miles from the young parents.

Giulia was thrilled in our first session: "It's such a wonderful experience! I'm sure my son will be very happy, in a few years, to know about his time in the womb. . . . Actually that's why we took so many pictures . . . To let him see them! It's really fantastic! I'm sure he'll enjoy it as a gift, an opportunity to let him know himself through our pictures . . . to let him see how much Federico and I have been waiting for him for so many months and how much happiness we felt fantasizing about him and making plans for his future . . . "

During the first videoconference, thanks to a free software that allows everyone to share images and music on the web, we were able to look at the same pictures, discuss them, work them through and make a selection. Giulia's baby was there, too, sleeping peacefully in her mother's arms. Giulia had done a preliminary choice of thirty-six pictures. In most of them, she was clearly pregnant and often alone (fig. 11.1), but in a close relationship with her baby in her womb (touching her body or her dress, for example, in such a way as to reveal its presence).

In some of the pictures Giulia was with her relatives or with Federico, her husband, who encouraged her to introduce other photos with family members and friends who had shared meaningful moments of their lives with them. Grandparents and great-grandmothers were included in the video as pivotal figures in the family's affective life during their baby's prenatal and postnatal life (fig. 11.2, 11.3, 11.4, 11.5). Giulia's sister, the baby's only aunt (fig. 11.6), was never to be left out either!

So, many pictures that were "doubles" of the original pics were discarded and a second picture session was scheduled in order for the parents to have enough time to select other images.

Many new pictures were introduced and discussed during that session: photos from the wedding, from holidays associated with the period when the baby was conceived or when the parents learned of his existence, from the moments when relatives and friends were anxiously waiting at the doors of the delivery room in the hospital, and, last but not least, pictures of Francesco after his birth (fig. 11.7).

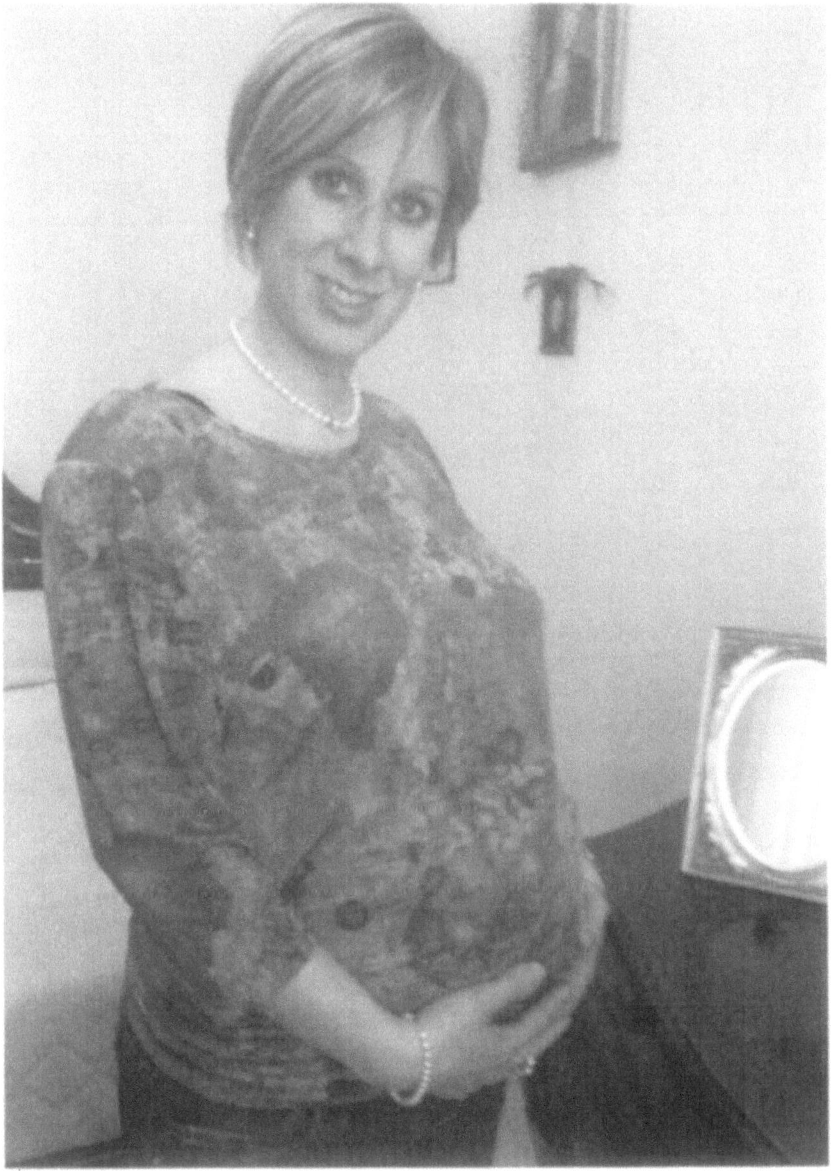

Figure 11.1. Giulia with her baby in the womb

Once again both young parents were so enthusiastic it was hard to make a selection (fifty-three pictures were chosen in the end) and discard the many "doubles" they had shown in the videoconference. In my countertransference I felt the themes of change and repetitiveness were central in this work of elaboration, just as it had happened in the first

Figure 11.2. The baby's paternal great-grandmother at the wedding

Clinic and Dreams Workshop. Conception, pregnancy, and all the transformations that take place during prenatal life unconsciously trigger anxiety. On the one side, the mother is afraid to lose her baby (abortion), on the other she is afraid to fall sick during pregnancy or to die at delivery. That is why, according to Fornari (1981), every mother unconsciously

Figure 11.3. The baby's paternal grandparents at the wedding

lives pregnancy in a psychodynamic scenario, which he called "primary paranoia." While Fornari theorized that this double anxiety has to be triangulated by the father, I personally believe that it is the afterbirth (precursor of the paternal imago) that actually plays the role of the third in this unconscious process (Nesci 1999). That is why parents might bring many "doubles" of the same picture. The discarding of these doubles, in the picture sessions, is an unconscious concrete repetition of the discarding of the afterbirth, after delivery! It was as if the parents were delivering the baby again, this time joyfully and without pain.

In the music session, Giulia immediately chose "Ma il cielo è sempre più blu" (literally, "Yet the sky is getting bluer and bluer . . ."), a song from 1975 by the Italian singer-songwriter Rino Gaetano. The lyrics are almost nonsensical, describing people in the act of facing life in the most varied of circumstances and emotional states. Yet beneath its apparent nonsense, the text reveals a forceful protest against the corruption of Italian politicians and leaders, against the mafia mentality, and so on. It is a poetic cry for the dream that in spite of all the horrible things that really happen every day (metaphorically speaking: in spite of all the primary paranoia surrounding pregnancy), hope remains with us (the baby will be delivered, will be happy, and have a wonderful life). This message is repeated over and over again in the song's refrain: "Yet the sky is bluer and bluer . . ."

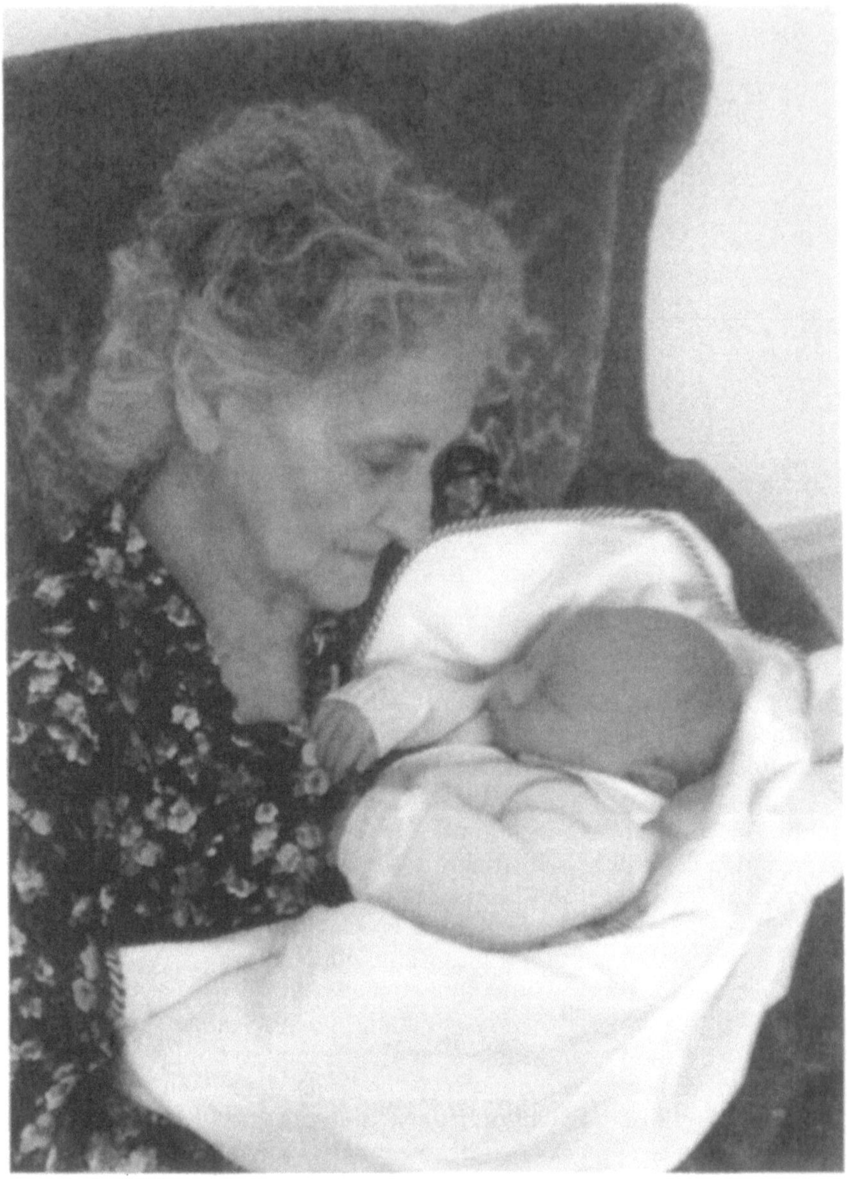

Figure 11.4. The baby's maternal great-grandmother

After we heard the song together in our videoconference music session, Giulia told me that she and Federico had started their relationship as friends, often talking about their respective unlucky love stories with their previous partners. They supported each other and, at the end, once they had taken their loads off, exchanged wishes for a "bluer sky," since

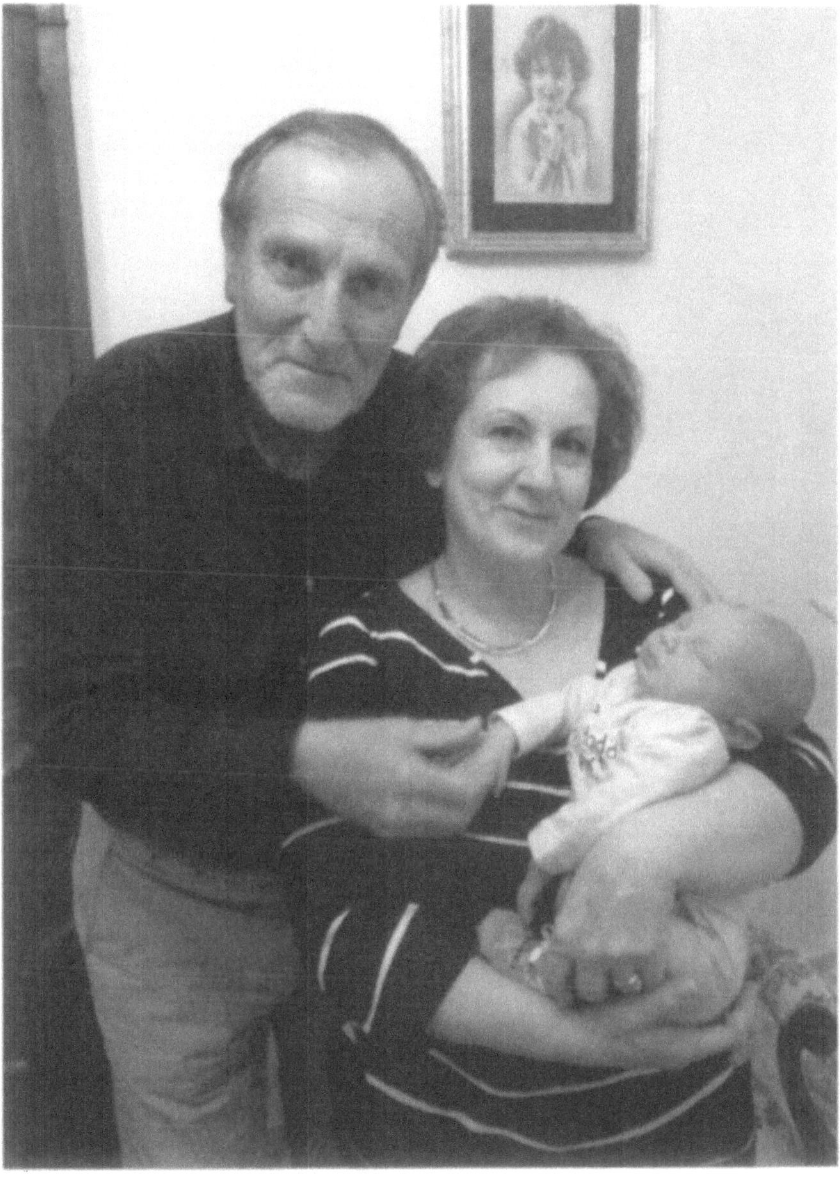

Figure 11.5. The baby's maternal grandparents

they both loved that song so much. In 2008, on the last day of the year, Giulia sent Federico a text message on the cell phone, wishing him that his sky would become bluer and bluer in the new year. They ended up getting together in 2009 and finally made their own skies bluer by leaving their previous partners, starting their engagement, and planning their

Figure 11.6. The baby's maternal aunt

wedding, which took place in 2010. Thus the song itself became the expression of their wish for happiness, for new horizons, leaving behind their previous years of unfulfillment and conflict. The refrain was so much a part of their lives that they asked one of their friends to sing it at the end of their wedding as they left the church and included it in a DVD

Figure 11.7. The baby

to be played in the delivery room when Giulia was giving birth to Francesco. That explains why this was the only song that occurred to them as the soundtrack for the memory object of the future which is destined to let their son know something about his parents during his prenatal life.

It was only after the screening session that I discovered one more root underlying Giulia's choice of the soundtrack. On Federico's birthday, before their marriage, she had organized a pizza party at a place with a large wall screen. Toward the end of the party, she projected a video showing all the meaningful moments of Federico's life, from his birth up to that moment, and the soundtrack, of course, was "Ma il cielo è sempre più blu . . ." Everyone was moved, and even the other people who happened to be eating there enjoyed the show and wished Federico a happy birthday!

THE BOOK COVER

In the very beginning, Amy King, the acquisitions editor of Jason Aronson, asked me if I had any suggestions or special ideas for the cover of my future book. Actually I did, although I didn't tell her immediately.

While I was lecturing on multimedia psychotherapy at my school, in Rome, a student brought in a beautiful picture of himself embracing his newborn child. I thought it would be good for expressing two ideas to my prospective readers: first, that multimedia psychotherapy is a new and joyful engagement although it has to do with mourning, since mourning (as we have seen) is part of human development and not only a process for death and grief; second, that my technique is like a new baby that comes to life and needs for a parent (the therapist of our Technological Age) to pick it up and embrace it.

Working with Giulia and Federico, experiencing their enthusiasm for the birth of their baby, I spontaneously thought they might be happy to have their son on the cover of a book that was going to be published in America. I asked them and discovered I was right. Then I remembered that Federico's father was the lucky owner of a Ferrari and a well-known restaurant (with a pool), so I suggested Giulia take a photo with the three of them—father, mother, and son—with their grandfather's beautiful car, the pool, and a "bluer and bluer" Italian sky. Once again they accepted enthusiastically and worked on it, but somehow failed to get the blue sky with the Ferrari and the pool! The dozen pictures they posted on our shared folder on the web had no sky at all in the background.

And so it happened that I took the photo myself of the blue sky (and a kite) with my cell phone on the shores of the Mediterranean, not far from Rome, and my new multimedia artist, Giorgio Porcaro, who had "freed" my son from the burden of patients' transference, liked it. In the end, my azure sky by the sea became the first and last image in the psychodynamic montage. Once again, teamwork is the main characteristic of multimedia psychotherapy in all its forms and expressions.

At the same time, we selected azure as the color for the background of the cover, while a short sequence of pictures of Giulia, Federico, and

Francesco was placed in the pole position at the center. A picture from a Sicilian cart (showing Columbus discovering the New World) was finally added to the cover, with the idea of communicating the anthropological continuity between old traditions and multimedia psychotherapy.

As of now, we have no idea about the outcome of producing a psychodynamic montage for pregnancy and a baby's perinatal life; Francesco is only two months old. Once more research on this application of my technique is carried out, we might envision multimedia psychotherapy as a possible complement to childbirth programs in the future. Intriguingly, still another application is appearing at the horizon of multimedia psychotherapy: producing memory objects to reinforce memory traces in patients suffering from Alzheimer's disease and/or other pathologies that affect memory. I will briefly hint at this to end my last chapter with hope for a metaphorical "New World" of discoveries in psychotherapy.

MEMORY OBJECTS FOR ALZHEIMER'S DISEASE

On July 2, 2010, the best alumni of SIPSI founded DREAMS, the first Italian nonprofit cooperative of psychotherapists (licensed medical doctors or psychologists) offering low-cost high-quality services to private and public health institutions. One of the first jobs our cooperative secured was to deliver psychological support to caregivers of Alzheimer's patients. At the moment, we are running a group program for the caregivers of patients followed by the *Centro Malattie dell'Invecchiamento* (CEMI), directed by Prof. Roberto Bernabei, a well-known gerontologist, at UCSC, in Rome. Our international institute (IIPRTHP), which supervises the members of DREAMS, is planning a study of multimedia psychotherapy aimed at producing memory objects that can help patients to maintain their capacity to remember and recognize their relatives. In fact, not being recognized anymore is one of the most tragic and painful experiences that caregivers of Alzheimer's patients shared with our psychotherapists during their group sessions at CEMI.

Our idea is to work with the caregivers to produce special memory objects integrating different sensorial inputs (using not only images and sounds but also clothes—and/or smelling or tasting substances) associated with people that the patient suffering from dementia might become unable to recognize with the progression of the illness.

The good news is that once the idea of multimedia psychotherapy is available, many possible applications inevitably come to mind!

EPILOGUE

The psychodynamic montage of multimedia psychotherapy lies within the philosophical frame of reference of narrative medicine (Good 1994), at a crossroads where different approaches or perspectives meet and integrate themselves naturally.

1. It is a psychodynamic endeavor, since unconscious fantasies must be acknowledged and worked through in the transference/countertransference dynamics in and out of the sessions.
2. It is a cognitive exercise, since the patient has to do some "homework," as Norman Clemens wrote in his introduction to my preliminary report published in the *Journal of Psychiatric Practice* (2009).
3. It is a systemic procedure, since relatives and friends are involved in the therapy in some way.
4. Finally, it is a form of art therapy as well, although (unlike most art therapies) the artist plays an autonomous role and has a twofold (distinct) relationship with the therapist and the art objects provided by the patient.

This complex process is even more complex if we consider it not only from the point of view of the subject as individual but also from that of the subject as group-individual. I will try to make this difference more understandable through a scene from the movie *Kaos*, created from the imagination of the Taviani brothers in 1984.

Kaos is not just "chaos" in ancient Greek; it is also the name of the native town of Nobel Prize–winner Luigi Pirandello, the famous Sicilian writer. In the film, Pirandello goes back to the home where his dead mother had lived. He feels a presence . . . Finally, his mother materializes, and they talk. Pirandello tells her he has been depressed since she died; he feels alone. He feels unseen by her eyes, and being unseen, he feels he does not exist: he feels as dead as she is. His mother replies that all these thoughts are too complicated. She thinks he should forget his individual personal depression, and learn to look at things also with the eyes of the unseen people (the group-individual) who don't see any more . . .

Out of the metaphor, the memory objects of multimedia psychotherapy tell a story to the depressed individual, integrating all previous identifications and repairing unsolved conflicts by the touching experience of musical harmony and visual transitions. On the other side, the side of the patient as group-individual, the memory objects of multimedia psychotherapy try to suggest to the patient a new way to look at things and use the "eyes" . . . The way suggested by Pirandello's dead mother in the scene of *Kaos*. The mother is an archetype (Jung 1934–1954); she doesn't (cannot) die. She goes on looking at her children eternally, the way only unseen people who see without eyes can do . . . She can call her "children" back (in dreams and "visitations") and can materialize as a phantom, like Pirandello's mother in the movie of the Taviani brothers. In Greek mythology, heroes do not die but turn into stars (the constellations) and look at us always, every night, from above. In Christianity,

Jesus Christ ascended to Heaven (as did Mary, mother of Christ, according to a dogma of the Catholic church), and we pray to them to look at us and protect us every day.

Out of the metaphor, the group-individual feels immortal. It feels that none of its objects of identification (throughout development along the whole life cycle) can disappear or die (although the child, the teenager, the young adult do actually change and turn into something else) and that they will be always be with us in the unconscious layers of our Self. Integrating these two perspectives is the very process of the cure.

An old story might be freely associated here, a story that reminds us that we are all "patients" since the day we were created as human beings. Here is my own translation from the Latin text by Pseudo-Hyginus, a Roman mythographer from the second century BC.

Once upon a time, as she was crossing a river, the goddess Cura (literally = Cure) saw some claylike mud, picked it up carefully, and shaped a human figure. Jove (Jupiter) came in. Cura asked him to give it a spirit, which Jove did easily. However, Jove denied her permission to choose its name since he believed that only he had the privilege to name the creature. While they were arguing, the goddess Tellus (Earth) claimed she should name the human figure since she had given it her body. Finally they all agreed to have Saturnus (Saturn, the god of time) be the judge of the matter. Here is the god's verdict: "You, Jove, will take back the spirit when the creature dies, since it is you who gave it; you, Tellus, will take back the body, since it is you who gave it; you, Cura, will take care of the creature throughout its life since it is you who took care of it from the very beginning. As far as its name is concerned, since there is a controversy, let it be called Homo, because from humble humus (fertile soil) it is made."

From an ethnopsychoanalytic perspective, we are all children of the goddess Cura, as long as we are alive; we are all creative, humble creatures who need someone to take care of us until the last breath of life . . . From this point of view, there is no "termination" in psychotherapy. Analysis is interminable not because we cannot be cured but precisely because we can.

Multimedia psychotherapy helps us in this regard. In fact, the memory objects of this new form of treatment are "open" to change and transformation. Any time, as the subject progresses and changes (and his/her mourning process develops accordingly), changes can be made to the concrete memory objects, working in new sessions and recurring one more time to the aid of the therapist and the multimedia artist. This potentially interminable process repairs and relieves the patient from mental pain thanks to the very fact of being imaginable as an ongoing process, something that can be carried out ad libitum.

As in my old childhood game, we can see ourselves, with no eyes, playing at building memory objects with our discarded film spools while singing, then tearing them down, singing another song, and building them up again and again, as long as we are alive on this Earth.

Bibliography

Akhtar, S., ed. (2001). *Three Faces of Mourning: Melancholia, Manic Defense, and Moving On*. Lanham: Jason Aronson.

Akhtar, S. (2003). Things: Developmental, Psychopathological, and Technical Aspects of Inanimate Objects. *Canadian Journal of Psychoanalysis* 11(1):1–44.

———. (2007). The Trauma of Geographical Dislocation: Leaving, Arriving, Mourning, and Becoming. In *The Geography of Meanings: Psychoanalytic Perspectives on Place, Space, Land, and Dislocation*, ed. M. T. Hooke and S. Akhtar. London: Karnak Books.

Ancona, L., Nesci, D. A., Poliseno, T. A., Averna, S., Mancuso, A. K., Ferrazzani, S., De Carolis, S., and Mancuso, M. (1992). Studying the Early Relationships in Prenatal Life: A Methodological Choice. *Acta Medica Romana* 29(2):395–399.

Averna, S., Nesci, D. A., Lafuenti, G., Valentini, P., Russo, A., and Ferro, F. M. (1990). Il gruppo sinciziale nelle gravidanze oltre termine "vere." In *Atti della SIGO*, pp. 233–234. Brescia: Clas International.

Baldazzi, V., Suppi, S., and Cicchetti, L. (2006). Pulcinella, Teresina e la Morte: una "Bagattella" per il Workshop "Cinema e Sogni" del 2006. *Doppio Sogno* 3:1–12. (Text available at http://www.doppio-sogno.it/numero3/ita/ValentinaBaldazziu.pdf and video available at http://www.doppio-sogno.it/numero3/baldazzi.htm).

Balint, E., Courtenay, M., Elder, A., Hull, S., and Julian, P. (1993). *The Doctor, the Patient and the Group: Balint Revisited*. London and New York: Routledge.

Balint, M., and Balint, E. (1957). *The Doctor, His Patient and the Illness*. London: Churchill Livingstone.

Bettelheim, B. (1954). *Symbolic Wounds: Puberty Rites and the Envious Male*. Glencoe: Free Press.

Bion, W. R. (1967). Notes on Memory and Desire. *Psycho-analytic Forum* 2(3):271–280.

Böhm, T. (1992). Turning points and Change in Psychoanalysis. *The International Journal of Psycho-Analysis* 73(4):675–684.

Briffault, R. (1927). *The Mothers: A Study of the Origins of Sentiments and Institutions*. New York: Macmillan.

Bynum, D. E. (1978). *The Daemon in the Wood: A Study of Oral Narrative Patterns*. Cambridge: Center for the Study of Oral Literature.

Canetti, E. (1962). *Crowds and Power*. New York: The Viking Press.

Carroll, K. M., and Nuro, K. F. (2002). One Size Cannot Fit All: A Stage Model for Psychotherapy Manual Development. *Clinical Psychology: Science and Practice* 9(4):396–406.

Clemens, N. A. (2009). Foreword to Multimedia Psychodynamic Psychotherapy: A Preliminary Report, by D. A. Nesci. *Journal of Psychiatric Practice* 15(3):211.

Coleridge, S .T. (1798). The Rime of the Ancient Mariner. In *Lyrical Ballads, with a Few Other Poems* by W. Wordsworth and S.T. Coleridge. London: J. & A. Arch.

Connolly, M. B., Crits-Christoph, P., Shappell, S., Barber, J. P., and Luborsky, L. (1998). Therapist Interventions in Early Sessions of Brief Supportive-Expressive Psychotherapy for Depression. *Journal of Psychotherapy Practice and Research* 7(4):290–300.

Davidson, J. R. (1985). The Shadow of Life: Psychosocial Explanation for Placenta Rituals. *Culture, Medicine, and Psychiatry* 9: 93–96.

Davis, M., and Nilan, R. (1989). *The Stanford Album: A Photographic History, 1885–1945*. Palo Alto: Stanford University Press.

Dreifuss-Kattan, E. (1990). *Cancer Stories: Creativity and Self-Repair*. Hillsdale, NJ: The Analytic Press.

Eco, U., and Sebeok, T. A., eds. (1983). *The Sign of Three: Dupin, Holmes, Peirce*. Bloomington: Indiana University Press.

Ehrenreich, P. (1890). *Beitrage zur Volkerkunde Brasiliens*. Berlin: W. Spemann.

Eliade, M. (1954). *Cosmos and History: The Myth of the Eternal Return*. Princeton, NJ: Princeton University Press.

Fachinelli, E. (1983). *Claustrofilia*. Milano: Adelphi.

Fazzi, M., and Nesci, D. A. (2008). L'angoscia del sopravvissuto: appunti di una psicoterapia individuale con una paziente oncologica off therapy. *Strumenti in Psico-Oncologia 1*. (Available at http://www.psychomedia.it/psic-onco/n1-08/fazzi-nesci.htm)

Fornari, F. (1981). *Il codice vivente—Femminilità e maternità nei sogni delle madri in gravidanza*. Torino: Bollati Boringhieri.

Frazer, J. G. (1915). *The Golden Bough: A Study in Magic and Religion*. London: MacMillan.

Freud, A. (1956). Psychoanalytic Knowledge Applied to the Rearing of Children. In *The Writings of Anna Freud*. Vol. 5, pp. 265–280. New York: International Universities Press.

Freud, S. (1886–1939). *The Standard Edition of the Complete Psychological Works of Sigmund Freud*. London: The Hogarth Press and the Institute of Psychoanalysis, 1953–1974.

———. (1900). *The Interpretation of Dreams*. Standard Edition 4–5.

———. (1901). *Childhood Memories and Screen Memories*. Standard Edition 6:43–52.

———. (1911). Letter to Jung 274 F. In *The Freud/Jung Letters*, ed. W. McGuire. London: The Hogarth Press and Routledge & Kegan Paul, 1974.

———. (1912). *Recommendations to Physicians Practicing Psycho-analysis*. Standard Edition 12:109–120.

———. (1913). *On Beginning the Treatment (Further Recommendations on the Technique of Psycho-analysis I)*. Standard Edition 12:121–144.

———. (1914). *Remembering, Repeating and Working-Through*. Standard Edition 12:147–156.

———. (1916–1917). *Introductory Lectures on Psycho-analysis*. Standard Edition 15–16.

———. (1917). *Mourning and Melancholia*. Standard Edition 14: 237–258.

———. (1919). *The Uncanny*. Standard Edition 17:217–256.

———. (1937). *Analysis Terminable and Interminable*. Standard Edition 23:216–253.

———. (1938). Constructions in Analysis. *The International Journal of Psycho-Analysis* 19(4):377–387.

Gaddini, E. (1953–1985). *Scritti*. Milano: Raffaello Cortina Editore.

Gaita, D. (1971). *Il pensiero del cuore: musica, simbolo, inconscio*. Milano: Bompiani.

Goldie, W. (1901). *Calabar and Its Mission*. Edinburgh & London: Elephant.

Good, B. J. (1994). *Medicine, Rationality and Experience: An Anthropological Perspective*. Cambridge: Cambridge University Press.

Jones, E. (1914). The Madonna's Conception through the Ear. In Jones E., *Essays in Applied Psychoanalysis*. London: The Hogarth Press, 1951, pp. 266–357.

Jung, C. G. (1934–1954). Archetypes of the Collective Unconscious. In Jung, C., *Collected Works of C. G. Jung*, Vol. 9, Part 1. 2nd ed., Princeton: Princeton University Press, 1968.

Kerényi, K. (1950). *Labyrinth-Studien*. Zürich: Rhein-Verlag.

Klein, M. (1946). Notes on Some Schizoid Mechanisms. *The International Journal of Psycho-Analysis* 27:99–110.

———. (1957). *Envy and Gratitude*. New York: Basic Books.

———. (1959). Our Adult World and Its Roots in Infancy. *Human Relations* 12:291–303.

Kohut, H. (1971). *The Analysis of the Self*. New York: International Universities Press.

———. (1984). *How Does Analysis Cure?* Chicago: University of Chicago Press.

Lafuenti, G., Nesci, D. A., Russo, A., Averna, S., Valentini, P., and Ferro, F. M. (1990). Differenze psicodinamiche tra gravidanze oltre termine 'vere' e 'presunte.' In *Atti della SIGO*, pp. 191–192. Brescia: Clas International.

Lawrence, W. G. (1991). Won from the Void and Formless Infinite: Experiences of Social Dreaming. *Free Associations* 2(22):254–266.
Mahler, M. S. (1961). On Sadness and Grief in Infancy and Childhood: Loss and Restitution of the Symbiotic Love Object. *The Psychoanalytic Study of the Child* 16:332–351.
———. (1966). Notes on the Development of Basic Moods: The Depressive Affect. In *Psychoanalysis—A General Psychology: Essays in Honor of Heinz Hartmann*, eds. R.M. Loewenstein, L.M., Newman, M., Shur, and A.J. Solnit, pp. 152–168. New York: International Universities Press.
———. (1968). *On Human Symbiosis and the Vicissitudes of Individuation*. Vol. 1. New York: International Universities Press.
Mahler, M. S., Pine, F., and Bergman, A. (1975). *The Psychological Birth of the Human Infant: Symbiosis and Individuation*. New York: Basic Books.
Maslach, C., and Goldberg, J. (1998). Prevention of Burnout: New Perspectives. *Applied and Preventive Psychology* 7:63–74.
Miyatake, T., Katayama, K., Takeda, Y., Nakashima, A., and Mizumoto, M. (2004). Is Death-Feigning Adaptive? Heritable Variation in Fitness Difference of Death-Feigning Behaviour. *Proceedings of the Royal Society Biological Sciences* 271(1554):2293–2296.
Nesci, D. A. (1991). *La notte bianca—Studio etnopsicanalitico del suicidio collettivo*. Roma: Armando Editore.
———. (1993). Entre la terre et le ciel: Quelques remarques sur l'usage du divan dans le setting psychanalytique. *Revue Canadienne de Psychanalyse* 1:61–72.
———. (1999). *The Lessons of Jonestown: An Ethnopsychoanalytic Study of Suicidal Communities*. Roma: Società Editrice Universo.
———. (2009). Multimedia Psychodynamic Psychotherapy: A Preliminary Report. *Journal of Psychiatric Practice* 15(3):211–215.
Nesci, D. A., Lafuenti, G., Averna, S., Russo, A., Valentini, P., Ferro, F. M., Ferrazzani, S., and De Carolis, S. (1990). L'imago placentare nelle gravidanze oltre termine 'vere'. In *Atti della SIGO*, pp. 189–190. Brescia: Clas International.
Nesci, D. A., and Nesci, F. A. (2008). Halo: Psicoanalisi di un videogioco. *Doppio Sogno* 6:1–14. (Available at http://www.doppio-sogno.it/numero6/ita/nesci1.pdf)
———. (2010). Un oggetto della memoria. *Doppio Sogno* 11. (Video available at http://www.doppio-sogno.it/numero11/OggettoMemoriaVideo.htm)
Nesci, D. A., Manollo, V. A., Laurenti, L., Piccirillo, N., Sica, S., Salutari, P., and Leone, G. (1998). L'impiego della levosulpiride nel trapianto di midollo osseo: risultati preliminari di un'esperienza di psichiatria di consultazione. *Psichiatria di Consultazione*, suppl. to n. 1:97–101.
Nesci, D. A., and Poliseno, T. A. (2004). Double Dream. Video presentation. 43rd IPA Congress, New Orleans (USA). Text published on *Doppio Sogno* 1:1–15. (Available at http://www.doppio-sogno.it/numero1/ita/nescipoliseno1201.pdf)
Nesci, D. A., Poliseno, T. A., and Averna, S. (2005). Il paradigma psicoanalitico nella formazione degli Operatori Sanitari: un nuovo "Rinascimento" culturale. *Doppio Sogno* 1:1–6. (Available at http://www.doppio-sogno.it/numero1/ita/nescipolisenoaverna801.pdf)
Nesci, D. A., Poliseno, T. A., Averna, S., Barra, A., Linardos, M., Salvatore, G., and Squillacioti, M. (2000). Gli interventi di supporto in Psico-Oncologia—i gruppi Balint. In *Psiconcologia*, eds. M.L. Bellani, G. Morasso, D. Amadori, W. Orrù, L. Grassi. Milano: Masson.
Nesci, D. A., Poliseno, T. A., Scafoglio, D., Fazzi, M., Palermo, E., and Pecci, A. P. (2008). Pulcinella e la morte: percorsi in Psico-Oncologia—Breve storia della terza edizione del format televisivo *Doppio Sogno*. *Doppio Sogno* 7:1 (introductive text available at http://www.doppio-sogno.it/numero7/ita/pulcinellaelamorte.pdf and video available at http://www.doppio-sogno.it/numero7.htm).
Ober, W. B. (1979). Notes on Placentophagy. *Bulletin of the New York Academy of Medicine* 55(6):591–599.
Ogden, T. H. (2005). On Psychoanalytic Supervision. *The International Journal of Psycho-Analysis* 86:1265–1280.

Ong, W. J. (1982). *Orality and Literacy: The Technologizing of the Word*. London and New York: Methuen.
Parens, H. (2001). We All Mourn: C'est la Condition Humane. In *Three Faces of Mourning: Melancholia, Manic Defense, and Moving On*. Ed. S. Akhtar, pp. 1–11. Lanham: Jason Aronson.
Peirce, C. S. (1867–1913). *The Essential Peirce, Selected Philosophical Writings*. Volume 1 and 2. Ed. N. Houser and C. J. W. Kloesel. Bloomington: Indiana University Press 1992–1998.
Perrot, E. et Vogt, E. (1913). *Poison de flèches et poison d'épreuve*. Paris: Vigot Frères.
Piontelli, A. (1992). *From Fetus to Child: An Observational and Psychoanalytic Study*. London, New York: Tavistock/Routledge.
Rank, O. (1924). *The Trauma of Birth*. New York: Richard Brunner, 1952.
Róheim, G. (1945a). *War, Crime, and the Covenant*. New York: Medical Journal Press.
———. (1945b). *The Eternal Ones of the Dream*. New York: International Universities Press.
Rosenberg, K., Trevathan, W. (1995). Bipedalism and Human Birth: The Obstetrical Dilemma Revisited. *Evolutionary Anthropology* 4(5):149–185.
Sade-Beck, L. (2004). Mourning and Memorial Culture on the Internet: The Israeli Case. *American Communication Journal* 7 (available at www.acjournal.org/holdings/vol7/iss1/liav_sade-beck/memorial_and_mourning.htm, accessed March 24, 2009).
Sartre, J. P. (1957). *Being and Nothingness*. London: Methuen.
Scarfone, D. (2006). A Matter of Time: Actual Time and the Production of the Past. *Psychoanalytic Quarterly* 75:807–834.
Sebeok, T. A. (1983) One, Two, Three Spells Uberty. In *The Sign of Three*. Ed. U. Eco and T. A. Sebeok. Bloomington: Indiana University Press.
Senatore, I. (2001). *Curare con il cinema*. Torino: Centro Scientifico Editore.
Settlage, C. F. (2001). Defenses Evoked by Early Childhood Loss: Their Impact on Life-Span Development. In *Three Faces of Mourning: Melancholia, Manic Defense, and Moving On*. Ed. S. Akhtar, pp. 47–94. Lanham: Jason Aronson.
Spencer, B., and Gillen, F .J. (1904). *The Northern Tribes of Central Australia*. London: McMillan.
Strehlow, C. (1908–1909). Die Aranda und Loritja Staemme in Zentral Australien. Francfort-sur-le-Main, quoted by G. Róheim in *The Eternal Ones of the Dream*. New York: International Universities Press.
Tylor, B. (1903). *Primitive Culture*. Vol. 2. London: McMillan.
Vacheret, C. (2000). *Photo, groupe et soin psychique*. Lyon: Presses Universitaires de Lyon.
van Gennep, A. (1909). *Les rites de passages*. Paris: Nourry.
Winnicott, D. W. (1951). Transitional Objects and Transitional Phenomena. *International Journal of Psycho-Analysis* 3:89–97, 1953.
Wright, K. (1991). *Vision and Separation between Mother and Baby*. London: Free Association Books.

Index

About the Author

Domenico A. Nesci, MD, is a psychiatrist, criminologist, and psychoanalyst (member of the International Psychoanalytic Association by virtue of full membership in the Canadian Psychoanalytic Society). He is on the faculty of the School of Medicine of the Università Cattolica del Sacro Cuore, president of the International Institute for Psychoanalytic Research and Training of Health Professionals (IIPRTHP) and co-director of the Scuola Internazionale di Psicoterapia nel Setting Istituzionale (SIPSI), in Rome, Italy. He taught at Stanford (Department of Psychology) and UCLA (Department of Political Science and Department of Psychiatry). For his teaching activities from 1999 to 2001, Dr. Nesci was awarded Distinguished Visiting Professor by the Psychiatric Clinical Faculty Association of UCLA.

www.ingramcontent.com/pod-product-compliance
Ingram Content Group UK Ltd.
Pitfield, Milton Keynes, MK11 3LW, UK
UKHW012039150926
475560UK00001B/82

9 780765 709134